The Critical Act

The Critical Act

Criticism and Community

Evan Watkins

New Haven and London   Yale University Press

1978

Designed by John O. C. McCrillis and set in IBM Press Roman type.
Printed in the United States of America by Halliday Lithograph, West
Hanover, Massachusetts.

Published in Great Britain, Europe, Africa, and Asia (except Japan) by
Yale University Press, Ltd., London. Distributed in Australia and New Zea-
land by Book & Film Services, Artarmon, N.S.W., Australia; and in Japan
by Harper & Row, Publishers, Tokyo Office.

Library of Congress Cataloging in Publication Data

Watkins, Evan, 1946–
  The critical act.
  Includes index.
  1. Criticism. 2. Poetics. I. Title.
PN81.W296   801'.95   78-3426
ISBN 0-300-02221-2

For Diane

Contents

Preface

This book began at the point when I became aware that I spent a great deal of time doing two different things. One was reading new poetry and the other was reading recent critical theory. For some time I rarely talked to the same people about both, and indeed found it convenient to separate them as much as possible. Each was interesting and difficult enough that I wasn't bothered by the implications of this division. The sticking point, finally, was that much of what I found exciting in both seemed to offer consistently different versions of recent literary history. The "common" opposition to the remains of New Critical precepts and modernist aesthetics was so immediately and finally different that it was as if "T. S. Eliot," for example, had become merely a chance nomination for two wholly discrete collections of phenomena. Thus it occurred to me at last that perhaps the most salient fact about contemporary poetics was less its rivalry with the "modern" than the way in which such rivalry disguised a remarkable duality within the "postmodern" itself.

However, a second and important fact has to do with how one makes sense of the sheer accumulation of scholarship around such figures as Eliot, Pound, Joyce, Yeats, Lawrence, and Faulkner. Surely much of the initial impetus for *Anatomy of Criticism* and, a decade later, *Validity in Interpretation* can be traced to the necessary recognition that nothing was to be gained merely by adding one more "insight" or "perception" to an aggregate quantity. Thus these books offer a systematic attempt to classify an existent body of scholarship as the chief task of critical theory. I assume the implicit corollary to be the futility of building up equally staggering amounts of commentary about even more recent authors. Thus the desire for establishing coherent first principles coalesced nicely with the promise for discovery latent in the successive waves of new thought arriving from the Continent. Recent literature could be left to fend for itself. At best it could enter critical discourse at any point when it might seem to validate the theoretical projections of formal models or when it seemed itself engaged in the formal recombination of literatry modes, such as the fiction of Coover, Barth, Pynchon, and others.

In its own way, "deconstructive" criticism, too, responds to the accumulation of scholarship, but with the demand that we demystify or unlearn the premises which make possible such accumulation rather than seek a coordinating framework to make sense of it. Thus it also responds to the dissonances set up within the systematic projects of critics such as Hirsch and Frye, to the separation between formal method and interpretive content, between the detached and contemplative posture of the critic and the actual process of reading, between the distinctively postmodern democratizing of literary accessibility and the often hermetically difficult modern works which provide the material for these procedures. Yet deconstruction still provides no real way of understanding recent literature. Indeed, in Harold Bloom's convenient formulation, it teaches rather the inevitability of misunderstanding, with all the fixity of interest in the weight of literature and scholarship that phrase implies. Deconstructive criticism needs both the scholarship and the myth of order it would demystify. Faced with new works, it can only invent an order it proposes to collapse.

The alternative seems to me a theory of literature that can elicit from recent poetry in particular the means of talking about and talking back to these developments in theory. This implies, first of all, a way of understanding poetry which can appreciate how it is critical as well as creative without at the same time turning poems into nothing more than engines of critical deconstruction, a validation of the current truism that one reads a poem by unlearning how it has been read by previous criticism. The effort of practical criticism then emerges as something far more important than material which theory can clarify and systemize, or even a "test case" to prove the efficacy of theory. I think it is perhaps the only way of allowing into theory the presence of another and distinctively different voice than one's own. Practical criticism prevents critical theory from lapsing into a massive and forbidding solipsism. Finally, my idea means shifting attention away from second-order interpretation—whether systematic, as in Frye, or deconstructive—with its necessary dependence on an accumulation of scholarship about past literature, and toward the difficulties inherent in reading and understanding new literature. I am convinced that while it is impossible to read recent poetry by extrapolating from what one already knows, an ability to understand new literature offers a genuine way into understanding literature of the past.

For a number of reasons I am uneasy with the convention that one thanks one's colleagues for their help in bringing a project to completion. More often than not, the most useful advice and criticism I received occurred indirectly, in reading portions of their work-in-progress, in discussion, in the constant and salutary exercise of making clear my objections to a particular line of reasoning, in short, as an audience to their work. Thus I like to think there is no less humility in my belief that the care and patience with which others read my manuscript had its ultimate effect through the profoundly reciprocal engagement my work provided with their own. "Completion" then becomes in a sense a misnomer. What I can present here is the way I have understood complex, intricate, and on-going discussions with Merle Brown, E. Fred Carlisle, A. C. Goodson, Alan Hollingsworth, Fredric Jameson, William Johnsen, Michael Koppisch, Roger Meiners, Bernard Paris, William Saunders, James Seaton, Linda Wagner, and Diane Wakoski. If their names are not always available in my footnotes, it is because my debt to their work is so comprehensive I often find it almost impossible to carve into discrete territories. To Merle Brown especially I owe a great deal. He is the teacher from whom I learned how very much I could expect from my teachers and the author from whom I learned how much I could expect from reading others. I don't mean, of course, to load him with all the responsibility for what follows, only to suggest again how my effort has been sustained by his own.

A somewhat different version of chapter 5 under the same title appeared in *boundary 2* 4 (1975-76): 933-45. A portion of chapter 8 under the title of "W. S. Merwin: A Critical Accompaniment" also appeared in *boundary 2* 4 (1975-76): 187-99. A shorter and somewhat different version of chapter 3 under the title "Criticism and Method: Hirsch, Frye, Barthes" appeared in *Soundings* 58, no. 2 (1975), 257-80. I wish to thank the editors for their permission to use this material. "On the Manner of Addressing Clouds" (©

I. Dialectic and the Myth of Structure

1

Introduction:
Poetics, Poetry, and the Practice of
Criticism

I

The idea that critical theory begins with the question of how we should study poems has been severely shaken by recent developments in criticism. The question was made to focus attention on the object of thought, on the individual poem, or on "the nature of literature." And like philosophy and other disciplines, criticism has learned to distrust any inquiry which seems to depend upon "metaphysical" assumptions. Kant's "Copernican Revolution" is perhaps only the most obvious example of the history I have in mind. As a result of this history, theory could no longer avoid a real consideration of the act of critical thinking, the way in which to a great extent the nature of the critical act determines the nature of the object being thought about. The new and intricate difficulties of modern literature made it even more abundantly clear that literature is by no means, if it ever was, a simple and static subject matter to be defined and explained by the theorist. Yet one should be aware of the risks inherent in a heightened theoretical consciousness becoming obsessed by its own procedures. Indeed, I wonder whether recent criticism hasn't actually intensified the assumption that literature forms a vast assemblage of raw material, opaque and intransigent, awaiting the clarity of the theorist's methodology to attain any order of intelligibility. For if the question, How should we study poems? is obscured by the requirement to study the methods of critical inquiry, then literature itself is relegated to an alien or at least irrational subject matter, menacing at the boundaries of critical thought. I see no way of returning to a naive form of direct interrogation: "Let's just begin again by looking hard at poems." But I do think it necessary to refuse from the beginning any assumption which has the effect of expelling literary works from the most immediate and primary questions of critical theory.

My idea is that another beginning can be made by in a sense reversing the traditional question, by asking instead how it is that poems can study us. This implies of course that a poem is more than an object of thought to be defined, explained, and interpreted. It must be understood as an object with a unique capacity to "talk back," to study in turn the critic who would analyze it. The immediate advantage is that the nature of the critical act thus would remain an essential consideration in the development of critical theory, but in a way that is mediated at every point by an attentiveness to the concerns evident in actual poems. The awareness that certain works of literature provide rigorous "test cases" for the adequacy of a theory is hardly new. However, such an assumption leaves the poem locked in time and place, its sinuous passages more or less visible and explicit, its corridors of meaning more or less available to be mapped by the critic, himself free to approach from any angle. What I am arguing is that genuine theoretical study begins at the point when theory allows a poem an analogous freedom of movement, a reciprocal ability to read and question the very terms of critical analysis.

A second and closely related idea is most often embodied in an easily recognizable phrase: "The poem tells us that . . . ," followed by the critic's interpretation of a particularly crucial passage or scene. Recent theory is a reminder that poems tell us nothing unless they are heard by the critic. It is the complexity of this critical act of attention which seems to me important. While it is true that a poem can tell us nothing unless we listen, it is equally true that unless criticism is conceded to be a massively solipsistic enterprise, the critic must be able to hear in the voice of the poem someone other than himself. "Dialectic" seems to be the best name to give such reciprocity. For the basic movement of dialectical thinking remains the process whereby subject and object exchange roles, where a static antinomy dissolves into the sheer relationality of a development with no fixed point of reference—neither the object itself, as in older theory, nor the critical act alone, as in more recent criticism—and no coordinates that can be mapped in advance.

"Dialectic" has a long and intricate philosophical history, some of which I shall try to include within the discussions that follow. Yet by my use of the term, I want to suggest as well a most intimate and experiential quality of one's encounter with literature, that eerie feeling at some point in the reading of a poem that one has already an audience for what is about to be spoken about the poem, an audience which is in fact the voice of the poem itself. The recovery of this experience, with all that it implies about theory and about poetry, seems to me the most pressing task to be undertaken by what I shall attempt to define in the pages that follow as a dialectical theory of criticism.

I think the most useful way to clarify my conception is by a brief examination of the change in direction of critical thought since the high point of the New Criticism. Indeed, it is now almost a truism that while critical theory has achieved a much greater degree of sophistication in the last three decades, in practice, when we talk about individual poems, we still sound like New Critics. However, if one has in mind the question of how poems study us, of what they can reveal about the presuppositions of critical theory, then the problem is not that recent theory has far outstripped practice, rather, it is the degree to which both theory and practice have undergone a dramatic transformation.

The most striking evidence for my claim lies in the relative lack of critical attention to the remarkable development of contemporary poetry. The finest work of the New Critics, after all, dealt with recent poetry; Leavis's *New Bearings in English Poetry*, for example, was written almost simultaneously with Eliot's publication of "Ash-Wednesday." And while a case could be made that the substance of Leavis's book, and *Revaluation* which followed, arose directly out of his reading of Pound and Eliot, I think it unlikely a similar argument could be made for *Figures of Capable Imagination*, even though Bloom seems one of the few critics aware of the existence of Geoffrey Hill or W. S. Merwin. Somewhat belatedly, a number of critics have discovered a similarity of intention in much recent fiction, but again, it would be difficult to conceive their work as

having derived its initial impulse from that fiction to the extent
the New Critics learned to define poetry by listening to the new
poems of Pound, Yeats, and Eliot. New Critical theory and practice
depended upon a close relationship to literature contemporaneous
with itself, and I think the disappearance of that relationship indicates less a concern for the best way to characterize literature as a
whole than a retreat by critical theory into an autogenetic consideration of its own procedures.

Nevertheless, there were real difficulties in a New Critical understanding of literary works that can't be minimized, no matter what
one thinks about the direction of more recent criticism. In *The New
Apologists for Poetry,* Murray Krieger argued that the decisive New
Critical commitment was to the individual poem as an autonomous
aesthetic object. The emphasis on autonomy means on the one hand
that the New Critics were in a position to realize the unique power
of the object of their critical thought. Yet, more clearly than his
predecessors, Krieger also recognized the problems engendered by
such a commitment: "Not the least of these, if one . . . is content
to follow where his theory leads, is that it denies him the right to
engage in the one activity for whose sake he bothers about theo-
rizing: the detailed technical analysis and criticism of specific works.
Indeed, such a theory makes it difficult for him to see how he can
even experience these works fully" (*NAP,* 138).* If autonomy is
defined in the absolute terms Krieger provides, then the poem is in
some way cut off both from "ordinary experience" and from every
critical attempt to characterize its unique nature. Any kind of dialectical reciprocity becomes as impossible to achieve as it would
be with the assumption that a poem is merely an object to be
interpreted.

Rather than "following where the theory leads," however, the
work of the New Critics represented a particularly acute stress
between theory and practice. In direct opposition to the theoretical
consequences Krieger describes, this commitment to the poem as
an autonomous object made for a richly experiential practice by
imposing upon the critic the task of making his own language

*See below, p. 237, for a list of the works cited in this chapter and the
abbreviations I have employed.

function in a double sense. He had to engage in an analysis of technical matters, but in a way that could suggest within the development of his criticism that elusive, implicit, shadowy movement of the poem at hand, something understood as profoundly different from his critical voice. Thus the critic's language would have to seem at times almost distorted by its double role, progressing by lapses in continuity and unexpected transitions as if it were being pulled in another direction by an invisible hand. As a result of this peculiar doubleness of language, an early essay by Leavis or R. P. Blackmur, for example, makes sense only to the degree one engages simultaneously in an active re-creation of the poem being discussed. Without the pressure of a recent and direct experience of Stevens's "On the Manner of Addressing Clouds," Blackmur's analysis will seem at worst incomprehensible and at best idiosyncratic, with no real, methodologically determined rationale.[1] The necessity to attend both to the poem and to the essay explains as well why the most scrupulous work with the OED can never yield that malapropism, "an Empsonian analysis." Despite the appearance of schematically ordered terms, Empson's criticism is impossible to duplicate merely by retracing his procedures. Thus while the New Critics' theory remains unsystematic and often contradictory, their critical practice at least suggests something about how poems study us, about what criticism is like that allows the presence of another voice within the critic's own thought.

I would chracterize the dominant direction of recent criticism as a movement from a theory of poetry—however muddled—to a "poetics" in a very special sense, and from the practice of criticism to the construction of systematic models of "poetic discourse," with perhaps the inevitable and secondary reaction to "demystify" or "deconstruct" those models. In sharp contrast to the New Criticism, these procedures are made possible by the belief in critical methodology as a way of neutralizing every tension between theory and practice and between criticism and poem. How should we study poems? thus becomes, How do we construct a methodology of critical inquiry? Traditionally, of course, a "poetics" develops methodologically in order to reduce or minimize the distance between theory and practice. In its new sense, however, "poetics" is a term that can be applied indifferently to theory, to practice, or to poetry itself. Joseph Riddel's preface to his recent study of William Carlos Williams, *The Inverted Bell,* offers a particularly striking argument for this indifference:

> If the Modern, or post-Modern, poem tends to be habitually a poem about poetry, a metapoetry, it is because it has discovered the function of poetry to be discovery. Poetics, in this sense, is the subject of the poem—in the sense, exactly, that Wallace Stevens could write that "Poetry is the subject of the poem." A poetics is the question from which the poem issues, the "difference" of which it is the utterance. A poetics is the initial freedom (or as I shall argue later, the "freeplay") in which the poetic act originates. A poetics may be described, then, only as the residue, the sign or trace, of some lost origin. It is the "subject" of the poem, that question of which the poem is a sign, and finally a profound questioning of the "origin" itself. [*IB,* xiii]

This is of course a late argument, already more concerned with "deconstruction" than with systematic description. But despite the rhetorical gestures toward "discovery" and "difference" and "profound questioning," Riddel's claim offers much comfort; it makes of critical theory the subject of every poem and thus escapes the difficult necessity of realizing in the voice of the poem something genuinely different from one's own professional concerns. Secondly, it permits the illusion that, in Riddel's words, "the demystification of certain critical habits" (*IB,* xiii) is the same as reading poetry, thereby doubly insuring that the boundaries of critical "discourse" are synonymous with the city limits of critical theory. The problem with the assertion that recent criticism possesses a greater theoretical sophistication than the New Criticism is that when a theory reaches this stage of autogenesis it is no longer a theory at all. It is a methodology which reduces the practice of criticism to the collection of particular "cases."

It should come as no surprise that Riddel makes the New Criticism his chief antagonist in *The Inverted Bell,* for if the New Critics pushed the tension between theory and practice almost to the breaking point, Riddel's "poetics" dissipates it entirely. His attack is directed at the conception of an autonomous poetic context, but not in a way which suggests he is aware of how this idea might engender results to challenge seriously his own beliefs. Rather, its nature reveals what is for him the same disturbing paradox found in Eliot's poetry, with its whirring, whirling evocation of a lost Word:

> What, in another context, I have called the "poetics of failure" applies here, for it is precisely a poetics of failure which characterizes this game of Modernism. Not "failure" in the aesthetic sense, however; for it is precisely in that moment when the ideal of an autotelic, autonomous poem realizes (if it could) its perfection that it calls attention to its separateness from life. It reveals the presence, the new Word it would capture, as no more than the ritual prize of the game: whether the achievement of stillness, or the illumination of a desired value. [*IB*, 271].

Like Eliot poetically, the New Critics were involved in an inevitably nostalgic attempt to recapture as an origin the presence of the Word within the mysterious perfection of aesthetic form, and for Riddel, at the very moment of success that origin must prove to be a mirage.

If one remembers the almost religious awe with which even I. A. Richards in his most neopositivistic moments tended to describe poetic "unity," Riddel's statement nevertheless looks like a serious charge. Yet one would expect the argument to be elicited from a consideration of how this peculiarly modern concern came into being and by an awareness of how "post-Modern" poetry attempts to feel its way out of the impasse. That would be to proceed theoretically, making one's language as consistent and coherent as possible while at the same time recognizing that it will be disrupted, distorted by a contact with the radically different kinds of language found in actual poems. In fact, however, the argument arises from another source altogether: "What I have been arguing, in a necessarily elliptical way, is that Eliot's poetry, and the poetics which stem from it, is analogous to the kind of interpretation Derrida associated with Lévi-Strauss" (*IB*, 270), that is, with Derrida's sense that the work of Lévi-Strauss remains contaminated by a nostalgia for the fiction of "presence" which has dominated all of Western metaphysics.[2] Thus regardless of whether Derrida is "right" or not, Riddel's own procedure becomes methodological rather than theoretical. The critique of the New Criticism serves as one possible application of the paradigm argument Derrida offers against Lévi-Strauss, and one can forget the difference between paradigm and particular case only by the most rigorous commitment to remaining safely within the boundaries of critical theory, by turning theory into method.

Likewise, in the portions of the book that seem to deal more directly with Williams, there is still no stress between the language of Williams's poems and a language which draws its energy from terms such as "difference," "freeplay," "sign," and "trace." Certainly no one can decide on principle that these or any other terms are inappropriate to criticism. Yet, unlike the language used by Leavis or Blackmur, which is elastically responsive both to its context in the essay and to the context of the poem, these words as Riddel employs them mean the same whether in relation to Williams, to Lévi-Strauss, or to the New Critics. Williams's poetry is not allowed to exert any counterpressure. Thus what Riddel's criticism engenders is the kind of static and contemplative distance from the poems which undoubtedly prompted the sly sarcasm of this review comment by a veteran Williams scholar: "Williams would have been interested in Riddel's approach. Williams was interested in everything . . ." (LW, 279). Of course it is a distance which has made possible, for Riddel and others, the freedom to appropriate concepts and terminology from the complex systems of continental thought—phenomenology, Marxism, and the dominant context of "structuralism" and "poststructuralism"—without the drag of continually engaging them with poems. At the same time, and as I suggested earlier, the result is an extreme theoretical self-consciousness which ignores actual literature and which in particular ignores what recent poetry has to tell us about the presuppositions inherent in critical theory.

For there are a number of new poetic talents in England and the United States who among themselves have at least begun to explore a quite different departure from the New Criticism than that represented by *The Inverted Bell*. In the 1963 version of his introduction to *Contemporary American Poetry*, Donald Hall offers some advice about how to read these new poems: "To read a poem of this sort, you must not try to translate the images into abstractions. They won't go. You must try to be open to them, to let them take you over and speak in their own language of feeling" (C, 33). Elsewhere in the preface, Hall makes clearer his opposition to the New Critical conception of the poem as an object of aesthetic contemplation. The criticism he imagines is more active, more willing to "smudge the slide" through its involvement with the poem, and less concerned with showing how emotions are "anchored" in a tough, paradoxical, impersonal structure of poetic language. For the discovery in these poems implies on the contrary that the "impersonal" element of poetry somehow inheres in its source in feeling, in a "general subjective life" which "corresponds to the old objective life of shared experience and knowledge" (C, 33). Thus, for Hall, the critic also must speak in such a way that his language is animated by the force of feeling which animates the language and imagery in the poem.

Clearly, Hall's "suggestion" raises more problems than it can resolve. Yet it seems to me to imply as well that the poetry of contemporaries—such as Robert Bly, James Wright, Galway Kinnell, W. S. Merwin, Charles Tomlinson, Geoffrey Hill, Jon Silkin, each in his different way—can offer at least a possibility for transforming the New Critical disjunction between theory and practice into a healthier relationship of *concordia discors*. Encouraged by a poetry which invites active re-creation of its development, which will not "stand still" to be looked at, the critical theorist would have a unique opportunity to study self-critically his own act of thinking about poems as well as "the poem itself." And no longer intimidated by a theory which seems to preclude articulating his experience with literature, the practicing critic could let his silent, creative listening to individual poems expand into a language whose inner impulsion becomes the minatory presence of other voices, other concerns, other beliefs than one's own within the otherwise settled system of critical theory. There would remain a tension between theory and practice, between a theory dominated by a self-conscious attentiveness to one's own thinking and a practice dominated by an other-conscious absorption in the expressiveness of the poem. However, this is not a distinction between "pure" forms of thought; each is forever "contaminated" by the other. And certainly it is not the crippling disjunction which makes it difficult to conceive how a New Critical analysis could be adequate to the poems Hall discusses.

II

There must be many ways to understand this poetry; no one should hope to dictate how a poem is read. The dialectical reciprocity I have insisted is the vital principle of both theory and practice surely can be achieved by a multiplicity of means. At the same time, however, a theory of poetry gains its precision in part from what it negates, from the way it is opposed to other forms of thinking about poetry. Thus, where I imagine many possibilities of individual performance, of the encounter between critic and poem, I must also make clear just how my idea of such community differs from the "structural poetics" found in Riddel and others. For me, the problem with any structural reading arises from the assumption that literature exists *only* to the extent that it is a "text," a structure of language being interpreted by a critic. Literature, Frye tells us, is dumb; only criticism can speak. More radically, the evolution of Barthes's commentary in *S/Z* works to convince us that disguised within Balzac's apparently "realistic" narrative is a "text" that comes into being only as a series of commentaries on itself, with Barthes's own taking its place in the series as a kind of commentary on the emergence of commentary. Barthes, that is, seems to take literally Derrida's admonition: "and whoever believes that one tracks down some *thing*?—one tracks down tracks" ("D" 158). The image of the critic as peripatetic detective dominates Derrida's own "Le Facteur de la vérité," and in a somewhat different way *The Anxiety of Influence* as well, where Bloom finds every poem to be in effect a deliberate "mis-detection" of an original, itself likewise displaced. In his review of *The Anxiety of Influence,* Paul De Man frankly suggests that "underneath, the book deals with the difficulty or, rather, the impossibility of reading and, by inference, with the indeterminacy of literary meaning" (PDM, 273).

It is hardly surprising, given this view of textuality, that reading as interpretation should come to seem an impossible enterprise or, to concede the attempt at a positive ideological thrust, an unrepressed chain of textual production. For if one attends to literature as a structure, a "text," it soon becomes obvious that any sense of activity or development or coherence must arise from one's own interpretive process and not from the "text itself." Once, that is, the poem is turned into a structure, the principle of development or coherence shifts from poem to reader. Even Frye will admit that while criticism must make the assumption of "total coherence" to its field of study, it is always with the awareness that the assumption is really necessary only to enable a criticism that would pretend to systematic knowledge. The next logical step is to realize that if in fact the poem as a structure has its "center" elsewhere, its principle of coherence in the interpretive process of criticism, then that interpretive process must be likewise open to the same question, the same "de-centering." Thus interpretation becomes an exercise in the indeterminacy of meaning, a process of textual production, or a series of "misreadings."

However, anything which is available to interpretation as an element of a poem's structure—its patterns of imagery, its archetypal relation to other poems, its axes of metaphoric and metonymic substitution, its "coded" language—belongs to what I would conceive as the antithetical moment of the poem; the structure is the poem's nonbeing. Once reduced to this structure, one can never expect to discover in a poem any principle of development or coherence. The being of a poem, on the other hand, is not its structure at all. It is the upsurge of feeling, the poem's *vis interna,* that power to blow the top of your head off by which Emily Dickinson said you recognize poetry, or the "electric flow" Ezra Pound sensed as necessary to every poem. In contrast to its nonbeing, its structure, the being of a poem is never available to be "tracked down"; neither a cipher nor a "some *thing,*" it is rather felt from within as the prehensive forward thrust of every line and every word. As Hall suggests, it is what "takes you over" as you read.

Nevertheless, even the presence of both being and nonbeing, feeling and structure in a poem remains an abstract conception. My own most disconcerting experiences as an undergraduate English major occurred in those classes where after spending three or four class sessions discussing, say, Joyce's enormously complex imagery in *Portrait,* the psychological development of Stephan, even—in rare moments—something like the drift of the Daedalus family toward lower-middle-class squalor, there followed one usually short class period devoted to establishing the fact that, after all, Joyce was a passionate writer. In his famous essay on modern literature, Lionel

Trilling points to just this futility, "teaching" students about the passion and power of Dostoevski, only to read paper after paper repeating the code phrases which would indicate a properly "deep" response to passion and power. Recognizing the being of a poem as its internal feeling prohibits reducing that poem to only a structure, and thus likewise the possibility of getting trapped within a perpetually dissolving chimera of interpretation. But it still leaves the poem understood as an abstract presence or, more exactly, an impossibly dualistic presence: a feeling realized from the inside out and a structure to be studied at a distance.

Even so cerebral an author as John Barth realizes that in his work he must be something more than a structural magician: "We tend to think of experiments as cold exercises in technique. My feeling about technique in art is that it has about the same value as technique in lovemaking. That is to say, heartfelt ineptitude has its appeal and so does heartless skill; but what you want is passionate virtuosity."[3] But exactly how "passion" and "technique" join together to make "virtuosity" remains unclear. For the most difficult quality of a poem to talk about is its becoming, which can be neither felt directly nor pointed to as a visible aspect of its structure. Feeling and structure as I have used these terms are opposites, yet like all abstract or unmediated oppositions if pushed far enough, the terms collapse into one another. The structure of a poem is a "presence" to the extent that, in Frye's words, it can be "spread out in conceptual space." In another sense, however, the being of a poem, too, is a presence, one to be felt rather than seen, immediately intuited rather than conceptualized. What brings both feeling and structure, being and nonbeing into existence is an act of poetic thinking which is also an act of making, which realizes the internal feeling of a poem only as it is being made into its very opposite, into structure. Apart from the act of thinking, neither feeling nor structure exists. As a "presence" to be examined "in itself" or felt "in itself," each is an abstraction.

Perhaps the most immediately experiential way to conceive this act is as a conversation. "Dialogue" is in some ways a more properly philosophical term to employ, but it carries with it as well so much sedimentation of meaning—just because it has a specific philosophical history, and because it has acquired also a spectrum of implications from its recent media usage—that it would detract from the commonness of the experience I wish to suggest. The poem becomes a poem through the poet's conversation with himself. This means to begin with that the poet is in reality two persons as different from each other as we ordinarily conceive two individuals to be. He is not just a "subject," a "transcendental ego," or a "psyche." For philosophical reasons, or in order to construct the data for experimental psychology, it often seems necessary to think of a person in these terms. Yet if we attend closely to our own experience, it is not very easy so to reduce oneself. In trying to write criticism of a poem, for example, the difficulty is that from the beginning one has an audience, seemingly never satisfied with whatever critical expression is achieved. This "audience," this "someone" who listens and who talks back and is listened to in return, surely can be as different from one's speaking voice as another listener would be. For that "someone" is already, and in a very simple and direct sense, "another listener."

My examples could be multiplied interminably. But the point is that in making the poem the poet activates these kinds of conversations in the most dramatically intense way rather than seeking to assuage their often painful nature. Like Galway Kinnell's hunter in "The Bear," he is not satisfied to speak as an observer of an action or a situation, or as one tiny part of something much larger than himself. His own being must swell to the size of the bear, or he must imagine himself like Blake's giant Los as he hammers out the very foundation of the language. If he were only a psyche, of course, flooding an alien world with his own emotions, such expansiveness would make him a monster, devouring everything he touches. However, "feeling" as I am using the word in contrast to "emotion" cannot be located within the boundaries arbitrarily imposed by the empirical conception of an individual. Feeling is prehensive, a contact with a world of objects, events, and other people, and thus it belongs to that world as much as to the individual psyche.[4] Further, the poet is not just a being, a subject. He is as well a listener, a translator, an intelligence who senses in just what way this immense force of feeling can come into existence as specific words, as a particular and determinate structure. This quality of his action, too, can be caricatured. As only a listener, only an intelligence, he would be like Milton's Satan, "squat like a toad" trying to translate Eve's tumult of vague desires into an act of eating the apple. In public appearances as he reads his poetry, the poet may choose to emphasize one or the other, portraying himself now as a creature of "vast" and "insatiable" appetites, now as a cramped, warped intelligence, turning every hope to ash, every feeling to a stony prose. It is only as we realize the poet's act of thinking to be more than the act of a psyche or an ego, to be a genuine conversation, a relation of speaking and listening between two people, that these caricatures recede.

All three "moments," its being, its nonbeing, and its becoming, are essential to the realized poem. Criticism which tries to capture only the feeling of a poem would in truth not be criticism at all but some form of mystic intuition whose actuality would arise from the way in which that feeling comes into existence within the critic's experience of it. And to that extent it would be an abstraction from the poem. Now, faced with the consummate delicacy of a poem such as this by W. S. Merwin,

Song of Man Chipping an Arrowhead

Little children you will all go
but the one you are hiding
will fly[5]

one's initial response may well be a kind of silent awe so strong as to make any expression of response, any attention to something other than the poem's immediate feeling, appear impertinently crude. Yet the poet has accepted his task. He has nerved feeling into the actuality of language, and if the critic would not be content with only an abstract appearance of immediacy, he must accept his as well.

On the other hand, criticism which attends only to the structural elements of a poem risks solipsism in a different way. Cut off from its being and its becoming, the structure of a poem seems eminently suitable for generalization. And of course there is a kind of excitement to be had through observing the agile intricacies of one's own mind as it folds structure after structure into homologous patterns. What else, after all, can be done with a structure alone except follow out one's flights of fancy about it? More sensibly, it could be argued that the critic studies the structural elements of a poem in themselves as a prelude to integrating that analysis of structure into some fuller sense of how the poem operates. But even here there is a problem. Is the structure "in itself" the "same" as the structure integrated with something else? If it is, what can it mean to say that the structure is really integral to the poem rather than simply a bonus complex of elements? And if it isn't the same, by what means does one then alter his structural analysis to accommodate this new entity which has emerged?

It is more difficult to imagine a criticism attending only to the becoming of a poem, only to the poet's conversation with himself which brings the feeling and structure of the poem into existence. Nevertheless, with a poet who is as finely self-aware as Dante in the *Commedia* or in a quite different way as Wallace Stevens in "Notes toward a Supreme Fiction," the possibility is certainly present. The problem is that these poems then begin to sound very much like critical thought. Because he is concentrating so hard on the poet's listening, on his self-critical judgment within the very act of making the poem, the critic slights the element of speaking; he slights the felt urgency of the original expressiveness which the poet's attentive listening translates into the language of the poem. As a result, that listening relinquishes its deft, light touch, its own uniquely creative play, and becomes almost ponderously criteriological. Poem and criticism seem to merge into one, and the critic finds himself either agreeing with or arguing with Stevens's epistemology in "Notes" at the expense of ignoring the drama of the whole poem.

III

Conceiving the poem as a fully dialectical act of thinking, as being, nonbeing, and becoming, provides I think at least a tentative theory to meet the criteria Hall suggests are necessary for reading much new poetry. Because the critic attends not only to a poem's structure but also to the being of the poem as feeling, he has a way of giving a more precise meaning to Hall's insistence that in these poems a "general subjective life" emerges which "corresponds to the old objective life of shared experience and knowledge." Further, one can talk about the elements of structure, about imagery for example, without trying to generalize about that structure, without turning the images into abstractions. For it would be possible to recognize such imagery as what gives the poem its particularity, its almost physical nature distinct from the body of every other poem. If structure in the abstract, considered in itself, is only the poem's non-being, when understood concretely as caught up in the act of poetic making, it is this unique and incomparable body. Finally, by the conception of a poem's becoming as a conversation, it is possible to account for what is perhaps the most curiously paradoxical quality of the poems to which Hall refers, the way in which they seem to be at once intimately personal and yet social. As I have suggested, the personal character of the poet's conversation cannot be reduced to psychic processes or some form of immediate subjectivity. But because it is a conversation, its very inwardness, its minute attentiveness to every detail of thought and gesture, is at the same time a kind of community, a social relationship which can undergo the difficult passage toward the inclusion of any larger community one wants to imagine. I shall try to show later, with Faulkner's novel *Absalom, Absalom!*, that this initial form of community provides the basis not only for a "lyric poetry" but also for the sense of "social reality" we reserve habitually only for novels.

Perhaps equally important, the idea of a poem as itself dialectical at least suggests an answer to my initial question, how it is that poems can study us. For it implies that the poet attends self-critically to his expression; he is his own first critic. Thus as one begins to articulate his ideas about a poem, he has the presence within the poem of another critical voice against which to measure his characterization. By listening to how the poet listens to himself, the critic learns a great deal about the assumptions he has made as critic in his effort of analysis. For example, if I ask myself what I must assume about the nature of the novel in order to assert that Shreve McCannon's version represents the most perceptive and accurate account of the Sutpens, I can of course read what other critics have said about *Absalom, Absalom!* on the grounds that I may well find an analysis which will reveal the flaws in my own. But with contemporary literature in particular, finding such criticism

may prove impossible. And if I have attended to *Absalom, Absalom!*
as a fully dialectical action, as being, nonbeing, and becoming, then
I should be aware of Faulkner's own presence over my shoulder, of
how and in what way Faulkner has heard critically both his own
voice and Shreve's. If I can discover as a result that Faulkner is far
from satisfied with Shreve's account, then the conclusion follows
that my own analysis of the novel's action is at least open to question as well.

I am convinced the experience I have described, often in quite
complex forms, is common indeed in the criticism of literature. I
would hesitate to put so much stress on it if it weren't. Theory,
however, has resisted strenuously the implications of such an experience. For unless one accepts the idea that in the very act of
making a poem the poet can be self-critical, and that such listening
is indeed part of the poem, then there is no justification whatsoever
for suggesting that "the poem itself" can correct a critical analysis.
We would be in the position E. D. Hirsch straightforwardly advances
in "Three Dimensions of Hermeneutics," of saying that "the text
compliantly changes its nature from one interpreter to another"
("Three," 247). Conversely, and for reasons I shall argue at length
in chapter 3, the experience of reciprocity in the reading of poetry
denies the corollary to which Hirsch is driven, that only the methodology of interpretation itself can guarantee any kind of validity.
While freeing the critic to concentrate on the nature of his own
inquiry, it likewise expels literature altogether from the problems
of critical theory.

So far I have sketched a theory in response to the question of how
poetry—and especially recent poetry—can study us. Yet the crucial
distinctions which can define this theory precisely remain in large
part still to be made. Clearly, some conception of poetic autonomy
is essential to a theory that claims for poetry the power to "talk
back" to critical analysis, to uncover the presuppositions within the
theory that would describe it. But just as clearly, any conception of
autonomy I present cannot imply the kind of absolute immediacy
invoked by Krieger's definition in *The New Apologists for Poetry.*
In order to be actual, I must argue that a poem possesses a relative
immediacy, that is, an immediacy caught up within a fully mediate
and dialectical act of thinking.

While realizing that the New Critics often seemed to refuse deliberately a systematic elaboration of critical theory, Krieger nevertheless
was able to demonstrate with some consistency that the aesthetics of
Benedetto Croce provides a powerful defense for a conception of
poetic autonomy very like what emerges from New Critical thought.
And because of his early and close association with another Italian
philosopher, Giovanni Gentile, Croce was certainly responsive to the
arguments that can be made for a conception of poetry as dialectical
in a way the New Critics could not have been. Together, the work of
the Italians forms the most intricate and sustained discussion of the
questions I want to raise in relation to a New Critical theory of
poetry. There are of course significant differences between Croce
and the New Critics which must be recognized, but the more complex philosophical awareness present in Croce's work makes it the
better means of achieving a necessary clarity.

While I have indicated already that my conception of the critical
act is most directly opposed to a methodological reduction of a
work of literature to its nonbeing, its structure, I have also suggested
like the "structuralists" a refusal of that "privilege" accorded to the
idea of a "constitutive subject" which dominates phenomenological criticism derived in particular from Husserl. Thus my argument
must develop on the one hand toward a more precise discrimination
between method and what I prefer to call criticism. E. D. Hirsch is
a crucial figure here, for as I shall argue he wavers between a phenomenological conception of intentionality and a structural conception of genre as the determinant of literary meaning. Frye, too, is
crucial; like Lévi-Strauss in a different context, he maintains the
possibility of separating a method from the larger philosophical
questions it would seem to entail. What I have to show is that in
both cases criticism is reduced to a methodology at any point when
it attempts to erect a set of procedures which claim to be self-
validating. The nature of criticism is profoundly relational; method
is solipsistic through and through.

On the other hand, this distinction between criticism and method
involves a more fundamental argument, occasioned by the "de-
centering" of subjectivity realized through the dominance of a
linguistic model in "structuralist" and "poststructuralist" thought.
It is hardly damaging to be labeled "solipsistic" when one's whole

enterprise questions the very nature of "subjectivity" and "inter-subjectivity" on which the charge is based. Thus I must conceive as sharply as possible the difference between a dialectical conception of the subject, of that exchange of roles which characterizes the critical act for me, and the primacy of language elaborated in alternative ways by Barthes and Derrida.

Of course in recent critical theory the more familiar use of "dialectic" originates with Marxist thought, and where I can distinguish clearly my own idea of the critical act from the development of critical methodologies, the task becomes more difficult with respect to recent Marxist criticism. For the work of critics such as Raymond Williams and Fredric Jameson demonstrates what is surely one of the most comprehensive alternatives to the dominance of structural methodologies in the study of literature. Further, my commitment to dialectical thinking makes it necessary for me to face a number of the charges directed at Marxist criticism: doesn't dialectical thinking by its very nature preclude any real attention to literary *form* as opposed to mere content, and as a consequence aren't Marxists singularly incapable of reading poetry? Doesn't it virtually obliterate any distinction between literature and other forms of expression? Doesn't it require the critic to become involved in considerations extraneous to an understanding of literature? Doesn't it condemn him to making insidious value judgments based on these extraliterary concerns? And finally, doesn't it in fact reduce literature to nothing more than a disguised hieroglyph of an underlying social reality?

In response to these questions, and to the work of Jameson and Williams, I want to develop in the second section of this book the implications of my conception of poetry and of criticism as forms of community, as ways of understanding a basic Marxist insight that dialectical thinking is social activity. The strength of Williams's criticism in particular has been his insistence on the complexity of relationship between literature and society. However, what seems to me new in the literature with which I am concerned is the awareness that social life does not precede the life of the poem but rather can be engendered as well in and through it, by means of that interior society which is, in fact, how the poem becomes a poem. One does not write poetry and do his living elsewhere.

A critical method, on the other hand, is managerial rather than social, a projection of "community" having more in common with the depersonalization of capital in a consumer society than with real relationships within and among individuals. The ideological thrust—explicit in the French, implicit in Frye—against the personal and the subjective, the "subject" as totalitarian "center," disguises the more subtly promiscuous authority generated by learning to subsume actual language, actual poems, and actual societies within the categories of the Symbolic, generic classification or the geological layers of *epistémés*. It is so easy to delight in the abstraction of imagining that our speaking abolishes "all interiority in that exterior that is so indifferent to my life, and so neutral" (*AK*, 210), for then one can manage to be absent when the response comes from another's voice. The literary version of this mechanism is that "distance" I spoke of between an autogenetic theory and a poem, arising from the desire to be free from the responsibility to other voices in and through the construction of language as an anonymous Other.

My own insistence on the question of how poems study us makes it essential to develop this theoretical argument into the criticism of particular works of literature and thus, hopefully, into that living critical community which seems to me the only real alternative to the anonymity promised by critical method. But where new literature can make new theories possible, it cannot "prove" the validity of a particular theory, any more than a theory can engender the understanding of an individual poem. The relation between theory and practice is far more intricate than any such mechanical model permits. Thus the essays in practical criticism which conclude each of the two sections of this book are intended neither as "case studies" nor as proof. Critical theory may gain its precision from the theoretical conceptions it opposes, but its reason for being derives from the reciprocal relation between individual poem and critical performance which it seeks to clarify. A theory if it is worth anything calls forth the necessity to become involved in the kind of response to literature which keeps one's thinking on the stretch, where theory can remain a means of movement rather than a skeleton worn on the outside or a protective armor against the intrusion of other voices. I think of recent literature as in its own

way comparable in richness and intricacy to the great period of
modern literature in the twenties, and any theory which lets one
advance even a little into this literature confirms a belief in poetry
as an essential human activity.

These essays in practical criticism are necessary for another reason
as well, since I am convinced one cannot purely theoretically oppose
a methodological conception of criticism. As I shall argue in my
third chapter, the strikingly new characteristic of recent method is
its nature as what might be called—to adopt, cacophonously, the
jargon prefix—"meta-method." It is a way of organizing other
methods, where theoretical opposition becomes limited to construct-
ing superior modes of organization—as for example Todorov's
critique of Frye's categories—or "deconstructing" in order to free
"the structurality of structure," as Derrida on Lévi-Strauss. In both
cases, "theoretical" critique is reduced to playing the game; it
becomes itself a methodology. The alternative must be an attempt
to conceive an integrally related theory and practice.

2

Poetic Autonomy

I

In its simplest form, I conceive the notion of poetic autonomy as implying that an individual poem is irreducible to a cause or norm outside itself, regardless of how systematically complex or detailed. This means, for example, that no matter what the heuristic power of a given psychological formulation, or what quantity of empirical data may become available, Conrad's *Lord Jim* would be itself discontinuous with whatever could be explained about Conrad's ambivalence toward the British Merchant Marine. Likewise, the novel would be discontinuous with even the most elaborate scheme of generic classification. Nor could it be conceived as the reflection of an existent social structure. Autonomy does not mean that these or any other considerations are necessarily irrelevant to *Lord Jim* or that they are in some way equivalently inappropriate. Perhaps most importantly, the idea of autonomy I am describing does not have to imply that the novel possesses some quantum of "insight" or "awareness" which just slips through the interstices of whatever conceptual net we throw over it. Rather, it is a way of insisting that the alterity of a poem or novel's existence results from a creative act which is self-limiting, which engenders the norms by which it can be understood and evaluated as a dialectical action. One is of course under no obligation to accept those norms as one's own; indeed, the best criticism often seems to me antagonistic. And just as obviously, one may begin and end *Lord Jim* with a particular theory of literature in mind. Yet if the novel truly has been read, it will not be the "same" theory after the reading as it was before. Like the novel itself, one's understanding will be discontinuous with the context that surrounds it.

Now, historically, a conception of poetic autonomy has been more complicated in a number of ways. In his *Estetica*, Benedetto Croce identifies autonomy with a concept of the uniquely individual character of artistic intuition. Not only is a poem irreducible to a conceptual system, but also the poem *qua* poem must be distinguished from intellectual activity of any kind by its quality of immediacy—its indivisible fusion of elements—and by the ineffable particularity of the knowledge it offers. The difference is crucial, for Croce's understanding involves the necessity to exclude, as I would not, any element of thoughtful, self-conscious attentiveness from the poem. Further, where my conception of poetic autonomy allows for the possibility of conceptual language, historical awareness, class interest, even generic concerns, to be actually involved within a poem, Croce must argue that these are all inexact and approximate ways of characterizing an artistic intuition ontologically distinct from and logically prior to them.

At least in places in *The Well-Wrought Urn*, Cleanth Brooks's argument for poetic autonomy results in a conclusion very like Croce's, even though Brooks's awareness of Croce's theory most likely came from the work of Wilbur Urban. The organic unity of a poem for Brooks arises from the uniquely self-referential quality of its language which does not allow the reader's attention to be transferred outside the poem. Thus any single word or phrase in a poem is qualitatively different from that word or phrase as it might be used in "ordinary language." Here is how Murray Krieger elaborates Brooks's point:

> The poet knows the inherent danger in his medium: that words struggle to mean things. He must, by the formal context he imposes on them prevent them from achieving their natural (that is, their nonpoetic) function. He must use every device at his command to block their direct pointing or he does not produce an aesthetic object. [*NAP*, 131] *

As this total and autonomous context, the poem is almost literally impervious to thought. One enters it by a kind of miracle, and once inside he cannot articulate his experience without stepping back

---

*See below, pp. 238–39, for a list of the works cited in this chapter and the abbreviations I have employed.

outside the poem. Similar to Croce's conclusion, any language the critic uses of necessity would be only approximate and inexact.

Northrop Frye, on the other hand, has taken Brooks's premise of the individual poem as a self-referential context in a direction which asks us to imagine all of literature as internally consistent, as comprising a "total form," an enormous self-referential context. However, the purpose of such expansion for Frye is to raise the possibility that the "axioms" of criticism can be derived from an "inductive survey" of the critic's field, this system of literature. Thus, rather than a means of distinguishing poetry from other activities or other forms of discourse, autonomy becomes in Frye's work a regulative concept for criticism, preserving its methodological purity from encroachment by other disciplines. The value of autonomy as a concept is methodological rather than criteriological; one assumes the autonomy of literature as a "total form" in order to sustain a systematically coherent critical enterprise.

Frye's radical change in emphasis is understandable to the extent that these other conceptions of autonomy—including my own— create an immediate and difficult problem for the critic: how can one talk about a poem? I remember an argument with Eliseo Vivas, concerning the means of critical response, brought to a sudden and dramatic halt by his quoting from "The Waste Land": "Oh keep the Dog far hence, that's friend to men,/Or with his nails he'll dig it up again!" After a pause, he asked if one really needed to talk about those lines. Having assimilated the received version of the New Criticism as an imposing edifice of "close reading" and thus prepared for quite a different argument, I was at a loss. Yet Vivas's challenge is indicative of a curious lack of continuity in New Critical practice. Even Empson, whose capacity for arrest on single words approaches the inexhaustible, leaves the impression of never having quite "seized on" the essential quality his analysis seems to strain toward making explicit. Or there is the crescendo of Blackmur's intricate discussion of Yeats's poems toward "A Deep-Sworn Vow" which culminates in his quoting the poem.[1] The point is missed if these examples illustrate only an inherent limitation in a critical practice dominated by the theoretical conviction that each individual poem represents an inviolable context. Rather, they arise from an experientially acute awareness that understanding a poem

seems to require at one and the same time a thoughtful attentiveness to the detail and complexity of language, with all that can be
made to imply, and as it were a step outside oneself, an almost
miraculous entry into the world of a poem where one is lost in
utterly rapt, intransitive attention.

Thus I would suggest further that in the definition of autonomy,
New Critical theory for the most part failed to understand these
paradoxical implications of its own practice. Here is Cleanth Brooks
in *The Well-Wrought Urn:*

> His [the poet's] task is finally to unify experience. He must
> return us to the unity of the experience itself as man knows it
> in his own experience. The poem, if it be a true poem is a
> simulacrum of reality—in this sense, at least, it is an "imita-
> tion"—by *being* an experience rather than any mere statement
> about experience or any mere abstraction from experience.
> [*WW,* 212-13].

The quotation comes from a chapter entitled "The Heresy of Paraphrase," and that title is indicative of Brooks's difficulty even before
one unravels the liturgical implications. For it assumes the critic's
"experience" *of* the poem should reproduce as closely as possible
the "experience" *in* the poem. To "listen to" or "to read"—"to
experience"—a poem means to repeat the poem. This sounds very
much like the psychological model proposed by I. A. Richards in
Principles of Literary Criticism, but there is a crucial difference. As
an aggressive empiricist, Richards assumes without question that
no two psychological states of experience will be exactly the same.
Brooks, however, is less concerned with psychological experience,
with what occurs in the poet's head or the reader's head, than with
"experience" as it is somehow "anchored" in the language of the
poem. Thus Brooks is committed in a way Richards is not to
the idea of an immediate poetic unity indissolubly linked with the
complexity of poetic language as self-referential.

Further, Richards argues that a failure in reading occurs when the
reader, for whatever reason, cannot approximate a *similar* state of
mind to the poet when the latter contemplates the finished poem.
For Brooks, on the other hand, failure arises from the imposition of
any other context, from the attempt to put "in other words" the

meaning of the poem. That is "the heresy of paraphrase." By definition, the self-referential quality of poetic language determines that
any other language will be unable to produce the same meaning,
whether or not the "experience" psychologically feels the same.
Analysis can be construed as a propaedeutic to genuine response, a
means of crossing off possible misconceptions, of teasing out the
implications of certain words and showing the relationships among
complicated patterns of imagery. But Brooks is consistent enough
not to be satisfied with this. Relying on the earlier work of both
Richards and Empson, he wants to find a way of connecting Empson's analysis of what Richards had called "free imagery" with
Richards's conclusion that the poem's total effect represents a
"harmony" or "balance" of opposing forces. For Brooks, this
unified whole must be the norm by which any analysis is carried
out; otherwise, the critic would have no way of knowing, for example, how far he could pursue the ambiguities of a particular word
before he cuts himself adrift from the poetic context as a whole.

However, if one's experience of the poem is conceived as essentially repetition, it would seem from Brooks's argument that
criticism inevitably divides into two antithetical acts: one immerses
himself in the experience of the poem as an aesthetic whole, and
then, abstractly and discursively, he tries to know something about
the discordant elements unified by the poem. Where the strength—
indeed, the existence—of New Critical practice at least suggests
that these two operations may be integrated, a theory such as
Brooks's sunders them completely. Thus there remains no way to
articulate within critical discourse itself an understanding of poetic
unity as a norm of judgment and, as a consequence, no real way
of justifying how and why one chooses to say this and not something else about a poem. As a means of judgment in the passage
quoted, Brooks is driven to suggest the idea that a poem is a "simulacrum of reality"—where "reality" seems to mean, alternatively, a chaos of "experience" which the poet unifies or a unity
we somehow already possess and to which the poet returns us.
Either way, the concept is sharply at odds with his own insistence
on an autonomous and self-referential poetic context which inaugurates "the heresy of paraphrase" that, in turn, makes necessary
for Brooks the idea of a poem as a "simulacrum of reality."

In the ten essays of practical criticism which compose the major portion of *The Well-Wrought Urn,* Brooks's activity as a critic is more complicated than these theoretical porpositions would indicate. For there he attends simultaneously to the context of the poem and to his own effort at articulating the connections among its elements. This means, in effect, that he listens to how he hears the poem, and it means his critical language comes to birth from at least two sources at once: the way he attempts to reproduce the poem and the way he listens to that heard poem. Yet, if Brooks were to recognize in theory such a double source, he would undoubtedly argue that the latter is deduced from the former, both temporally and logically. And is this by any means certain? Granting for the moment the questionable hypothesis that listening is no more than a kind of immediate reproduction of another's speech within oneself, there still remains the presupposition of another activity which listens to and compares the "original" to the "reproduction" at every point. Nor could this silent listening be construed as merely reflective or unproductive, for it is the act wherein both original and reproduction can be understood as indeed "original" and "reproduction." It "produces" the existence of both. And by this point, indeed, the terminology has become virtually meaningless.

Thus one apparent resolution to the whole dilemma would be to follow the lead of much contemporary criticism and step outside the problem. However one conceives the nature of poetry or the "experience" of poetry, criticism at least should be methodologically coherent. Indeed, in *Anatomy,* Frye argues that there are two essentially different mental operations involved. Either one reads for the incommunicable, personal—and, one supposes, "autonomous"—experience of the poem, or one does systematic criticism realting each poem to the "total form" of literature. Brooks's theoretical hedging, the drag introduced into his theoretical chapters by the practical criticism preceding them, is effectively eliminated. The only functional meaning of autonomy becomes the perpetuation of critical homogeneity. As I have suggested, Riddel's conception of "poetics" is more radical. For he infers that both poem and critical discourse discover some form of this gap or discontinuity within themselves and so are really the "same," "about" the same "subject," the same distance from an "origin" or an "original." Whatever the surface structure of a poem might seem to imply, its underlying form engages the identical problematic as critical theory. "Poetic autonomy" is nothing but a fiction of Modernism. The next chapter will be taken up with a critique of these possibilities, but to anticipate briefly, I want to argue that, rather than escape, these "resolutions" simply displace the difficulties Brooks faces into an even more intransigent paradox.

A second resolution would be to admit some form of judgment, some capacity for self-critical listening into the very nature of a poem. This is of course what is required by the theory of poetry I sketched in chapter 1. Insofar as it is genuinely poetic, a poem will be dominated and unified by the first "moment" in its dialectic, by feeling, by the upswell of being which suffuses all the disparate elements in its articulated body. Yet in order to become actual, a poem would have to include as well the poet's listening to this originative expressiveness. However exalted one's sense of the creative act, the poet remains most thoughtful and self-conscious in his effort. A poem is autonomous to the extent that its action cannot be predicted on the basis of any context outside itself. But because that action is dialectical and not immediate, the critic has a means of access to a poem in a way that is not miraculous. For the very making of a poem is the unfolding of its immediacy into a kind of critical question through the poet's listening to his speech. And one realizes such implicit interrogation as analogous to his own activity. Thus there is no ontological gap between how the poet makes the poem and how the critic reads it. Further, the critic has a rationale for his attentiveness to the complexity of language in a poem which Brooks insists is necessary. His critical analysis simply expands and clarifies what the poet has been engaged in already. The difference is that the unity of the critical act is weighted toward the mediating moment of a dialectic rather than toward the immediate, that is, toward the relationships which develop out of that initial community of speaking and listening through which the poem becomes a poem.

Yet any resolution which designates poetry as "dialectical" must threaten the sense of a poem as possessing that immediacy which, in Eliot's phrase, communicates before it is understood. And for

Brooks at least, it would break open the poem's context; it would
make impossible any conception of a poem as an autonomous aesthetic object, existing in some way "before" or "beneath" the level
of statement *about* "experience." Thus a poem would appear to be
directly available to "nonaesthetic" criteria of judgment, to norms
outside itself. One can't have it both ways, he could argue. Either a
poem represents an immediate fusion of language and meaning,
form and content in an aesthetic whole, or it becomes simply one
among many other kinds of human discourse.

A third resolution corresponds most closely to the development of
Croce's critical theory. In his *Estetica,* Croce too wants to make as
sharp a distinction as possible between art and other activities.
Thinking itself is understood as the process of making such distinctions, and only artistic intuition is free from this process. It is
immediate and individual, prior to the distinctions introduced by
intellectual activity. However, Croce's studies in Vico, Marx, and
Hegel and his emergent friendship with Italy's other influential
neo-idealistic philosopher, Giovanni Gentile, convinced him of
the necessity to rethink his very conception of thinking. The result
is that by the *Breviario* of 1913 the nature of "distinction" has
changed dramatically. Intuition is understood as directed immediately toward an a priori synthesis of feeling and image, but mediately and indirectly toward something else as well, toward critical
judgment. A poem possesses all the sensuous immediacy Brooks
might wish, yet it also generates out of its very nature a necessity
for such judgment. And Croce can claim to be maintaining a real
distinction between poem and criticism because, in his new theory,
"distinction" must imply as well a dialectical unity. In his best work,
Croce will remain faithful to this double intention: to distinguish in
kind between poetry and criticism, and to integrate them within the
unity of the Spirit.

Clearly, then, Croce wants to distinguish artistic activity from
other activities, and just as clearly he wants to imagine it as part
of a coherent whole. The problem, the real division within the
theory adumbrated in the *Breviario,* and developed further in
Nuovi saggi di estetica, is between his attempts to distinguish and
his attempts to integrate. In the *Breviario* at least, he continues to
think of an individual poem as distinct; it is intuitive, immediate,

and nondialectical. Nevertheless, his emphasis on integration reminds him that this intuition must become part of a dialectical process. Thus he can distinguish *a* poem from *a* critical judgment, and he can integrate the *concept* of intuition with the *concept* of judgment through the "circle" of the Spirit, but without realizing that these are still two different operations. Because his understanding of poetic autonomy confuses the concept of intuition with an individually existent poem, he cannot discover any real reason why a poem and a critical judgment are intrinsically and necessarily related. If the "resolution" evident in Croce's work were confined solely to critical theory, the burden of argument would be easier. Croce could be made to work against Croce to demonstrate my own position.

Yet in one important sense this double quality does not need to be elicited from Croce's work by his critic. For Croce was himself engaged continually as a practicing literary critic. Indeed, no other philosopher of comparable stature has achieved such a rich and diverse response to such a multiplicity of literary works. As a result, one already listens to Croce with, as it were, a double ear. To be sure, it is necessary to attend to his attempt at developing a precise, conceptual understanding of the nature of poetry and criticism. But in this theoretical work, one hears as well the essays in practical criticism—qualifying, resisting, exploring the resonances set in motion, adumbrating the next shift in his theory—and through them the voices and rhythms of the literary works he writes about. This complicates considerably the task of any critical argument against Croce's conception of autonomy, but it is also what distinguishes a genuine theory such as Croce's from merely the elaboration of a methodology.

II

Although the differences between Croce's early literary criticism and a book such as *The Well-Wrought Urn* are perhaps more immediately obvious than the similarities, Croce nevertheless shared with Brooks and other New Critics a certain reluctance to think critically about his own act of thinking about a work of literature. The poem is *there,* to be grasped in its entirety, as free as possible from interference by the critic's preoccupations. It is not inconceivable to imagine Croce defending his criticism as Wordsworth defends his poems: "I have at all times endeavored to look steadily at my subject" ("PLB," 338). Yet from the beginning Croce's was a more philosophically motivated reluctance. If one conceives both a radical distinction between artistic intuition and intellectual activity and a necessity for the critic to become rapt within the intuitive, individual nature of the poem, then there is a kind of menacing detachment in being self-reflective about one's activity as a critic.

Further, to the extent that thinking is understood as a process of making distinctions, it must possess as well a quality of certitude which, for the sake of clarity, refuses to consider those larger questions of the relationships among what has been divided already. In contrast, the breathtaking quality of Croce's definition of intuition, even in the *Estetica,* is that it resolves nothing, guarantees nothing in advance. Where logical thought, for example, might *begin* from a distinction between the subject and the object of perception, intuition holds in suspense the elements of an experience which, in its wholeness, beggars the distinction at the source. Thus, as late as the *Breviario,* Croce will argue emphatically: "As soon as reflection or judgment develops out of that state of ideality [art as "pure intuition"] art vanishes and dies. It dies in the artist, who changes from artist and becomes his own critic; it dies in the spectator or listener, who from rapt contemplator of art changes into thoughtful observer of life" (*GA,* 15).

Now the countermovement in Croce's thinking, as he strove to become not only a critic but also a historian and a philosopher, was the necessity to integrate all his basic concepts. Indeed, the problem introduced as historical in the first chapter of his 1906 essay, "Ciò che è vivo e ciò che è morto della filosofia di Hegel," has much to do with Croce's own intellectual history:

> Yet in investigating reality, our thought finds itself facing not only distinct, but also opposed concepts. . . . As has been said, two distinct concepts nevertheless can be united in their very distinctness; two opposite concepts seem to exclude one another. . . . Instead of the concrete universal, the organic reality sought after, thought seems everywhere to run against two universals, the one facing the other, the one menacing the other. ["VMH," 8–9]

For in the *Lineamenti di una logica come scienza del concetto puro* which preceded "Ciò che è vivo," Croce had argued that artistic intuition and logical thought are "distincts," each a concept in and of itself, and at the same time related through a "nexus" or "gradation" of distincts. But it is not hard to realize how they must have come to seem more like opposed concepts, each threatening to exclude the other. For one is said to provide knowledge of the individual, the other of the universal; one is indivisible, the other the very fount of distinction; one is immediate, the other discursive. Caught within such divisiveness, there is little room for someone who wants to engage in practical criticism and also think critically about literature in relation to history, philosophy, and moral behavior.

Thus one can anticipate Croce's aesthetics beginning to develop in several related directions. On the one hand, and already in the 1906 essay on Hegel, he will try to develop a more flexible conception of thinking, one which does not exclude the individual richness and texture of intuition. After "Ciò che è vivo," it would no longer be possible for Croce to make the statement that a philosophical concept is the "same" concept no matter how it is expressed. On the other hand, intuition begins to assume a real complexity, to become an active making as well as a passive kind of knowledge. And under the influence of De Sanctis, he was led to abandon his conception of criticism as effectively another work of art, a poem which reproduces a poem. Instead, he will argue that criticism is a synthesis of "taste" and judgment, of the critic's capacity to re-create the poem as it is with his capacity to judge the aesthetic success or failure of intuition.

For Croce, Hegel's great discovery was a dialectical thinking which realized:

> The opposites are not illusion and unity is not an illusion. Opposites are opposed to each other, but they are not opposed to unity, since true and concrete unity is precisely the unity or synthesis of opposites. It is not immobility but movement; it is not fixed and static but developmental. The philosophical concept is the concrete universal, and therefore a thinking of reality as at once united and divided. Only in this way does

philosophical truth correspond to poetic truth, and the pulse
[*palpito*] of thought to the pulse of things. ["VMH," 14-15]

The important point is that Croce is thinking not only about Hegel
but also about the problems in his own theory. That is, he conceives
his very exposition of Hegel as already caught up in his critical
relation to Hegel's dialectic. His title may tell us that he will impartially distinguish "what is living" from "what is dead" in Hegel,
but his way of proceeding demonstrates a quality of self-reflection
he had denied to himself as literary critic. To be sure, there is a
difference between writing about a philosopher and writing about
a work of art, but the exciting quality of "Ciò che è vivo" comes
through as Croce's new willingness to attend to his own theory
in relation to what he is thinking about. The proof of this inheres
in the necessity for questioning Croce's thinking almost from the
beginning of the essay; there is no need to wait until the exposition
of Hegel has been concluded in order to sense the pressure of Croce's
response to Hegel and to ask, for example, how a statement such as
"The opposites are not illusion" should be interpreted. Does Croce
understand Hegel to mean that within the synthesis opposites are no
illusion, or does he intend to claim that in and of themselves opposing concepts are real?

The importance of the question becomes clearer as one follows
Croce's argument to its conclusion, that a theory of distincts is
present in Hegel but confused with an erroneous dialectic of opposites. Here is how Croce explains the former: "In the theory of
distincts, every concept—and let the concept be a—is at once distinct
from and united with the concept that is superior to it in degree,
concept b. Thus (beginning the exposition of the relation) if a is posited without b, b cannot be posited without a" ("VMH," 59). If, in
Croce's example, a is artistic intuition, then we must suppose it real
in and of itself. Philosophy, on the other hand, concept b, exists as a
mere abstraction unless its means of expression are artistic: "In fact,
no philosophy exists save through the words, images, metaphors,
linguistic forms and symbols which are its artistic side. . . . an un-
expressed philosophy is not conceivable: man thinks in speech"
("VMH," 60).

Now in Hegel's dialectic of opposites, on the other hand, Croce concludes that *neither* term of the opposition exists independently. Apart from Becoming, Being and Not-Being "are not two concepts but two abstractions" ("VMH," 61). Consequently, Becoming cannot possibly be a genuine synthesis; it can neither "suppress" nor "conserve" what doesn't exist to begin with. It is only within a nexus of distincts that one can affirm concept *a* as real. Then, when *a* enters into a relation with concept *b*, it is "suppressed" as distinct but "conserved" through the relation with *b* wherein *b* becomes concretely real as well. For Croce, Hegel understood well enough the necessity to conceive reality "as at once united and divided," but such a possibility can be realized only if the dialectic of opposites is more strictly formulated as a nexus of distincts. Otherwise, it provides merely a unity, a monotonic Becoming as real.

Nevertheless, it remained for Croce's fellow philosopher, Giovanni Gentile, to develop this insight into Hegel. For as Merle Brown has argued in his study of neo-idealisitc aesthetics, the conceptual difficulty which vitiates "Ciò che è vivo" is Croce's failure to realize how a dialectic of opposites differs from positing a contradiction. Thus Croce explains the nexus of distincts as superior to Hegel's dialectic to the extent that a "synthesis" of abstract contradictories affirms nothing, whereas a nexus of *a* and *b* can result in a new entity compounded of both. A genuinely dialectical thought, however, understands that the negation of *a* as the antithetical moment of the dialectic implies much more than merely the absence of *a*:

> For example, if the thesis is unity, the antithesis is, to begin with, not-unity. Croce would go no further, but for the dialectic to move it is necessary to recognize not-unity to be multiplicity, which is not the contradictory of unity but is what I am calling its opposite. To reason out the synthesis of unity and multiplicity is not so simple or so sterile as reasoning out the synthesis of unity and not-unity, which would no doubt be simply unity all over, with something of the "life-urge" added to it. [*NIA*, 61]

It is the difference between visualizing the presence or absence of unity and conceiving a relation between unity and that multiplicity without which both "unity" and "synthesis" are meaningless concepts.

Further, had Croce thought more carefully about his own act of thinking which constructs the nexus of distincts, he would have realized that a vital element is missing. For suppose one grants the argument that philosophy joins logical thought and artistic intuition. How then is intuition as complete in itself to be integrated with philosophy as the union of intuition and logical thought? Only mystically, one feels: "And the universal spirit passes from *a* to *b* and from *b* to *a*, through no other necessity than that of its own external nature, which is to be at once art and philosophy, theory and praxis, or however else it may determine itself" ("VMH," 63). Croce brings his nexus of distincts into contact with Hegel's dialectic of opposites, and the result is to indicate with sharp clarity the differences between them. That is, Croce attends both to his theory and to Hegel's, but he is unable to turn this awareness back on itself in a way which implicates his own present act of thinking. Even though he is making a major modification in the nexus of distincts, both it and the dialectic of opposites are conceived as already the object of his thought. That object, in truth, is more complicated than it had ever been before; it is not a "simple" object at all, but the relation between two forms of thought. The problem remains that Croce stares so intently at this complex object that he ignores his act of thinking about the relation.

His failure is the more disheartening because he had good reason to suspect Hegel's overly rapid passage from art to philosophy. By beginning in the *Phenomenology* from a notion of "sensible certainty," Croce argues that Hegel has in fact bypassed genuine artistic activity without realizing it. Even in the simplest perception, "sensible certainty" is already mingled with some form of intellectual reflection, "and it is only natural that that first reflection should prove itself imperfect and be surpassed" ("VMH," 82). Croce's experience as a literary critic was more than adequate to dispense with any comparison of art to this abstract perception. Yet one can agree with Croce about the experiential richness of each individual poem without drawing the conclusion that

> art is, precisely, subject without predicate, but in a way that is altogether different from the nothingness and void of the thing-in-itself and of the thing without properties. It is intuition

without intellectual reference; it is the feeling [*fremito*] which a poem communicates, through which there opens a vision of reality which we cannot render in intellectual terms and which we do not possess except in singing or in re-singing, in creating it. ["VMH," 82]

For in order to make his point that a poem possesses a fullness of being which cannot be conceived on the order of an incomplete perception, Croce equates this individually existent poem he is imagining with a *concept* of intuition that necessarily excludes all "intellectual reference."

However, to the extent that Croce's insistence on distinguishing the experiential wholeness and immediacy of art from logical thought takes the form of positing these as radically different kinds of activities, it is tempting to argue that his theory arises from a more fundamental error. His defense of intuition is mistakenly directed against the "inevitably" abstract nature of philosophical thought, when in fact his genuine antagonist should be the historical circumstance of a bourgeois ideology marked precisely by its reification of thought into separate and unrelated "areas." For it is against *this* abstractness that the ideal of art as inclusive of the most disparate human experience takes on any value. Had Croce been more aware of the distortion as historical, his distinctions would have been less rigid, and he would have been less concerned with a conception of poetic autonomy itself derived from the very forms of reification he should be opposing. The difficulty is that such an argument lacks any real specificity of reference to the actual context of Italian thought from which Croce's theory emerges and is thus itself an idealization.[2] Further, it seriously undervalues the importance of Croce's work as a practicing literary critic. Like Marx before him, and in a far more intricate and sustained way, Croce realized that exhilaration one feels in the presence of art as occasioned by an activity that simply cannot be comprehended as a pale shadow of something else. Thus inadequate as his distinctions and his conception of autonomy may be, they were not mere ideological reflexes but genuinely responsive to and interpretive of his experience as a critic of literature.

And by the *Breviario* of 1913, Croce has himself come to the conclusion that not only does poetry include elements of theoretical and practical activity, but also its very nature engenders a movement from artistic intuition to logical thought. The *Breviario* is not an easy book to read, however, for a number of reasons. Although never delivered, the four essays were intended as a series of lectures, and that must account for their occasionally almost gnomic brevity. Further, as Gian N. G. Orsini points out, by the time he came to write the *Breviario,* Croce had behind him not only the *Estetica* but also the *Logica,* the *Filosofia della pratica,* and a more or less continuous discussion with his colleagues about the questions raised in the *Breviario.* Thus the positions Croce takes are not nearly so dogmatic as one might think from reading nothing of his work but the English translation. Yet Croce himself indicates in his foreword that he has attempted to deepen and sharpen his ideas in the *Breviario,* and these changes seem to me to occasion the real difficulty in understanding.

Art is defined in the *Breviario* as the "*aesthetic a priori* synthesis of feeling and image within intuition" (*GA*, 31). The "image" which had been conceived in the *Estetica* as the essential nature of intuition is now but one element in the artistic synthesis, and the difference is crucial. For insofar as "image" was identical with the indivisibility of intuition, there was no way for Croce to introduce any kind of complexity or development into his definition of art. It is little wonder his critical preferences tended toward short, essentially "imagistic" poems or lines rather than the intricate work of Ariosto or Shakespeare about whom he would later write perhaps his finest criticism. The definition in the *Breviario,* however, does allow Croce to think of poetry as complex, because "image" must imply always "a nexus of images, there existing no images-in-isolation, any more than thoughts-in-isolation" (*GA*, 27). Likewise, he can understand poetry as an active making, a creation of images rather than merely the passive kind of knowledge suggested by the static concept of an "image."

"Feeling" is the other element in the artistic synthesis, and it is what gives poetry its simplicity, its indivisible unity. Croce often uses the word *aspirazione* and even *fremito* as well as *sentimento* to characterize what I am calling "feeling," for he understood artistic feeling neither as passive desires nor as a sudden outburst of emotion. It is rather a longing, a reaching outward, an almost physical prehensiveness; it is a *stato d'animo* not yet concentrated on a specific goal of practical action or the emotional conflicts among possible courses of action:

> What we admire in genuine works of art is the perfect imaginative form that a state of mind assumes there; and this is called the life, unity, compactness, and fullness of the work of art. What displeases us in spurious and poor works of art is the unresolved conflict of many different states of mind—their stratification or mixture or vacillating manner—which acquires an apparent unity from the sheer will of the author, who for such purposes avails himself of some scheme or abstract idea or an extra-aesthetic outburst of the passions. [*GA*, 25]

All the complexity of images in a genuine poem have their reason for being in this fundamental feeling. Thus the choices made by the poet in the act of creation are always inclusive rather than exclusive. Within the single, dominant feeling of the play, Shakespeare for example can elaborate all the complexity of character and action which involve Othello, Iago, and Desdemona without having had to "take sides" by excluding anything.

In the third lecture of the *Breviario*, "The Place of Art," Croce explicates his "philosophy of the spirit" as the process of a "circle" which passes through three "stages" or "levels": the aesthetic a priori synthesis; the logical a priori synthesis of subject and predicate, or representation and concept; and the practical a priori synthesis of knowledge and action. This last becomes "always a new feeling, a new desiring . . . a new lyric, a new art" (*GA*, 56), thus "closing" the circle. The most difficult aspect of the *Breviario* is Croce's attempt to integrate these "levels," particularly insofar as the definition of art as intuition is now said to generate within itself a kind of dialectical ferment which makes it something more than an immediate identity:

> Was man *qua* artist driven toward image alone? Toward *image* and toward *something else* at the same time. Toward image insofar as man is artist, and toward something else insofar as artist is man: toward image at the first level [of the process].

But, since the first level is connected with the second and third
levels, he was also driven toward the latter too, although immediately toward the first, while mediately toward the second and
third. Now that the first level has been reached, the second
emerges right behind it, and from something aimed at indirectly
becomes something of direct concern. And so a new requirement
presents itself, and a new process is initiated. [*GA*, 51; translator's interpolation]

As he is at pains to explain in the next paragraph, this movement
does not imply that a "faculty" of intuition "yields its place" to a
second faculty of judgment. Rather, the activity of intuition engenders a kind of immediate "satisfaction" but at the same time a
"dissatisfaction," an almost peripheral awareness of incompleteness
within the very unity of intuition.

   And this is of course the critical point in the argument where
Croce's thinking suggests simultaneously two contradictory resolutions. One can infer that he means nothing more than that art as
complete in itself, like the concept of art in "Ciò che è vivo,"
nevertheless leaves the artist to some degree dissatisfied with his
effort. Thus Foscolo, in Croce's example, "no longer gives form to
the image because he has already done so. Nor does he fancy, but
perceives and reports. . . . Thus, the lyrical image is changed, for
him and for us, into an item of autobiography, or into a *perception*"
(*GA*, 53), a judgment. In temporal succession, the artist first com-
pletes his intuition in the synthesis of feeling and image, then he
is driven to judge his own labor. As itself an active synthesis, intuition would involve the same triumph over its contradictory as in
"Ciò che è vivo," where intuition is said to be the conquest of
beauty over ugliness. The problem with this resolution is that it
can work only within a theory of art as passive knowledge such
as Croce elaborated in the *Estetica,* for in reality there is nothing
very active about it. No matter what determinate content Croce
tries to provide for "ugliness," it reduces to "not-beauty," and
the "synthesis" of such contradictories merely realizes the thesis all
over again. Thus not only would there be no real reason to imagine
an artist "driven" to judge his labor, but also one could question
why he *labors* in the first place. Without a sure sense of how "oppo-

sition" includes and goes beyond "contradiction," any idea of an active synthesis loses its meaning.

On the other hand, in the first long passage quoted, Croce seems equally insistent that within the very activity of creation itself, the artist aims "directly" at the making of an image but "indirectly" at judgment and practical action as well. Rather than a clean, temporal division, one would have to say that the philosophical and practical elements in a poem are dominated and harmonized by the immediacy of feeling. This conjecture is supported by a startling passage a little further on: "Of all the various syntheses we have distinguished in succession—aesthetic synthesis, logical synthesis, practical synthesis—the sole real one is the *synthesis of syntheses*: the Spirit, which is the true Absolute, the *actus purus*" (*GA*, 57). For if Croce means what he says here, he must abandon any notion of a distinct activity as real in and of itself. The "nexus of distincts" would be dissolved into the sheer relationality of a dialectic of the Spirit. This does not imply, of course, that Croce would give up any effort at making distinctions:

> Those who used to see or continue to see art in terms of concept, history, mathematics, type, morality, pleasure, and every other thing are right because there are within it (by virtue of the unity of the spirit) these and all other things. In fact, this existence of all of them, together with the persistent onesidedness of art (as well as of any other particular form) which tends at the same time to reduce them to one alone, explains the passage from one form to another, the fulfillment of one form in the other, and development. Still, those very persons are also wrong (in virtue of the aspect of distinction, which is inseparable from unity) because of the manner in which they reveal the aforesaid things: all abstractly on a par, or in confusion. [*GA*, 57]

Distinction is necessary if unity is to have any meaning. Croce's point in this elliptical passage is that each of the "levels" in the circle is "onesided"; intuition, logic, or praxis in turn includes and dominates the others, depending upon whether one's immediate goal is the making of a poem, writing history, or storming a barricade. Thus there could be a development from one level to another—

as intuition, for example, becomes a subordinate element in the unity of judgment—but also and more importantly a development within the very nature of each. Rather than a "triumph" over its contradictory, intuition would become a dialectic of genuine opposites which we might describe as follows.

The essence of art is lyric; it is the moment of feeling, of utter oneness, of indivisibility which can provide an experiential basis for both Vico and Marx's speculations about the metaphorical relation between art and the "childhood" of the race. But no feeling exists unless it is expressed, and expression involves as well the making of an image or, more precisely, a "nexus" of images, of objectified parts which can be distinguished from each other. In this antithetical moment, the work of art is all multiplicity; it is what one is attending to when he speaks of "the world of the poem," an imagined complex of images, characters, events, and so forth. As Croce reminds us again and again, these "moments" are inseparable. Intuition is a synthesis, and thus "their relation alone is artistic, that is, their unity, understood not as an abstract and lifeless unity, but that concrete and living one which constitutes the *a priori* synthesis" (*GA,* 31). Rather than the triumph of beauty over ugliness, the active quality of intuition would result from the necessity to integrate feeling as the moment of oneness with feeling as the multiplicity of expression, to realize art as both simple and complex. These opposites would be identified dialectically and not immediately, through an intuition which holds the Absolute within the relativity of the individual poem.

Yet there is a difficulty here as well, for insofar as Croce insists that intuition is a *relation,* it must be *mediate;* it must imply some way of sensing within artistic activity itself just how feeling splits into images as it comes into existence, such that the act can be unified as an expressive whole. And Croce's teleology has determined already that the very making of a poem is an immediate goal, only latterly and indirectly involved with mediation in any form. Further, there is nothing in the *Breviario* to indicate that Croce has realized an act of thinking flexible enough to perform the delicate task of judgment required by conceiving of intuition as a genuine relation of opposites. The choice of "intuition" itself seems to preclude such a possibility. Thus his assertion in the fourth

lecture that critical judgment "may be reduced to the following
very brief proposition . . . 'There is a work of art a'—or its corresponding negative—'There is not a work of art a' " (*GA*, 74) suggests
a logic of distinction as rigid as that which cripples the argument of
"Ciò che è vivo." For the judgment of relation is thus after the
fact, needing

> first of all, as every judgment, a subject (the intution of the
> work of art a), to arrive at which requires the effort of exegesis
> and creative reproduction, together with the discriminating
> power of taste. . . . In addition, it implies, as every judgment
> does, a predicate, a category, and in this instance the category
> of art, which must be embodied in the judgment, thereby
> becoming the concept of art. [*GA*, 74]

The passage does indeed represent a genuine advance over his earlier
notion that the critic effectively makes another poem about the
poem. But the emphasis is still on a situation such as this: first there
is the intuition of the work of art, and then, with this subject now
a given, there is the act of judgment which relates subject and
predicate.

Croce's sensitivity as a practicing literary critic quite rightly forces
him to resist any pressure from his own argument to include such
a ponderous and mechanical act within the deft lightness of intuition. Later, in fact, when he decides that Dante engages in such
judgments in the *Commedia,* Croce simply dismisses them as "non-
poetic" aspects of the poem. As a result, however, Croce has no way
of conceiving what could mediate between "feeling" and "image" as
long as they are thought of as real opposites. Nor does he have any
way of distinguishing intuition as a relation, a synthesis, from that
lyric feeling which is the thesis of his incipient dialectic. Thus as the
definition of intuition as an a priori synthesis continues, it begins
to sound less and less like a genuine synthesis and more like yet
another assertion of immediate identity:

> It is immaterial, therefore, or it is a matter of mere terminologi-
> cal convenience, to describe art as content or form, provided
> that it is always understood that content is given form and
> form is given content, that feeling is a feeling which is formed

[into "image," although at another point in the *Breviario,* so
convoluted does Croce's discussion become, the terms of this
formulation are reversed] , and form is a form which is felt.
[*GA,* 31]

Without opposition of some kind, synthesis is impossible. Croce may
insist that intuition is both simple and complex, whole and multiple,
a kind of knowing and a kind of making, but one is left with no
real sense of how these qualities are to be integrated, or if in fact
they aren't conceived as pretty much the same to begin with.

III

If one is sympathetic to Croce, and to the necessity for maintaining a conception of poetic autonomy, it must seem as though I have
been overly ingenious in emphasizing those elements in his work
which could lead in the direction I want to go at the expense of the
coherence which would obtain from adhering more closely to
Croce's stated objectives. Conversely, a willingness to forgo any
concept of poetic autonomy leads to the conclusion that a thought
as muddled as Croce's should be put resolutely behind us. My
defense is that Croce's own thinking is better than the critics on
both sides. His consistency inheres in his refusal to let go of either
aspect of a most difficult paradox: each individual poem is autonomous, and the critic is responsible for bringing the poem into the
terms of his own discourse. On the one hand, Croce is convinced
that poetic autonomy is a necessary concept, that poetry is not
merely a heightened version of history or philosophy. On the other
hand, poems are made by humans and can be humanly understood
within the norms of history. In the formula stated in the *Breviario:*
"The critic is not *artifex additus artifici* but *philosophus additus
artifici.* His task is not realized until the image acquired is preserved
and transcended at the same time" (*GA,* 73). The critic does not
approach a poem as a temple of the gods, and he is capable of
articulating his experience of a poem within his critical judgment.

I have suggested that one can begin to resolve the paradox only
by realizing an equivocation in Croce's conception of poetic autonomy, his confusion of a concept of intuition with an individually
existent poem. Croce's theory in the *Breviario* lets him conceive of

individual poems, individual acts of judgment, and individual praxis and imagine a "circle" which includes as levels or stages the form of each of these activities. But it does not allow him to conceive his own present act of thinking which leaps the gap between individual poem and circle by predicating a concept of intuition to each poem. Such judgment is already objectified as one stage in the circle. Or alternatively, it is projected as a kind of given, an "actus purus" or "synthesis of syntheses" that is of course indistinguishable from the image of the circle itself. Philosophically the problem returns to Croce's failure in "Ciò che è vivo" and even in the *Logica* to understand dialectic as more than a synthesis of contradictories. As long as one thinks of thesis and antithesis as contradictory, they remain distinct from one's present act of thinking about them. They are the object of thought. Dialectical opposition, on the other hand, involves the development of thinking only within the oppositions being thought about. It is, again, the difference between visualizing *a* and not-*a* as contradictory and understanding that one's thinking develops by negating itself, by realizing itself in its own opposite.

In contrast to Croce, almost from the beginning of his "actual idealism" in the lectures collected as *La Riforma della dialettica hegeliana* of 1913 and the *Teoria generale dello spirito come atto puro* of 1916, Giovanni Gentile had concentrated on the "pure act" as the only genuinely real concept. Gentile learned much from "Ciò che è vivo." But where Croce had attempted to incorporate Hegel's dialectic of opposites into a nexus of distincts, Gentile went directly to the heart of the problem Croce had discerned: Hegel's failure to demonstrate a genuine difference between Being and Not-Being. Hegel had claimed his system to be an "objective idealism," and thus he argued that while one could recognize a difference between Being and Not-Being as a matter of felt, subjective opinion, subjectivity was to be excluded from this most elemental stage of the dialectic. Yet, "objectively," what possible difference could exist between Being as pure indeterminacy and Not-Being as the absence of determinate content? The attempt to introduce Becoming as an active synthesis of Being and Not-Being can result only in a form of ambivalence, with Becoming as the principle of activity opposed either to Being or to Not-Being indiscriminately.

Gentile's "reform" of the dialectic "begins" from the act of think-

ing as a mediate synthesis rather than beginning from the concept
of Being as Hegel had attempted. For Gentile, this act of thinking,
pensiero pensante as the dialectical identification of thought and
action, is the only fully concrete concept. The subject as mediate
self, as the act of thinking, knows itself as the immediate subject
in the act of becoming its opposite, a not-self. As a criticism of
Hegel, Gentile insisted that his "reform" could be understood
initially on experiential grounds. For however one describes the
concepts of Being and Not-Being, "all these words mean nothing so
long as the concepts are accepted as existing independently, and we
are not told who equates the opposites and who identifies them in
the synthesis. So long as the drama which is described does not find
the actors or the protagonists to make it real in their performance, it
has no meaning" (*PA,* 123). It was not for nothing that Gentile
had studied Marx seriously as a philosopher concerned with realizing
Hegel's dialectical logic within the real activity of individuals.

Although Gentile almost always spoke of his theory as a dialectic
of the "subject," it is only in a special sense which suggests the
inadequacy of dualistic teminologies such as "subject" and "object"
for dialectical thinking. He had no intention of suspending the concepts of Being and Not-Being, along with Hegel's entire elaborate
sequence of categories, from a Cartesian cogito which reasons
from the fact of its immediately given nature to the existence of an
"objective" world. Unlike French thought, which even now must
exert all the violence of its language against such Cartesianism,
Gentile's philosophical predecessor was Vico, not Descartes. Pensiero
pensante is the reciprocal relation between subject and object in
the act of becoming. Thus it is as much "object" as "subject," or
more exactly, it is the act wherein the actors are ceaselessly becoming their identities. The subject "is" a subject only to the extent
that it is also an object, and the object "is" an object only to the
extent that it is also a subject. Alternatively, in terms more familiar
from Marxist thought, the mediate subject is so completely the
producer of history that one recognizes his immediate self only
in relation to what is not this self, to the product of that history.
Anything conceived immediately, as "in itself," represents an
abstraction from the relationality of pensiero pensante. Thus the
"subject" to which Gentile attributes so much is the negation of

immediate subjectivity and the negation of presupposed objectivity. The immediate subject exists only insofar as it objectifies its Being as its Not-Being. Unlike Hegel, who equated even this form of objectification with alienation, Gentile's theory insists that any "subject" is abstract which does not undergo such development. At least in this important sense, Gentile's dialectic of the "subject" represents a more "objective" idealism than Hegel's.

The public debate between Croce and Gentile concentrated on the differences in their way of thinking, on Croce's nexus of distincts in contrast to Gentile's dialectic. Yet, clearly, the argument had a number of implications for aesthetics which Croce himself was the first to realize fully in several of the essays collected with the *Breviario* in *Nuovi saggi di estetica.* The importance of these essays can be inferred from that fact that Croce was engaged simultaneously as a practicing critic with some of the greatest poets in our literature: Ariosto, Shakespeare, Goethe, Corneille, and Dante. Although he was never one to be satisfied with a purely theoretical discussion of literature, it may be supposed nevertheless that the temerity to embark upon such projects arose from a newly earned serenity and confidence that the theory he was developing could be put to severe tests. In more ways than one, the period from 1913 to 1921, when his study of Dante was published, proved to be perhaps the most vital and exuberantly creative of his long career, despite the difficulties he faced in advocating Italian neutrality during World War I. His friendly opposition to Gentile's "actual idealism" resulted in a number of sharp exchanges. But it also shaped an entirely new direction in Italian intellectual life, and it afforded him an opportunity to make his affirmations as precisely and clearly as possible without engendering the animosity which would later develop from the division between fascist and antifascist, from Croce's political exile and his grimly necessary determination to make himself a party of one. The tragedy is that Italy's political situation developed more rapidly than either could foresee, eventually forcing Gentile on the one hand into the most grotesque perversions of his own thinking to justify an initial allegiance to Mussolini, and Croce on the other to resist fascism at the expense of embedding himself that much deeper in the forms of thought he was on the verge of transcending at this point in his career.

"Precision" and "clarity," however, are not the characteristics one finds attributed to the three crucial essays in *Nuovi saggi di estetica:* "Il Carattere di totalità dell'espressione artistica" and "La Riforma della storia artistica e letteraria," first published in 1917, and "L'Arte come creazione e la creazione come fare" in 1918. In his *Neo-Idealistic Aesthetics,* Brown summarizes Croce's tactics in the following way:

> Croce writes always with an immediate audience in mind and he has a number of polemical points which he wishes to keep in the foreground. Even though thinking much like an actualist, Croce will arrange his thoughts so that he appears to be opposing actualism; and, although he is making a drastic change in his aesthetics, he is committed to the position that he is doing no more than deepening his own thought. Unless one discounts his journalistic tactics, his thought will inevitably appear contradictory and full of arguments proving nothing. [*NIA,* 124; "actualism," of course, names the philosophy of Gentile and his followers]

More directly, even a very sympathetic critic such as Gian N. G. Orsini finds "Il Carattere di totalità" to be constructed around a manifest contradiction: "We seem to have reached an impasse: for Croce, art now is something like judgment, and yet it still is not judgment" (*BC,* 214).

To his own satisfaction, Croce could keep aesthetic activity free from judgment as long as he conceived of art as directed at knowledge of the individual, and even with the vague kind of universality attributed to art in the *Breviario.* But as Orsini rightly points out, once he acknowledges "a character of totality" to artistic expression, Croce must implicate that activity in the nexus of problems previously relegated to historical thought. For by "universality" or "totality" Croce does not imply either an empirical conception of an infinite number of elements or a transcendent and static norm, outside of history. The former fails to include the act of thinking which posits such an infinite field, and the latter cannot comprehend the way in which a "transcendent" norm becomes actual only within the historically determinant moment. Thus, when he had attempted to define the relation between "individual" and "universal" in the

Filosofia della pratica, Croce had concluded that the individual is not one finite, limited self in contact with other limited selves but rather "the historical situation of the universal at every moment of time" (quoted in *BC,* 211). That is, the individual is also universal to the extent that he is self-limiting; the particularity of the individual exists only in relation to the whole of which he is aware. Properly, there are three terms involved rather than two. The individual is the synthesis of particularity and universality. Yet, clearly, the activity which relates these terms is conceived as a form of historical judgment and thus excluded from artistic activity prior to "Il Carattere di totalità." And as I have suggested, there remains something very mechancial and abstract about Croce's conception of judgment in the *Breviario* as that which joins representation and concept, particular and universal. If he is to realize the crucial insight in "Il Carattere di totalità" that artistic expression involves "the difficult passage from immediate feeling to its mediation and resolution in art" ("CT," 122), then he must develop a form of judgment which can provide the necessary dynamic for this passage and avoid being the mechanical linkage of two essentially different elements.

Similar to the argument in the *Breviario,* the poem is said to begin in an immediate feeling, an *aspirazione,* a longing. But where in the *Breviario* there was no good reason why this artistic feeling wouldn't be like any other feeling except that by definition it was inclusive rather than exclusive, Croce now wants to recognize another element of the artist's activity. It is what he calls "the love of cosmic harmony" or the "character of totality" that turns this immediate feeling with which the poem begins into a kind of problem, a source of dissatisfaction as well as satisfaction. Thus, throughout his expressive act, the poet is asking himself what his entire cosmos, all the images he is in the act of creating, would be like if they were dominated and unified by his immediate feeling: "Expression and language are not merely manifestations or reflections of feeling . . . or even the remaking of feeling by means of a concept, which is a false idealization. Rather, expression is the posing and the resolution of a problem, a question which pure feeling in its immediate life neither resolves nor even asks" ("ACF," 150).

As caught up in artistic activity, this drive toward "harmony" is also a feeling; it involves no concept or predicate affixed ex post facto to the immediacy of intuition. Yet it is at the same time a judgment, what Croce calls an "auroral" form of knowing, for it operates as a "self-correction," a "self-limitation" ("CT," 128). It is the artist's way of criticizing himself, or refusing to exclude other feelings and actions from the immediate and dominant feeling of his creation. Most importantly, as a mediate development and resolution, the expressive act now possesses for Croce the internal dynamic so lacking in the argument of the *Breviario*. The artist is driven to judge his labor, not because it has been completed and the logic of Croce's "circle" requires him to take the next step, but because a kind of dissatisfaction is intrinsic to the creative act itself. The "love of cosmic harmony" moves the artist to a continual questioning at every step of the way, a "difficult passage" toward the resolution and integration of immediate feeling with the multiplicity of images in the poem.

Brown has argued that "if one were not opposed to actualism" as Croce claims to be, then this theory of art as cosmic could be described as very similar to Gentile's dialectic:

> The immediate feeling with which the poem begins is the thesis; it is the immediate subject. Its antithesis is the whole multiple world of the poem, all the feelings and images which the ruling feeling is in the process of dominating. The synthesis, the mediate subject, the *pensiero pensante,* is the sense of cosmic harmony, aesthetic coherence itself; it is that awareness by means of which one determines at every point of the dialectic whether the objective moment is adequate to the immediate subject, is its identical opposite, is dominating the multiplicity of the object as the unifying feeling. [*NIA*, 134]

However, Brown's translation of Croce's theory into actualistic terms obscures a genuine disagreement. For, in theory, Gentile could understand the difference between poem and criticism to emerge from the recognition of how an individual poem is dominated and unified by the moment of immediacy. Because one simply does not possess the clarity of distinction offered by Croce's concept of the "circle," it would be necessary to determine in each individual act whether it is thus poetic or whether it is dominated by the mediate moment, by the act of thinking. The mere presence of conceptual language or historical judgment would not be sufficient to make the distinction.

Yet, at this point in his thinking, Gentile in fact tended to reduce every action to an almost formulaic reenactment of his pensiero pensante. Thus, in a passage Brown quotes from the *Sommario di pedagogia,* Gentile argues that "the book which is read is not . . . the book of the first author, but the *book of the reader.* In other words, every book can be said to have as many authors as it has readers" (quoted in *NIA,* 155). Brown senses that such an argument "rests too heavily upon the act of comprehension and slights the act of assertion" (*NIA,* 156), that, like Hegel, Gentile reduces art too quickly to a form of philosophy. But on the basis of his understanding in "Il Carattere di totalità," Croce could point to the passage as an indication of Gentile's failure to realize that if in truth poetry as distinguished from criticism is unified by immediate feeling, then an act of poetic thinking is simply not the same as an act of critical thinking. It may well be a form of judgment and hence a relation, a mediation. But it will not operate judgmentally in the way judgment develops in the critical act. Dante's *Commedia* is not immediately identical with how one reads the *Commedia.*

This seems to me the import of a crucial argument at the beginning of "Il Carattere di totalità:"

> In sum, with the theory of art as judgment one does indeed avoid the faults of immobility and transcendence, but not that other fault of an oversimplified understanding of what constitutes knowledge [*del semplicismo gnoseologico*] which in this case takes the form of an excessive logicism, perhaps even reinventing a new and more or less latent form of transcendence. But regardless, it certainly denies to art its unique nature. ["CT," 120]

Gentile is not named, but it seems obvious that it is his work to which Croce refers. And indeed, what better way of describing the tendency found even in the argument Brown quotes from that much later book, the *Sommario,* than as a "latent form of transcendence" which exalts the abstract concept of pensiero pensante at the expense of the actors who "make it real in their performance?"

Croce's early insight is borne out as well by H. S. Harris's sympathetic study of Gentile. For Harris finds not only a personal or temperamental but also a philosophical problem in Gentile's massive *Sistema di logica* to be precisely the "doctrine of the 'eternal solitude of the Spirit'" (*GG,* 255), where the word "solitude" measures the distance from that very experiential ground Gentile had claimed for his "reform" of the Hegelian dialectic. Croce was already sensitive to such a tendency in Gentile's work, and I think his awareness can explain why, to Orsini, the theory elaborated in "Il Carattere di totalità" seems to offer art as simultaneously judgment and not-judgment.

It is, in fact, only if one grants a certain clarity and precision to Croce's argument in *Nuovi saggi di estetica* that a more fundamental question can be raised, and perhaps only at this point, arguably the furthest development in Croce's theory of literature. For the problem has to do with the conceptual limitation of idealism in any form when, by its own internal dialectic, the world of Becoming is identified with a vision of human thought illuminating every recess of its density. The classic example is Hegel's concept of the Absolute Idea, that secure philosophical vantage point from which one contemplates the whole of history. The deeper flaw in Gentile's *Sistema di logica* participates in this same "transcendence," as does the argument in the *Sommario* where Gentile identifies pensiero pensante with, in effect, a completed action, a present thinking which finds itself perfectly mirrored in its own past. The development of Croce's thinking in *Nuovi saggi di estetica* is perhaps less radical but equally suspect. For the way he continues to think of poetic autonomy—as indeed the very term "cosmic harmony"—betrays just such a bias toward the contemplative, toward the serenely beneficent gaze possible now only to aesthetic activity as Croce understands it, and which in fact names for him the essential quality of Ariosto's great poem. It is a vision where even the coruscating fire of irony burns like the stars in a sympathetic heaven, as in this most memorable passage Brown quotes from the essay on Ariosto:

> one may call Ariosto's irony similar to the eye of God who observes the movement of creation, of all creation, loving

everything equally, both good and evil, greatness and small-
ness, loving creation both in man and in a grain of sand, because
he has made all, and taking in nothing but the harmony itself,
the eternal dialectic, the rhythm and the harmony. [*ASC*,
46–47; quoted in *NIA*, 141]

It should be said immediately that Croce's form of aesthetic contemplation as epitomized here has little in common with what
Georg Lukács in *History and Class Consciousness* diagnoses as
the structural inability of bourgeois thought to free itself from
the reified spectacle of the thing-in-itself. There is nothing menacing or threatening, no dark interiors, in Croce's poetic cosmos; it
reflects the smile of a nature who returns, not to a "thing-in-itself,"
but to what he has made into art as a source of replenishment and
strength, as one dreams in order to make wakefulness again possible.
Yet it is necessary to recognize as well the corresponding failure
to accommodate the possibility of a poetic action which exposes
its own development at every point to the uncertain stress of choice
and conflict, to even those matters of technique, of argument,
of conceptualization which Croce continues to find extra-aesthetic,
whose inclusion would mean for him the collapse of poetic autonomy
into a fully social and historical context. Thus the autonomy, the
distinctiveness of poetic activity as Croce conceives it, comes at
the expense of making the "self-correcting" judgment implicit in
the poet's sense of "cosmic harmony" so delicate an affair that it
must be defended continually against any encroachment that would
cloud its contemplative gaze. Poetry, as Wallace Stevens said, may
well be "a finikin thing of air," but surely it is not so fragile as
Croce would have us believe.

While his estrangement from Croce had long been realized as
irrevocable, Gentile's *La Filosofia dell'arte* should be understood
in direct relation to *Nuovi saggi di estetica.* For it is not only the
rectification of the problem in Gentile's own work which Croce
had discerned much earlier but also a way of releasing the concept
of poetic autonomy from the last vestiges of contemplative removal
still retained in Croce's thought. With his newly insistent argument
for the social character of *pensiero pensante*, Gentile's understanding
of literature has nothing contemplative about it. That bias toward

the visual (I am anticipating briefly my discussion in chapter 6)—still embedded in such terms as "point of view," "approach," "distance/ proximity," Lukács's "perspective," even J. -P. Sartre's way of evoking class consciousness as a force in art—corresponds in Gentile's thinking to genuine artistic activity as alienated labor to free labor in *Capital*. Thus, rather than the result of marking out an exclusively aesthetic province, poetic autonomy becomes, as it should, both interpretive of aesthetic experience and a constitutive measure of artistic freedom from and antagonism to the demands of commodity structure. I am not suggesting that there is no way of distinguishing a poem from any other human action, only that poetic autonomy as I understand it is creative of such distinctions and not the other way around.

3

Criticism and Method:
Hirsch, Frye, Barthes, Derrida

I

A traditional conception of methodology as a means of organizing the content of experience into meaningful patterns implies that such organization is at once provisional and heuristic. It is heuristic to the extent that it enables one to anticipate how a new content may be systematically interpreted without at the same time pre-determining the patterns of intelligibility which will emerge. And it is provisional insofar as the method always could be modified by evidence arising from an outside source. Even Husserl, who granted enormous privilege to the "phenomenological method," was quite explicit that it required a "ground" independent of the elaboration of phenomenological analysis itself. Thus the very idea of method implied a certain openness to change, but at the expense of positing an existent realm—of the "irrational," of pure "matter" or pure "experience," or perhaps most explicitly, of the "thing-in-itself"— forever just beyond the limits of methodology. In literary criticism, it is perhaps the idea of "approaches" to literature which most fully embodies this dilemma involved in the construction of a methodology. The very word "approach," on the one hand, has come to imply at least a minimum organization, a tentative and schematic way of accounting for both a range of data and for one's own descriptive procedures. On the other, of course, it is always an approach to *something else* and thus always partial and always subject to correction by the fullness of the object or the experience being described.

There are at least two ways critical theory has attempted to go beyond the dilemma inherent in the idea of an "approach" to literature. What I am calling "criticism" in the title to this chapter means any act which frees the poem from its status as merely an object of thought to be "approached," defined, explained, and interpreted. Thus I suggested in chapter 1 that the first move is to imagine a dialectical criticism which resolves the antinomy of "approach" and "object" by allowing a poem the power to "approach" the critic in return. In chapter 2, I argued further that at the point when one becomes truly conscious of his own act of thinking, the critical act itself assumes a kind of dialectical reciprocity. The crucial idea here is hardly new; it involves a critique very similar to the one Hegel directed at Kant, and which Marx directed at Hegel himself, where a static and contemplative relation to the object of thought dissolves into the movement of dialectic.

However, the most difficult quality of dialectical thinking, and hence of criticism which purports to be dialectical, is its lack of finality. This means that, in one sense at least, with every new work of literature the critic is obligated to begin all over again. Indeed, Merleau-Ponty, for example, was so sensitive to this inconclusiveness that in *The Visible and the Invisible* he rejected any possible thematization of experience, presumably even the kind I offered in my first chapter, describing poetry as itself a dialectical act of being, nonbeing, and becoming. Certainly he was right to the extent that one thereby risks inventing a formula through which every poem is marched. Dialectical criticism simply cannot be "applied" to poems. My own feeling, however, is that Merleau-Ponty's extreme position commits dialectical thinking to what is perhaps another and more insidious version of the very problem he would escape. Even the refusal of formula and of thematization cannot be accomplished once and for all, nor is it possible to imagine the sense in which one "begins all over again" with each new work as a fell swoop which clears away the debris of accumulated experience. It means rather that one is obligated to think through his experience, his formulas, and his biases each time, in the knowledge that what worked once may never work again. Thus the move from theory to practice is the re-creation of a theory of poetry within the norms of understanding dictated by an individual poem, with the result that theory is born again in a form impossible to determine in advance. Theory commits one to an idea of poetry but not to the means of reading individual poems; it is a source of belief, but one which must be challenged with each new poem.

I think I am justified in calling the second alternative "method," for it concentrates on the possibility of freeing methodology itself from a "ground" in an independent object. Nevertheless, this is "method" in a special sense. For the goal is the organization of other methods rather than "raw data" of any sort, and the promise is that methodology can thereby assume the status of a self-regulatory and self-contained system. Thus one doesn't do away with the notion of "data," as my dialectical conception of criticism implies, but rather suspends its efficacy, allows its existence only as already caught up within a kind of first-order interpretive operation which becomes, in turn, the material for the second-order operation that is the proper function of method. Where a traditional conception of methodology posits at its limit a realm of "experience" or "raw material" and where a dialectical criticism is violated by each new poem being considered, this conception would enable a methodology capable of preserving its procedures intact.

As a result of attempts to elaborate such "meta-method," the dominant focus of attention in critical theory for the last twenty years at least has been the interpretation of interpretation, the means of finding a "ground" for one's interpretive effort within the activity of interpretation itself rather than in "the nature of literature." The necessity for defining an idea such as poetic autonomy, which occupied my argument in the last chapter, is thereby simply sidestepped as a "philosophical question" having little to do with the real problems of method. Such avoidance makes it somewhat less than surprising that the common feature among the new methodologies is an initial division of some sort which frees the critic from any consideration of this and other questions.

At the very beginning of *Validity in Interpretation,* E. D. Hirsch distinguishes meaning from significance, and the subsequent argument depends absolutely on the intransigence with which that division is conceived. Even the sense in which the division itself has significance—else why bother?—is for Hirsch tangential. His goal is a logic of validation designed to adjudicate objectively among various constructions of textual meaning. Such logic is not "mere" method; its task is to determine which "guess" or "pseudomethod" has produced the most probably correct results. Northrop Frye at the beginning of *Anatomy of Criticism* argues that criticism must choose as a goal the knowledge of literature as something wholly distinct from value judgments about individual works, and only knowledge based on a conception of a total form of literature can be certain. Thus his contempt for "taking a stand": "One's definite position is one's weakness, the source of one's liability to error and prejudice, and to gain adherents to a definite position is only to multiply one's weakness like an infection" (*AC*, 19).* *Anatomy* is not to be construed as merely one more method, one more "position" which, heaven forbid, invites error. Rather, it is to be the means whereby all particular methods may be integrated. Roland Barthes, likewise, has nothing but contempt for the "academic" historical method as being the product of a vested interest in a particular social structure. Linguistics, on the other hand, offers the possibility for a "general form" of discourse and a "criticism of criticisms" (*CE*, 275) based on the distinction between the "system" of a text and its "message."

But any method grounded in a basic distinction has involved always a paradox, and one that is especially crucial for methodologies such as these which claim to be self-regulatory, independent both from "experience" and from philosophy. The classic way to pose the problem asks by what means the "fundamental" distinction is effected and who institutes the means; what is the origin of the distinction? This predisposes the answer toward a philosophy of reflection and toward a formulation such as Kant's antinomy:

> *Thesis:* The judgment of taste is not based upon concepts; for otherwise it would admit of a dispute (would be determinable by proofs).

> *Antithesis:* The judgment of taste is based upon concepts; for otherwise, in spite of its diversity, we could not quarrel about it (we could not claim for our judgment the necessary assent of others).

The resolution reveals the means by which the judgment of taste can be distinguished from other forms of thought, and ultimately the

*See below, pp. 240–41, for a list of the works cited in this chapter and the abbreviations I have employed.

procedure comes to rest—and here Husserl joins Kant—in the unity
of the subject as the substantial origin of all distinction.

As I have implicitly suggested, Italian criticism in the early part
of the twentieth century developed the first integral theory and
practice to challenge the assumptions in reflective thought. For the
very way in which the question is asked—What is the origin of
distinction?—itself presupposes a distinction which then cannot be
explained. It is impossible for a reflective philosphy to account
for its most elemental relation, between the self-identity of a necessary subject, a thinking substance, and the multiplicity and contingency of what is being thought about. Croce's response, as he
progressed from the "nexus of distincts" in his earlier work to the
theory of "cosmic harmony" in *Nuovi saggi di estetica,* was to
realize that any thinking through of a methodological distinction
must involve its own activity in the resolution. Thus the relation
between unity and multiplicity, necessity and contingency, includes
and goes beyond any distinction. Gentile took the next step, arguing
for an actual rather than a substantial origin, for a dialectically
unifying act of thinking which develops only through its critical
alterity to itself. The idea of an actual origin was the basis for my
conception of poetic autonomy in chapter 2. For Gentile, the only
necessity is in this act of thinking, not an imaginary thinking substance or an imaginary object already there to be thought about.
Thought is contingency in the act of becoming necessary by
recognizing its own limitations. But because its origin is actual
rather than substantial, this movement never can be stilled; thought
never attains the security of taking full possession of its impassioned
inner development by a reflective process of objectification. Necessity inheres in the very insecurity of the act of becoming rather
than always being deferred in the illusory fullness and security of
a *telos* lying just beyond the horizon of thought.

While Croce's aesthetics, at least, has been valuable to the theoretical elaboration of the New Criticism by Eliseo Vivas and Murray
Krieger, the forms of contemporary criticism with which I am concerned here have developed a quite different criticism of reflective
philosophy and a quite different resolution than that represented
by Croce and Gentile. The criticism is directed at the arbitrariness
of a substantial subject as the source of distinction. Why not a

further subject which reflects on the first subject, so that we may truly have knowledge of it, and then still a further subject which reflects on the first two—a *partes extra partes* series ad infinitum? The resolution is to stay within the confines of reflective thought by beginning with a radical separation between what is necessary and what is contingent, but to do so by substituting a conception of a virtual for a substantial origin. I am going to argue that this is the operative force in the work of Hirsch, Frye, and Barthes and that it is the means by which they hope to institute a methodological formalism that can be self-regulatory. It is a resolution at once clarified and contested from within by the work of Jacques Derrida, but in a way which fails to realize a genuine alternative.

I take my definition of "virtual" from another discipline, but one in which its meaning has been recognized most explicitly, in Lévi-Strauss's *The Raw and the Cooked:*

> But unlike philosophical reflection, which claims to go back to its own source ["directly" is understood in the French text], the reflections we are dealing with here concern rays whose only source is hypothetical [*virtuel* is the French word at this point, and I have preserved a literal translation]. Divergence of sequences and themes is a fundamental characteristic of mythological thought, which manifests itself as an irradiation; by measuring the directions and angles of the rays, we are led to postulate their common origin, as an ideal point on which those deflected by the structure of the myth would have converged had they not started, precisely, from some other point and remained parallel throughout their entire course. [*RC,* 5-6]

This "ideal point" leads to a structure elaborated by the observer, intended to approximate as closely as possible the movement of the mythic material but at a necessary remove from it, a virtual distance. A little further on, Lévi-Strauss explains why this must be so and how he has responded to it:

> As the myths themselves are based on secondary codes (the primary codes being those that provide the substance of language [*ceux en quoi consiste le langage*]), the present work is put forward as a tentative draft of a tertiary code, which is intended

to ensure the reciprocal translatability of several myths. This is
why it would not be wrong to consider this book itself as a
myth: it is, as it were, the myth of mythology. [*RC*, 12]

A claim for a "real," substantial origin would be an arbitrary imposition by the observer on the material of myth. On the other hand,
a methodology which could trace the relationships among the forms
of myth by assuming a mythic shape itself would be far more important, even though it could claim only a methodological and not a
truth value. Almost at the end of the book, the initial break with
the conception of a substantial origin is emphatically affirmed:

> And if it is now asked to what final meaning these mutually
> significative means are referring—since in the last resort and in
> their totality they must refer to something—the only reply to
> emerge from this study is that myths signify the mind [*l'esprit*]
> that evolves them by making use of the world of which it is itself
> a part. [*RC*, 341]

Myth signifies the making of myth, and to halt the process at any
one point, at the subject or at the world, claiming it as an origin,
would be nothing more than an arbitrary imposition.

The advantage of a virtual origin for a methodology of literary
criticism is that it can appear to sanction a founding distinction—
and the impersonal objectivity of knowledge which can follow from
that distinction—by avoiding the need to explain the "real" relation
between a necessary and self-identical subject and a contingent,
multiple world. There is no longer any "real" subject, any author, or
any critic. However, my argument is that while this new sense of
method thereby escapes the dilemma imposed by an older conception, the disjunction between the method and its "content," in
fact an essential division is displaced into the mechanisms of the
method itself which a hypothesis of a virtual origin merely defers
rather than resolves. This displacement can be understood best by
imagining a sequence which I find reveals with increasing clarity
the presuppositions and limitations of the effort: rather than a
"subject," there is in Hirsch the concept of "type" which subsumes a distinction between authorial intentionality and literary

convention; in Frye, a concept of "archetype" which conceals an attempt to conflate classificatory and dialectical thought; in Barthes, a relation between "metalanguage" and "object-language" which is resolved into a division between an inclusive "space" of *écriture* and a temporal process of exclusion; and finally, in Derrida, a critique of structural opposition, or division, itself which culminates in a hypostasis of Language as a wholly anonymous Other.

Now despite their manifold differences, the central concern in both Hirsch and Frye is to develop a concept which can provide a determinate goal for literary criticism as a progressive and systematic discipline. This goal is conceived as the point at which no further change or transformation is permitted; it is stable and self-identical. Hirsch, for example, admits a potential infinity of interpretive constructions of meaning: "There are no methods for making guesses, no rules for generating insights" (*VI*, 203). But interpretation as a discipline represents the attempt to determine a means of eliminating error by taking as its material these very interpretive constructions rather than the text itself, the relation of author to text, or the relation of text to reader. A method based on the text along dissolves into the vagaries of "semantic autonomy"; one based on the relation of author to text into the necessarily inconclusive attempts to determine with certainty the psychology of the author; and one based on the relation of text to reader into the relativism of mere taste. Hirsch's effort is to be limited to what happens after the "guesswork" of understanding: "the discipline of interpretation is founded, then, not on a methodology of construction but on a logic of validation" (*VI*, 207). Already constructed meanings are what can be known, not the way in which those meanings came into existence. Thus "meaning" is what I have defined as "virtual," resulting from an ideal goal at an absolute remove from the problematic context of originating meaning, from the attempt to understand how meaning is originated, and from the significance or value of the meaning.

Similarly, Frye has no explicit intention of decreeing one definitive method for the critic to employ: "The presence of incommunicable experience in the center of criticism will always keep criticism an art, as long as the critic recognizes that criticism comes out of it but cannot be built on it" (*AC*, 27–28). Knowledge of literature

is "built on" a "central hypothesis" which can explain its own
conceptual framework:

> Its materials, the masterpieces of literature, are not yet regarded
> as phenomena to be explained in terms of a conceptual frame-
> work *which criticism alone possesses.* They are still regarded as
> somehow constituting the framework of structure of criticism
> as well. I suggest that it is time for criticism to leap to a new
> ground from which it can discover what the organizing or con-
> taining forms of its conceptual framework are. [*AC,* 15–16;
> my italics]

This "new ground" for knowledge, like Hirsch's "meaning," is
thus virtual, existing at a remove from the substance of its effort.
Understanding literature is potentially an infinite task; what can
be known is the virtual framework that renders such understanding
intelligible and communicable.

However, an awareness of the work of Roland Barthes as the next
step in my sequence makes clear a crucial problem engendered by
these conceptions. If meaning or knowledge is virtual—if it exists at
a remove from the doubtful context of significance or value—are all
discourses on a text equivalent? How can a methodology perform
the task of judgment? Without self-contradiction, I do not think the
question can be posed this way by either Hirsch or Frye. For it is
precisely the concept of "judgment" which has been put out of play
by the initial distinctions meaning/significance and knowledge/value-
judgments to the extent that these distinctions project a notion of
"type" or "archetype" as an "identity," a point at which difference,
and hence the necessity to choose, has been eliminated.

For Barthes, as for Lévi-Strauss in *The Raw and the Cooked,* the
possibility of "really" achieving such an identity is by its very
nature impossible, implying nothing more than a return to the
arbitrariness of a substantial subject as the undifferentiated source
of distinction. While this substitution of "virtual" for "substantial"
may put at a distance any explanation of the relationship between
subject and world—between author and text and between reader
and text—it must face still the problem of explaining the relation
between necessity and contingency, self-identity and multiplicity.
The conception of a necessary and stable identity such as repre-

sented by "type" or "archetype" becomes merely a hypostasis of
the paradox and not a resolution. Thus Barthes must be content
with a "presence," an identity that is always deferred, a metalanguage which fails in the very moment of its successful determination by introducing a movement of difference into the heart of its
identity in a way that cannot be accounted for, only repeated ad
infinitum. With the ideas of "repetition" and "difference," or
"deferral" (différance), one is of course already involved with the
work of Derrida, where, as if by magic, the apparently solid and
static structure of self-validating methodologies is shaken through
and through. Yet, as I shall argue, it is at the expense of reintro-
ducing within the very system of thought that would repudiate them
a kind of "history" and a kind of "subjectivity" which dialectic
understands and which suggest the limitations of simply "stepping
aside" from the problems generated by these concepts in the way
proposed by the reduction of criticism to method.

II

The immediate problem Hirsch faces in *Validity in Intepretation*
is to define meaning in such a way as to preserve the clear implication of self-identity: "*Meaning* is that which is represented by the
text; it is what the author meant by his use of a particular sign
sequence; it is what the signs represent. *Significance,* on the other
hand, names a relationship between that meaning and a person, or
a conception, or a situation, or indeed anything imaginable" (*VI,* 8).
Yet even here meaning, too, is a relation; it is that which must be
re-presented in language, even if not necessarily the same language
each time. Meaning occurs at the juncture of "a particular sign
sequence" and an author's intention. The striking gesture which
inaugurates the actual argument of *Validity in Interpretation* is
Hirsch's attempt to neutralize this duality by conceiving meaning
within the concept of *type* as an "identity" which shares in both
terms of an opposition but never belongs wholly to either one: "It
is essential to emphasize the concept of type since it is only through
this concept that verbal meaning can be (as it is) a determinate
object of consciousness and yet transcend (as it does) the actual
contents of consciousness" (*VI,* 49). A type cannot be a purely
linguistic construct, a sign, even though it "signifies" the content

of the work. But neither can it be a kind of "mental signifier," for it is itself "chosen" by an act of consciousness. It is to be conceived as "outside" this opposition and, indeed, as the identity which "mediates" and "governs" it: "Between the enormously broad systems of types and possibilities that constitute a language, and the individual speech acts that have made it and continue to make it, there are mediating type concepts which govern particular utterances as meaningful wholes" (*VI*, 111).

Thus, as it pertains to verbal meaning, Hirsch's type stands in a critical relation to the three traditional conceptions of type: as ontological, that is, as constitutive or heuristic; as a merely formal means of classification; and as historically determined. Hirsch diverges from the German tradition of hermeneutics in Heidegger and Gadamer because of this last requirement. To admit a historical constitution would be to allow all the forms of contingency which Hirsch wishes to exclude:

> The historicity of all interpretations is an undoubted fact, because the historical givens with which an interpreter must reckon—the language and the concerns of his audience—vary from age to age. However, this by no means implies that the meaning of a text varies from age to age, or that anybody who has done whatever is required to understand that meaning, understands a different meaning from his predecessors of an earlier age. [*VI*, 137]

He also must remain outside neo-Kantian thought by denying that type is constitutive of, or a heuristic instrument pointing to, a substantial reality:

> On the other hand, the incongruity between the complete explicitness of things and the incomplete explicitness of our conceptions about them does not necessarily obtain when the thing we are concerned to know is a verbal meaning. Here full congruity [between type and meaning] is possible because meanings, being themselves types, are capable of being fully known. [*VI*, 273]

Yet the refusal of these traditional sanctions for the concept of type in no way implies something merely arbitrary, a means of classification: ". . . for purposes of classification it matters very little whether we use Roman numerals, the weeks of the year, or the phases of the moon" (*VI*, iii), but type matters so much that it cannot be resolved even into a function of *langue*. Saussure's concept is based upon the assumption that the relation between signifier and signified in the sign is always purely arbitrary, and for Hirsch the relation between author's intention and sign sequence in a type cannot be arbitrary in any way.

Having put aside these traditional senses of type, the question remains as to what means a logic of validation can employ to determine one type as more valid than another. The answer is a double one, given in a way that reveals the effaced duality of consciousness and language at the heart of the definition of type. On the one hand, meaning is said to be "an affair of consciousness" (*VI*, 37). The words are mere "physical tokens" apart from the consciousness of the author or the interpreter, and "only one interpretive problem can be answered with objectivity: 'What, in all probability, did the author mean to convey?'" (*VI*, 207). On the other hand, it is a type, in its particularity as a specific genre, "a sense of the whole," which constitutes every utterance:

> A genre conception is constitutive of speaking as well as of interpretation, and *it is by virtue of this that the genre concept sheds its arbitrary and variable character.* . . . it is obvious that not only understanding but also speaking must be governed and constituted by a sense of the whole utterance. [*VI*, 78; my italics]

The author "wills" *this* particular meaning rather than that one, but this very spoken meaning is itself constituted not by the author but by a sense of type as generic. Thus the validity of an interpreter's construction of meaning depends upon his having acted *as if* the author were a substantial subject who inaugurated *this* meaning for his text and simultaneously *as if* the language of the text formed a linguistic system to be understood independently of the author, although neither, strictly speaking, is accurate. What can be accurate is a concept of type which somehow subsumes and actualizes these two operations within itself as an "identity" of the two, existing independently of the interpreter's critical judgment. If type cannot perform this function, then the authority for determining one construction of meaning as more valid than another remains arbitrary.

Now, even granting that there is to be an absolute gap between "psychic processes" and intended meaning—in order to avoid a regression into the dubious territory of the psychology of the author—the logic of validation in any given case can never indicate exactly where that gap occurs because one of the two terms remains in principle unknowable. It is an impenetrable psyche, the subject of mere "guesswork." For Hirsch, the generic conventions of language are what can be known. But these conventions cannot originate the authorial will-to-speak-meaning—and hence meaning itself—in any particular case. Thus, far from being immediately accessible, type is in effect a no-man's-land between an unknowable psyche with its mysterious will-to-mean and mere "physical tokens," the already-spoken-meaning, arranged in patterns by various interpretive monads which approach them. What everybody sees is said to be the "same," a typal identity of the author's will-to-mean and the already-spoken-meaning, but nobody can know for sure what it is he sees, this elusive "speaking" type which conjoins them. And he can hardly be expected to know what another sees.

It is not a question of a continuum, of one type being recognized as more probable than another. The absolute necessity and non-arbitrariness of type as a general concept is immediately identical with the absolute contingency of any particular type, the arbitrariness of the interpreter who steps into no-man's-land and asserts that in *this* case the will-to-mean and the already-spoken-meaning represent *this* type. The immediate identity of necessity and contingency is the only self-identity possible in *Validity in Interpretation.* Thus there is no way to judge the validity of an interpretive conclusion; all constructions of meaning are equal.

The point of a more recent essay, "Three Dimensions of Hermeneutics," is that all discourses on the meaning of a text are in fact equivalent unless there is a prior agreement between interpreters on an ethical norm. If meaning is to be an analytical concept, then all meanings are "equally real":

> One meaning of a text can have no higher claim than another
> on the grounds that it derives from the "nature of interpreta-

tion," for all interpreted meanings are ontologically equal; they are all equally real. When we discriminate between legitimate and illegitimate meanings in "Lycidas," for example, we cannot claim merely to be describing the nature of Milton's text, for the text compliantly changes its nature from one interpreter to another. ["Three," 246–47]

If a norm is agreed upon, then there is still the possibility for an objective reconstruction of meaning within the agreed-upon principle, and Hirsch attempts to make a case for authorial meaning as the one we *should* embrace. But for Hirsch to have given up so much is to lose any way of absolutely distinguishing meaning from significance, even though he does try to formulate such a principle:

An interpreter is always playing two roles simultaneously—as speaker (or re-speaker) of meaning and as listener to meaning. Both moments are necessary, for if the text is not "spoken" (construed) it cannot be "heard," and if it is not heard, it cannot have been, for the interpreter, spoken. Meaning is what an interpreter actualizes from a text; significance is that actual speaking as heard in a chosen and variable context of the interpreter's experiential world. ["Three," 250].

This is a good statement with which to begin to conceive the relation between meaning and significance as necessary and prior to their distinction, but it will not work to enforce an absolute division on which to base a theory of "objective" intepretation. After having engaged in the activity of both speaking and listening to myself speak, can I then reflect on my utterance and logically divide it into a moment of speaking (meaning) and a moment of listening (significance) which are utterly distinct? Even if I could, then my act of reflection on the original utterance as I try to understand it would itself be both a speaking and a listening. Thus meaning never could be wholly free from the radically unstable context of significance in the way Hirsch desires, for each act that would divide meaning from significance would necessarily be compounded of both. And such a series of contingent constructions is precisely the problem which the substitution of a virtual for a

substantial origin of interpretation in *Validity in Interpretation*
was to have eliminated.

I have said that Northrop Frye shares with Hirsch a central concern for criticism as a progressive and systematic discipline and that
the concept of archetype, like type, projects an identity which is
to efface the necessity for individual judgment by providing the
possibility of a self-regulating system. Nevertheless, "archetype" is
not merely a transposition of the problem Hirsch faces to a new
level of inquiry. The etymological distinction between type and
archetype suggests the possibility, but the underlying development
of Frye's thinking results from a tension between two fundamentally
different ways of conceiving the origination of criticism, a problem
Hirsch feels he has displaced at the very beginning of his effort as
all "guesswork" (hence he can say of Frye's thought that it belongs
to "some theory about man" [*VI*, 110 n.], as if his own didn't).

Here is Frye at the end of "The Road of Excess:"

> In Blake there is no either/or dialectic where one must be either
> a detached spectator or a preoccupied actor. Hence there is no
> division, though there may be a distinction, between the creative
> power of shaping the form and the critical power of seeing the
> world it belongs to. Any division instantly makes art barbaric
> and the knowledge of it pedantic—a bound Orc and a bewildered
> Urizen, to use Blake's symbols. The vision inspires the act, and
> the act realizes the vision. This is the most thorough-going view
> of the partnership of creation and criticism in literature I know,
> but for me, though other views may seem more reasonable and
> more plausible for a time, it is in the long run the only one that
> will hold. ["RE," 174]

What Frye characterizes as an "either/or dialectic" is obviously not
dialectical at all, but the seminal operation of classificatory thought.
Classes can be made by definition mutually exclusive. This individual
animal is either a sheep or a goat; this poetic image is either apocalyptic or demonic. The critic is either a disinterested spectator or a
partisan polemicist. Implicit in the comment on Blake, on the other
hand, is at least an incipient dialectic whose implications are profoundly different from what one typically associates with Frye's
theoretical system. Criticism of Blake, such as Frye's own *Fearful*

Symmetry, hardly could be content with placing a poem of his within an exclusive class of poems. Instead, it would have to show how all the poem's rich individuality is a concrete realization of a universal form and how Blake's creating the poem is at once a making and a knowing, creation and criticism. These opposites would be identified dialectically and not immediately, as genuine opposites within the unity of a dialectical action. As Frye states, "there is no division, though there may be a distinction."

My examples, of course, are not random but are intended to reveal the unresolved conflict within the concept of archetype. As a dialectical principle, it would describe that flash of recognition which transports the critic beyond himself and into the most elemental feeling of the poem, where poet and critic see the world of the poem with the same eyes and touch its objects with the same hands. Frye knows all too well that such recognition cannot be direct and that certainly literature cnanot be taught directly. Yet even in Frye's descriptions of this moment, it is not thereby conceived as an immediacy contained within the mediate development of a dialectic. Literature "is there to serve mankind," a "power to be possessed," and the experience of such a power is incommunicable. Thus it is more like a substance, a first term or goal in a series than a moment in a full dialectical action.

Indeed, in *Anatomy* the archetype as the basis for criticism is conceived as original in the sense of a first pattern or model rather than as originative, and this is a classificatory principle. The argument of *Anatomy* proceeds by the either/or categories of "direct experience" and criticism, value judgments and knowledge, "commentary" (allegory) and criticism (archetypal), making and knowing, existential projection and intrinsic categories. Individual essays are organized in the same way, such as "Theory of Myths" with its division into apocalyptic and demonic imagery. Archetype becomes itself nothing more than a general category. "Recognition," too, assumes a different meaning. It signifies the critical realization of an identity between any particular work and the total form of literature, the most general pattern criticism can articulate for the shape of literature as a whole.

Cogent criticism of Frye's thinking as a schema of classification is not hard to find. The best examples are William Wimsatt's 1965

English Institute essay and Tzvetan Todorov's first chapter in *The Fantastic*. These are apposite because they reach a remarkably similar conclusion in radically opposed ways. For Wimsatt, Frye's archetypal patterns may indeed represent true patterns: "But in that sense they are also truistic, simplistic, and uninteresting" ("NF," 93). In order even to pretend to accuracy, they must be such prodigious abstractions from particular works that they are irrelevant. Frye then simply reimposes these abstract patterns on the text as if he had discovered the deeply originative central form which explains all the detail in the work, as if we could explain *King Lear* by saying that, like all men, Lear was born and in *x* amount of time died, the ultimate form of the seasonal cycle. The absurdity of such reasoning, Wimsatt continues, means that Frye must then decorate these clichés with his "Hallowe'en cast of characters and the mazes of their cyclic action" ("NF," 96), the result of which may be more specific but also wildly idiosyncratic, arbitrary, and in fact contradictory in places.

Todorov agrees that Frye provides an arbitrary schema, but he proposes to explain the reason for it in a different way. Frye directly opposes structuralist thought, according to Todorov, by an acceptance of this postulate: "The *structures* formed by literary phenomena *manifest* themselves at the level of those *phenomena*—i.e., those structures are directly observable" (*F*, 17). Thus while Wimsatt sees Frye as abstracting from the density of a work, Todorov suggests that Frye is operating under the delusion that those structures are not abstractions at all. In the line, "Rocks, moss, stonecrop, iron, merds," for example, we are to see the *structure* of demonic imagery rather than the *structure* of apocalyptic imagery in exactly the same way as we see "moss" rather than, say, "dew." Words and imagery exist on the same level as the structure of words and imagery.

For Todorov, the first result is that Frye must forgo the very methodological certainty he seeks to achieve: "One of the words most often encountered in *Anatomy* is surely the word 'often' and its synonyms" (*F*, 18). More seriously, if structure and phenomena exist on the same level, if there is not an "ideal" or "virtual" distance between them, one has no means of elaborating a coherent structure except by arbitrary choice, never knowing whether the object of one's choice was a genuine structure or a local image: "It might even be said that the man who classifies cannot do his job so well: his classification is arbitrary, for it does not rest on an explicit theory—it is a little like those pre-Linnean classifications of living organisms which readily constructed a category of all animals which scratch themselves . . ." (*F*, 19; Todorov's ellipsis).

As devastating as these criticisms are, neither Wimsatt nor Todorov attends to the peculiar status accorded classification in the movement of Frye's thinking. For all the grandiose pretensions to scientific detachment and to making his theoretical assumptions schematically explicit, *Anatomy* nevertheless should be read as an act of a human mind and not merely the systematic product of that mind. The problem is that *Anatomy* is composed of two incipient and contradictory actions, neither of which is fully realized. The ambiguity is here:

> In looking at a picture, we may stand close to it and analyze the details of brush work and palette knife. This corresponds roughly to the rhetorical analysis of the new critics in literature. At a little distance back, the design comes into clearer view, and we study rather the content represented: this is the best distance for realistic Dutch pictures, for example, where we are in a sense reading the picture. The further back we go, the more conscious we are of the organizing design. At a great distance from, say, a Madonna, we can see nothing but the archetype of the Madonna, a large centripetal blue mass with a contrasting point of interest at its center. In the criticism of literature, too, we often have to "stand back" from the poem to see its archetypal organization. [*AC*, 140]

Now for Wimsatt, Frye "backs up" only to abstract patterns from the specificity of the work. The process is analogous to the optical illusion of the "inductive survey" in the "Polemical Introduction" to *Anatomy*, one unfortunately still being repeated as late as *The Critical Path*. Todorov, on the other hand, would understand the procedure as an attempt to gain a perspective on what is actually there in the work, not a generalized shadow merging into all other works. One's perspective will change as he gets closer or moves further away, but the work remains the same, and what we see remains equally "in" the work.

My argument is that the passage I have quoted from *Anatomy* is itself intended to operate as an "ideal" or "virtual" mimesis of the originative recognition which generates the archetype as a dialectical principle. This originative recognition is wordless; the original (the model) mimesis is communicable. The virtual origin of criticism in the process of "backing up" is mimetically identical with an originative "passing into" the work, like a mirror image. Thus there is to be an omega point, an implicit identity of archetype as originative and archetype as original, and ultimately an identity of dialectical and classificatory thought. The nonarbitrariness of archetypal organization does not derive from an "inductive survey" with all its connotations of nineteenth-century scientism which Wimsatt and Todorov rightly expose. Rather, that "survey" itself is a second-order operation, at once at an absolute remove from the experience of literature and yet mystically at one with it. It is as if Frye would direct criticism to its actual origin, in the sense in which I used that term at the beginning of this essay, by projecting the possibility of an identity between the substantive "power" of literature and the virtual imitation of that power which is the "objective" structure of literature as a total form.

One wants to say that such a position cannot be criticized rationally; it is an article of faith, to be justified if at all by the practical consequences it may have. Yet the claims Frye makes for his criticisms are those of an autodidact, and the consummate arrogance with which he characterizes other critical positions makes some form of criticism a necessity. R. G. Collingwood has demonstrated convincingly the incompatibility of classifactory and dialectical thought; one is based on substance, the other on act. And in *Anatomy*, an effaced dialectic is no better than none at all. Here is the climactic assertion of identity in the "Theory of Symbols":

> Thus the center of the literary universe is whatever poem we happen to be reading. One step further, and the poem appears as a microcosm of all literature, an individual manifestation of the total order of words. Anagogically, then, the symbol is a monad, all symbols being united in a single infinite and eternal verbal symbol which is, as *dianoia,* the Logos, and, as *mythos,* total creative act. [*AC,* 121]

As with biological specimens, each new work becomes nothing more than an immediate manifestation of the class "Literature," and the meaning of "total creative act" is reduced to something like the truism that new frogs get born. Todorov makes a distinction Frye never quite achieves: "Now there is a qualitative difference as to the meanings of the terms 'genre' and 'specimen,' depending on whether they are applied to natural beings or to works of the mind" (*F*, 5). One can only hope that the statement I quoted at the beginning of this discussion is not the end, after all, to "The Road of Excess," for to believe it would require abandoning a classificatory methodology for good.

III

Structural thought understands its object as if that object were a deduction from language. But unlike Descartes, who undertook to deduce the existence of the physical world from the apodictic certitude invested in the Cogito, Barthes—and more radically, Derrida—would show how the primacy of a linguistic model uncovers a structure of uncertainty at the very root of meaning. One is never "outside" language, in a "privileged" position to decide, to *judge*, whether meaning is or is not initially verbal. Thus, rather than a "theory of language"—where the very syntax of the phrase describes what is to be avoided—structural thinking announces itself through a necessary complication of terminology which indicates its object only to the extent that that object comes to birth as itself an ambiguously signified and signifying system within an infinite construction of language. The advantage to such a sudden access of terminology is not, as Robert Scholes has argued, a more precise way to name the specificity of literary phenomena. For the very possibility of critical "naming" is forbidden by the insistence that the work of literature is not an existent, an immediately given object of analysis whose status in Being proves so elusive in this passage from *The Well-Wrought Urn* which I quoted in my second chapter:

> His [the poet's] task is finally to unify experience. He must return us to the unity of the experience itself as man knows it in his own experience. The poem if it be a true poem is a simula-

crum of reality—in this sense, at least, it is an "imitation"—by
being an experience rather than any mere statement about
experience or any mere abstraction from experience. [*WW*,
212-13]

Structural thought formalizes, *as a feature of language,* this endlessly
shifting "experience" and its uncertainty over which Brooks vainly
attempts to posit some prior control.

Now the importance of Saussure and linguistics for a structuralist
understanding of literature does not lie so much in the distinction
between synchrony and diachrony, although this argument has been
advanced impressively by Fredric Jameson in *The Prison-House of
Language,* or in the attempt at reintegration in Jakobson or Ben-
veniste. It lies rather in the result of one of Saussure's central insights, that language is a system of differences, a result which trans-
poses "to say" as an act of speech, of *parole,* into a differential
configuration of acoustic space, into *langue.* This is not to suggest
that words, like things, are separated *in* space; it is almost the
reverse. Any object becomes intelligible to the extent that it can be
seen within a virtual relationship of mutually implicatory differences. "We shall be concerned here with the death of myths, not
in time but in space" ("HMD," 269), runs the opening sentence of
a recent essay by Lévi-Strauss.

In the work of Merleau-Ponty, phenomenology was forced to
integrate the temporal transformations of the subject into the
development of history in a way which precluded both the distanced objectivity that reduced history to a spectacle of processive
change and the truism of neohistoricism that man is *in* time. But
what if transformation could be conceived spatially rather than
temporally or, to put it more exactly, if space could become itself
a differential structure of transformation? Then if the essence of
transformation was difference as *distance* rather than difference as
process, would it not be the case that a certain distanced objectivity
was not only possible but necessary in order to describe accurately
the object of study? The distinction between synchrony and diachrony is useful as a means to this end, this change in the very
notion of transformation itself which is the fundamental mode of
structuralist research in the work of Roland Barthes.

The concept of an identity at the center of both Hirsch's and Frye's thought avoids the need to explain the movement of transformation as such. Change, movement, contingency are measured against an ideal point of stability, a point where no further change or substitution is permitted. While Barthes, like Hirsch and Frye, projects the possibility of a "criticism of criticisms" to order the various interpretive "codes" by which a work of literature may be described, his subject is gathered from what remains implicit in their work, the movement of transformation and not the product of it. An identity as product or goal, even a potential one, is a return to substance and its categories, a regression from structuralism to a taxonomy of the kind of Todorov discerns in Frye's *Anatomy*. At the same time, Barthes need not implicate the critic in the same way Gentile must in his actualist aesthetics or Merleau-Ponty in his development of phenomenology. If transformation is a matter of difference as distance, then the critic is obliged to elaborate—to "lose" himself, to distance himself—a virtual structure which remains at a distance from its material.

The importance of difference has not always been a crucial factor in Barthes's thought. Even in an interview printed as the last essay in *Critical Essays*, Barthes is arguing that difference is the "motor" only of diachrony and not of genuine history. Paradoxically, history is synchronic, an intelligible form that can be exhaustively studied as opposed to the merely temporal process of diachronic change. Yet there has always been implicit in Barthes's work a sense that the synchronic itself is invaded by a doubleness, a "duplicity" which is not so easily characterized. In "Literature and Metalanguage" (1959) he writes: "And then, probably with the first shocks to the good conscience of the bourgeoisie, literature began to regard itself as double: at once object and scrutiny of that object, utterance and utterance of that utterance, literature object and metaliterature" (*CE*, 97). In a later essay in *Critical Essays*, Barthes elaborates the consequences of this doubleness for the critic:

> . . . simultaneously an insistent proposition of meaning and a stubbornly fugitive meaning, literature is indeed only a *language*, i.e. a system of signs; its being is not in its message but in this "system." And thereby the critic is not responsible for recon-

structing the work's message but only its system, just as the
linguist is not responsible for deciphering the sentence's meaning
but for establishing the formal structure which permits this
meaning to be transmitted. It is by acknowledging itself as no
more than a language (or more precisely, a metalanguage) that
criticism can be—paradoxically but authentically—both objective
and subjective, historical and existential, totalitarian and liberal.
[*CE*, 259-60]

Literature is only a language, but in a way that accentuates the
doubleness of language rather than projecting a more clearly manifest synchronic form. The difficulty in studying literature is not
in deciphering a *message* but in accounting for the duplicity of the
system formed by the sign sequence. Difference as distancing, as a
simultaneous tracing and effacing of meaning, has become the
"motor" not of diachrony but of a synchronic system "in motion."
The language system of a text has a content which can be perceived consecutively or diachronically, something like what Frye
posits in "Myth, Fiction, and Displacement" as the "power of
continuity" which keeps us reading until the end. However, Frye
jumps immediately to the recognition of an identity between the
particular work and the total form of literature once the critic has
"frozen" the work to examine its parts as a simultaneous presence,
a stable synchronic system. Barthes, on the other hand, argues that
the system of a particular text as a whole is itself a signifier which
has as its signified another kind of "content," an insistence that is
literature *of a particular kind.* Thus this signified becomes in its
turn another sign system which at once signifies a system of literature even as it effaces that insistence by stubbornly refusing to
be subsumed into it.
Barthes's *S/Z,* a "commentary" on Balzac's story "Sarrasine,"
shows the extent to which Barthes is willing to push his understanding of the double functioning of a language system. "Sarrasine" is a
frame story, told by a narrator in order to seduce a listener, much
as Balzac can be understood as "seducing" the reader into an acceptance of the "realistic" credibility of his story by the device of the
frame. In the story told by the narrator, the artist—Sarrasine—is
intent on consummating his desire with Zambinella, a *castrato* opera

singer whom Sarrasine through most of the story thinks a woman. When he discovers Zambinella's true identity, he attempts to destroy the statue he had made of him/her. But the story ends in catastrophe, the "message" of the statue having been the loss of a desired object, Zambinella, just as the creation of the statue has been made possible by Sarrasine's "embrace" of castration. Within the frame, narrator and listener then take leave of each other, their physical desire unconsummated except in the ambiguity of the system of the frame signifying as a message the duplicitous system of creation/ castration in the story, itself signifying as a message the system of Sarrasine's statue, in turn signifying a *lost* message, a *lost* object of desire. Through his elaboration of the five "codes" by which "Sarrasine" can be approached, Barthes would read the text of the Balzac story into the text of all literature, as he reads the transformational structure of the story into the reader, who must be "divided into two subjects, into two cultures, into two languages, *into two hearing-spaces*" (*S/Z,* 150; my italics). The loss of nuclear self becomes the necessary distance to constitute the reader's understanding of "Sarrasine."

This procedure describes perhaps the fullest sense in which a critical metalanguage is paradoxical, in the way first suggested in *Critical Essays,* as "both objective and subjective, historical and existential, totalitarian and liberal." The critic is required to demonstrate exhaustively the language system of the text, to "saturate" it as fully as possible by transforming it into the language object of his own metalanguage. He is not free to choose this incident or this "symbol" as *the* meaning. Thus his work is objective and totalitarian. Yet he also must recognize that the text is never a "simple" language object; it, too, is a system which signifies another object. In exposing this distance within the text itself, the critic invariably exposes the distance between his metalanguage and the language of the text. That is, he destroys his own metalanguage through the very act by which he elaborates it. His work can represent only a "suspended objectivity," a virtual totality which must always liberally admit other possibilities, even its own supersession. Thus, paradoxically, it is only by maintaining and recognizing a certain distance between himself and the text that he can be said to have been in any way "complete." Rather than "interiority" or a self-

contained system, "completeness" means being implicated in the
distancing of transformation. A "criticism of criticisms" henceforth
must be the "process" (my quotation marks here are to indicate
that such "process" is spatial and not temporal) of transformation
rather than an attempt at determining an immediate identity, or
even the stability of a synchronic system.

The peculiarly regressive structure entailed is clearest in this
remarkable concluding passage to *Système de la mode,* a passage
which Fredric Jameson uses in *The Prison-House of Language* to
mark his most damaging criticism of structuralism:

> It is a relation [between the "system-object" of the text and
> the metalanguage of the critic] which is at once transitory
> [*éphémère*] and necessary, because human knowledge can
> participate in the becoming of the world only through a series
> of successive metalanguages, each one of which is alienated in
> the instant that determines it. This dialectic again can be ex-
> pressed in formal terms: in speaking of the rhetorical signified in
> his own metalanguage, the analyst inaugurates (or reassumes) an
> infinite science: for should it happen for someone (another, or
> himself later on) to undertake an analysis of his writing and to
> attempt to reveal its latent content, it would be necessary for
> this someone to have recourse to a new metalanguage, which
> would in his turn expose him: a day will inevitably come when
> structural analysis will pass to the rank of a language object
> and be absorbed into a superior system that will explain it in
> turn. This infinite construction is not sophisticated: it accounts
> for the transitory and, as it were, suspended objectivity of
> research and confirms what might be called the Heraclitean
> characteristics of human knowledge, at every point when by its
> object it is condemned to fuse [*confondre*] truth and language.
> This is a necessity which structuralism precisely tries to under-
> stand, that is to say [*de parler*] : the semiologist is he who
> expresses his future death in the same terms by which he has
> named and understood the world. [*SM*, 293; partially quoted
> in *PH*, 208, in a slightly different translation]

And here is Jameson's comment on the passage: "Thus synchronic
certainty dissolves into the pathos of relativistic historicism: and

this because a theory of models cannot recognize itself for a model without undoing the very premises on which it is itself founded" (*PH*, 208). With the passage from Barthes as evidence, Jameson is able to convey with particular force the paradox I suggested in the introduction to this essay. Where a traditional concept of method or "model" is caught in the duality between its own procedures and a content which arises from "outside" the method, this new concept of methodology attempts to overcome the duality by taking as its "content" other methods. Barthes, however, has been forced to realize that such a "theory of models" merely displaces an initial duality into the mechanisms of the method itself, and a "method of methods" cannot recognize itself as such without denying the very possibility it was inaugurated to achieve.

But it is possible to be even more precise. "This infinite construction is not sophisticated"—the implications of this statement are of primary concern, for as I have suggested also, temporal difference has in fact been displaced by spatial distance in Barthes's thought, and the distinction is significant. In his paper delivered at the 1966 Johns Hopkins conference, Barthes argues that

> just as temporality, person, and diathesis define the positional field of the subject, so modern literature is trying, through various experiments, to establish a new status in writing for the agent of writing. The meaning or goal of this effort is to substitute the instance of discourse for the instance of reality (or the referent). . . . The field of the writer is nothing but writing itself, not as the pure "form" conceived by an aesthetic of art for art's sake, but, much more radically, as the only area [*espace*] for the one who writes. ["TW," 144; translator's interpolation]

A little bit later, he restates the goal of the effort:

> We are all trying, with different methods, styles, perhaps even prejudices, to get to the core of this linguistic pact [*pacte de parole*] which unites the writer and the other, so that—and this is a contradiction which will never be sufficiently pondered— each moment of discourse is both absolutely new and absolutely understood. ["TW," 144; translator's interpolation]

There is to be an identical *space* where what is new and what is understood, the writer and the other, necessity and contingency—all of which make up the infinite construction of distancing—can be understood as somehow at one. If difference is conceived temporally, the differential movement becomes a mark of exclusion, even if the exclusion is hidden in the illusive continuity of the "referent" sustained by the "realistic" novel. But if, on the other hand, difference is spatial, a transformation, a distancing, each "instance" can be inclusive rather than exclusive. The differential as distance can be part of the very idea of space; it is, in fact, the intelligibility of the idea of the "same" space. While Hirsch and Frye in their own ways could project an identity only by positing an ideal point where difference disappears, Barthes holds forth the possibility of an identity as the mutually implicatory distancing everywhere in the act of writing, a "space" of discourse that can be all-inclusive. It is this reasoning which underlies the "absolutely plural text" posited in *S/Z*.

Unlike Frye's total form which is contingent on the lack of difference, the immediate identity between any particular work and the whole of literature, Barthes's ideal text depends upon each individual text as different, existing at a distance from the others. So in the beginning of *S/Z* he can criticize any attempt to derive "a great narrative structure" that comprehends all texts because the individual text "thereby loses its difference." To insist on the differences among individual texts means to particpate in an infinite construction of the identity of all texts within an "instance" of discourse which need not posit an arbitrary and determinate goal that collapses all distance and difference.

The ambiguity in Barthes's work which allows Jameson's critique is that such a possibility does not thereby "overcome" temporality. In the passage from *Système de la mode,* the ambiguity is even in the use of a phrase such as "a day will inevitably come." An "instance" of discourse as a space, a distancing, implies a simultaneous presence of distances, and distance can be presence only through the presupposition of an unambiguous present, one uncomplicated by the presence of past or future. That is the reason "this infinite construction" *cannot* be sophisticated. To return to *S/Z*, "the division of listeners" is possible because the distance within the listener, the effect of two listeners, is everywhere *present* to constitute this distancing *presence*. Presence is difference as it elides the difference between presence and present. The very act of positing an infinite identity of transformational distance determines the closure of temporality in the present, the result of which is the "relativistic historicism" Jameson finds at the end of *Système de la mode* as each closed, present moment mechanically passes into the next closed present. Every message is a message of loss, because the inclusiveness of a spatial, transformational system signifies always the exclusiveness of the temporal moment in a movement of signification impossible to account for. In order to escape the substantialist implications of a systematic identity, Barthes objectifies the temporal moment as itself a substantial and uncomplicated identity.

Thus it is that even in Barthes there remains the impossibility of explaining a most elemental relation: how are difference as temporalization and difference as distancing conjoined? To imply a radical division between them—one exclusive, the other inclusive— is a judgment that never can be accounted for within the closure of the distinction itself. Any methodology inaugurated by a distinction which effaces the insecurity of such judgment at its center is condemned by its very nature to recapitulate the disjunctive origin ad infinitum. Barthes seems to me to know this ambiguity so well that to insist any more on the point is a redunancy. What can be insisted on is another element of risk, one which is less that of refusing any meaning *as such* than of reducing the very structure of uncertainty which haunts meaning from the beginning for Barthes. For if judgment is always deferred, the opposition between "certainty" and "uncertainty"—and their more ideologically charged variations—collapses. Unless some "certainty" of judgment remains a possibility, any critique implied through the structural necessity of "uncertainty" remains empty. What begins as a radical epistemological break between an infinite construction of terminological systems and the older conception of the work of literature as an existent reality is itself transformed by its own momentum into merely a virtual or procedural distinction. The two, as it were, become accomplices, each the *différance* of the other.

But before so precipitously entering into a kind of "deconstruction"—and into *différance* as both a spacing and a temporalizing—it is necessary to recover more precisely the nature of the critique

Derrida directs at the very concept of "structure." For if it is "successful," that is, if "deconstruction" is indeed a procedure for
unmasking binary opposition, for perpetuating "uncertainty" as
différance, then the conceptions of methodology which I have
criticized can themselves be reappropriated to perform a legitimately
self-critical function. On the other hand, we must suspect that the
critique is too powerful, that it sets in motion within the operation
of structural thought itself those very problems which structuralism
has proposed to reduce.

IV

In truth, the originality of Derrida's reading of Lévi-Strauss in
"Structure, Sign, and Play" is less in his recognition "that the
metaphysical reduction of the sign needed the opposition it was
reducing" ("SSP," 251) than in his reformulation of the terms of
an older philosophy such that the difficulties it engenders can be
understood to persist within structural thought itself. By the argument which implies that the oppositions between mind and body,
subject and object, identity and multiplicity, intelligible and sensible
are themselves versions of a single problematic expressed in the
concept of "center" or of "presence," he is able to show how the
latter concept remains implicated in the work of Lévi-Strauss even
though Lévi-Strauss has attempted explicitly to avoid being trapped
by the older dualisms:

> When Lévi-Strauss says in the preface to *The Raw and the
> Cooked* that he has "sought to transcend the opposition be-
> tween the sensible and the intelligible by placing [himself] from
> the very beginning at the level of signs," the necessity, the force,
> and the legitimacy of his act cannot make us forget that the
> concept of the sign cannot in itself surpass or bypass this oppo-
> sition between the sensible and the intelligible.

There are in fact two reasons it cannot, the first of which is described as the passage continues:

> The concept of the sign is determined by this opposition:
> through and throughout the totality of its history and by its
> system. But we cannot do without the concept of the sign, we

cannot give up this metaphysical complicity without also giving
up the critique we are directing against this complicity, without
the risk of erasing difference [altogether] in the self-identity of
a signified reducing into itself its signifier, or, what amounts to
the same thing, simply expelling it outside itself. ["SSP," 250–
51; translator's interpolations]

"Sign" has implied always the existence of an intelligible "meaning" to which the sign itself, as pure sound, refers. What is signified
in this way thus becomes a kind of "center" which determines the
coherence of language, yet precedes or follows the sign as a fundamental ground, limiting the freeplay of signification. However, if
as Saussure argued the elements of signification are constituted by
the system of differences wherein each sign is inscribed rather than
by this "presence" of a signified both inside and outside language,
then it becomes necessary to conceive of language as having no
center. For both signifier and signified are involved in difference;
there is no fullness of presence, no transcendental signified apart
from differences. This new concept of "sign" thus operates as a
powerful criticism of the opposition between sensible and intelligible. Nevertheless, it needs the opposition. For otherwise, and
without the presence of the opposition in the background, it would
seem now as if everything were being rendered as merely intelligible.
That is, one would "erase" difference by "the self-identity of a
signified reducing into itself its signifier, or, what amounts to the
same thing, simply expelling it outside itself."
   Perhaps more important, however, is the status of the critique
itself once the opposition between sensible and intelligible is understood to involve the contradictory coherence of a "center" at
once "inside" and "outside" the structure of signification. Because
it can reveal the endless play of gaps, relays, detours which make up
signification and which had been disguised by the various overlays
of metaphysical concepts, language becomes a "privileged" mode
of explanation for a structural thought such as Lévi-Strauss's. Yet if
language is not to become itself only another center, a fundamental
or ground "code" of explanation, it cannot exist simultaneously
inside and outside the systems of thought it would displace, even
though these systems are to be criticized continually by the opera-

tion of language. Thus the new concept of "sign" needs the opposition between sensible and intelligible not only in order to define its irreducible difference but also to avoid perpetuating the same contradictory condition of coherence which determines the opposition in the first place.

Sometimes Derrida is betrayed into thinking of "script," of "writing," in a way which suggests he is caught up within these paradoxes in the same way as Lévi-Strauss, as for example in this passage from *Grammatologie* which Fredric Jameson quotes to make the argument: "'Script, letter, sensible inscription have always been considered in the Western tradition as body and matter external to spirit, to breath, to the Word and to Logos. And the problem of the soul and the body is *doubtless* derived from the problem of script to which it *seems*—inversely—to lend its own metaphors'" (*PH,* 183; Jameson's italics). This does appear very much like a continuation of the history Derrida would contest, transforming the force of desire for "presence" from one center to another. De-centering the contradiction within the concept of structure operates by *re-centering* metaphysics within the "problematic" of language, where the contradiction of a self-presence in speech is revealed by re-centering language within a concept of "script." To counteract this settling in of concepts, Derrida attempts to conserve the freeplay of freeplay by inscribing it within a series of substitutions: protowriting, trace, *différance,* supplement, *pharmakon,* hymen, and so on. "There is nothing," he says about *différance,* "kerygmatic about this 'word' so long as we can perceive its reduction to a lower-case letter" ("D," 159), and the statement holds *a fortiori* for the other "words" as well. The "center" is always already invaded by a play of substitution.

On the other hand, structuralism as represented in Lévi-Strauss—and, as I have argued, in Barthes as well—moves as it were by a kind of tilt from "presence" to "absence" and back again, as "as-if" center to a noncenter and back. Recognizing through the reliance on a linguistic model that the very concept of a centered structure is contradictory, structuralism nevertheless reduces freeplay to merely "an interplay of absence and presence" ("SSP," 264). The certainty of being-in-presence is undermined by the uncertainty of absence, but only to the extent that one grants, as Lévi-Strauss, a kind of methodological value to the certainty of a virtual center or, as Barthes, a "suspended objectivity." What language offers for Derrida, on the other hand, is not the mirage of a first-order explanatory code with its symmetrical determination of the loss of a center. The freeplay of signification is at the same time the signification of an endless freeplay as that which is "older" than presence/absence, as "the joyous affirmation of the freeplay of the world and without truth, without origin. . . . *This affirmation then determines the non-center otherwise than as loss of the center*" ("SSP," 264). Freeplay must be understood as in some sense an "uncertainty" which yet "precedes" or "produces" the very possibility of certainty/uncertainty, presence/absence. Rather than symmetrical opposition, it is the means of showing how the terms of an opposition are the "same" without being an identity; it is the differance of their difference.

Now the risk engendered by Derrida's critique of "structure" is the reappearance within it of the very "metaphysical" concepts structural thought has done its best to repudiate: history and subjectivity. Although in some ways having elaborated an argument similar to Derrida's, Foucault simply refuses any such possibility in a rather amusing passage from his introduction to the English translation of *Les Mots et les choses*.[1] Derrida, however, is more rigorous, even going so far in "Differance" as to suggest that "if the word 'history' did not carry with it the theme of a final repression of differance, we could say that differences alone could be 'historical' through and through and from the start" ("D," 141). And writing on Lévi-Strauss in the essay from which I have been quoting, he acknowledges the necessity of a certain "tension" between freeplay and history: "One can therefore describe what is peculiar to the structural organization only by not taking into account, in the very moment of his description, its past conditions: by failing to pose the problem of the passage from one structure to another, by putting history into parentheses" ("SSP," 263).

This "tension" is a result of a historical demand for continuity, for understanding a new structure on the basis of how it develops out of the past, and a demand for specificity which can posit no such basis, no transcendent ground that includes both the old structure and the new. The question is whether "tension" can be an adequate indication of what is involved. For by determining everything which "comes before" the "rupture" marked by the advent of a new structural organization as of a piece in its difference from the new structure, the very description of that new structure thereby constitutes in the same act the past as past in a certain way. That is, the necessary specificity of the description constitutes history as a monolithic past over against the "tension" between historical continuity and freeplay. Without a history as a continuous whole, as "that which comes before," there could be no absolute rupture, no absolute difference. Thus the tension between history and freeplay is itself played against a background of a monolithic past, and "history" is put "into parentheses" by an act which remains historical through and through. What Derrida calls in Lévi-Strauss "an ethic of nostalgia" is more exactly a historical gaze fixated on a past which is determined by that very gaze.

Now the striking characteristic of Derrida's "freeplay" is its appearance as a new structure in just this contradictory sense. For everything which "comes before" this "rupture"—"this moment . . . in which language invaded the universal problematic"—represents for Derrida an unbroken continuity of the metaphysics of presence. And even granting Derrida's argument that presence requires freeplay as a condition for its possibility, it is necessary to add that freeplay requires a continuous *history* of presence as a condition for its possibility. This is the ultimately damaging realization which lurks within the full context of the passage in "Differance" from which I quoted earlier:

> On the other hand, these differences [which make up language] are themselves *effects*. They have not fallen from the sky ready made; they are no more inscribed in a *topos noētos* than they are prescribed in the wax of the brain. If the word "history" did not carry with it the theme of a final repression of differance, we could say that differences alone could be "historical" through and through and from the start. ["D," 141]

Two conclusions can be drawn. The first is Derrida's own, that presence always and already differs from itself. Differance is this disruption, "older" than presence. However, if it is the necessity imposed by differance which tells us that "differences alone could be 'historical' through and through," then it follows that a "history" of presence free from repression must as well differ from itself, and not merely through the substitution of one center, one fiction of presence for another. For unless what "comes before" the rupture marked by the thinking of differance is *other than* a continuous whole, unless the thinking of presence in Kant, in Hegel, and in Husserl can be made to differ radically and profoundly, differance remains an "effect" of the historical act which differs differance from the history of presence by constituting that history as a monolith, as "what comes before."

Yet if this "history"—of presence-which-differs-from-itself—also must differ from itself, it makes no sense to speak of rupture. There would be no more—and no less—difference between reading Derrida and Husserl than between reading Husserl and Kant, except through the repression which figures forth a structure of structurality: from a differential "noncenter" of freeplay, one imagines a "before" as an unbroken history of desire for presence and an "after" as the joyous affirmation of an endlessly shifting ground on which one stands to look backward without anxiety at the monolith in the distance, again, surreptitiously constituted by that very gaze. Either one imagines a "history" of absolute difference, where of necessity Husserl no more than Derrida would remain trapped by a metaphysics of presence, or one constitutes a monolithic history of desire for presence by differing differance from presence. Thus it is that in order to arrive at the genuinely original specificity of structural thought, Derrida must conceive a tension between differance and presence against the background of a continuous past, a continuous metaphysics of presence.

Once before, in his long and brilliant analysis of Husserl, Derrida had attempted to come to terms with these implications of his "deconstruction" of presence, as it is involved not only with history but with subjectivity as well. I shall presume familiarity with Derrida's critique and enter at a crucial pitch of argument:

> Even while repressing difference by assigning it to the exteriority of the signifiers, Husserl could not fail to recognize its work at the origin of sense and presence. Taking auto-affection as the exercise of the voice, auto-affection supposed that a pure differ-

> ence comes to divide self-presence. In this pure difference is
> rooted the possibility of everything we think we can exclude
> from auto-affection: space, the outside, the world, the body,
> etc. [*SP*, 82]

Husserl had conceived the act of "hearing oneself speak" as a unique
kind of "auto-affection." Like auto-affection in general, this heard
speech signifies a realm of ideality whose elements are capable of
being repeated as each time the same. Yet where every other operation of auto-affection achieved this universality only to the extent
that it "passed through" exteriority—the whole world of objects,
of space, of the body—Husserl nevertheless specified the possibility
of a pure speech, a subject which preserves full self-presence within
the unique auto-affection of the speaking voice as it excludes this
exterior multiplicity from its operation.

But Derrida continues:

> As soon as it is admitted that auto-affection is the condition for
> self-presence, no pure transcendental reduction is possible. But
> it was necessary to pass through the transcendental reduction in
> order to grasp this difference in what is closest to it—which can-
> not mean grasping it in its identity, its purity, or its origin, for
> it has none. We come closest to it in the movement of differance.
> [*SP*, 82]

What is crucial here is that *Husserl's own analysis* is made to under-
mine the identity of self-presence. It is not as if Husserl's "metaphysics of presence" exists in a simple, unsophisticated moment
of a past at once constituted by and differed from Derrida's realization of "differance." Unlike Barthes's thinking, Derrida's "construction" is indeed "sophisticated," for his "deconstruction" is
made to appear within the very movement of Husserl's argument. If
self-presence has as its condition of possibility an auto-affection that
signifies universally, through the advent of all that is exterior to the
transcendental subject, then there is no "ground" for the purity of
self-presence and no pure multiplicity which comes to break up
the self-proximity of the voice: "This movement of differance is
not something that happens to a subject; it produces a subject. Auto-
affection is not a modality of experience that characterizes a being

that would already be itself (*autos*). It produces sameness as self-relation within self-difference; it produces sameness as the non-identical" (*SP*, 82).

I do not think it necessary to pause and enforce the cogency of Derrida's argument in relation to a problem in Husserl's thinking, for the problem is not unfamiliar. It is what I have noted as the impossibility for a reflective thought to explain its most elemental relation, between the self-identity of a necessary subject and the multiplicity of what is being thought about. The originality of Derrida's reading arises from the transformation of the problem into a question of language: "The voice is the being which is present to itself in the form of universality, as con-sciousness; the voice *is* consciousness" (*SP*, 79–80). How, then, and within the terms of this transformation, is "self-relation within self-difference" conceived; in just what way does it contest the "privilege" accorded to the subject in Husserl's thought while yet refusing to assign that thought to a simple and determinate moment of the past? The answer is neither immediate nor obvious, for clearly Derrida cannot be content to impose a radically different philosophical system onto Husserl's phenomenology. He must continue, as he has to this point, in the attempt to elicit from Husserl himself the terms of a critique.

However, the difficulty of the task becomes more apparent a little further on, in the discussion of the relationship between "intention" as a meaning-to-say and "intuition" as the immediate grasp of the object signified in intention. Now for Derrida, Husserl's premises should lead to the conclusion that the very structure of signification requires that these be kept distinct. It is not necessary, for example, that one "intuit" an object of perception in order that a statement about perception be meaningful. If I say, "I see a particular person by the window" (Derrida's example), I "really" do not have to see a person, nor does a person have to be there, in order that another understand what I mean, what I intend to say. Indeed, Derrida concludes, the possibility of signification *as such* requires the possibility of an absence of intuition: "the total absence of the subject and object of a statement—the death of the writer and/or the disappearance of the objects he was able to describe— does not prevent a text from 'meaning' something. On the contrary, this possibility gives birth to meaning as such, gives it out to be heard and read" (*SP*, 93).

Yet the strain is evident to the extent that Derrida's argument has begun to assume the form of dangerously exclusive alternatives: either intention and intuition are coincident, in which case language is secondary and derivative; or they are disjunctive, and the structure of signification requires the absence of intuition. Thus as Derrida describes the relation between intention and intuition, there is a certain inevitable distortion to the extent that they have begun to function like signifier and signified. That is, rather than continuing to translate Husserl's thinking in a way sensitive to the resonances set up within his use of intention and intuition, one is made to feel the presence of a radically different conceptual system *operating upon Husserl*. Husserl's *thinking* becomes a *thought;* it recedes into a past, an object, mere error to be rectified. Likewise, what is posited as the "death" of the subject gains its force from the self-proximity of the voice being made to depend upon the exteriority of writing, and thus a fortiori the subject or "consciousness" upon its own absence, its own death. But inversely, and by the same premises, the drama in question has been reduced already. For the "death" in question is no more than *anonymity*.

Now having accepted the exteriority of the sign as anonymous, Derrida is astonished when Husserl claims that "'In solitary speech the meaning (*Bedeutung*) of 'I' is essentially realized in the immediate idea of one's own personality, which is also the meaning (*Bedeutung*) of the word in communicated speech. Each man has his own I-presentation (and with it an individual notion of I) and that is why the word's meaning (*Bedeutung*) differs from person to person'" (*SP*, 94-95). This statement implies that the intention to mean in the saying of "I" is inseparable from the intuition of "I" as the being-present. And for Derrida, it should be no more necessary to intuit an I-object in order to say "I" and be understood than it would be necessary that a person really be by the window in order that the statement "I see a particular person by the window" be understood. The condition of possibility for the saying of "I" remains the absence of subject and object, the perfect "anonymity of the written *I*" (*SP*, 97).

The question is why a thinking which has argued for "difference," for an "auto-affection" which "produces sameness as self-relation within self-difference," should be astonished in just this way at Husserl's "meaning" of "I": "One cannot help being astonished at this *individual concept* and this *'Bedeutung'* which differs with each individual" (*SP,* 95 n.). Is the point really the breakup of the self-identical "subject" which Husserl presupposes, or is it rather *to preserve at all costs* the anonymity of written language? Surely to oppose directly Husserl's "I" as realized in the immediate intuition of individual personality, in the self-as-object immediately present to the self-as-subject, one again should apply to Husserl's own concept of auto-affection. The result would be to insist upon "this *'Bedeutung'*" as that "which differs *in* each individual," as a movement of auto-affection "prior to" the "I" conceived as self-presence, as a being already itself. In this way one criticizes the "privilege" of the subject, of immediate self-identity, without at the same time presupposing the equation of exteriority with the universal and the anonymous. For there is no a priori requirement—*beyond the central and thereby metaphysical necessity imposed by a particular conception of language*—that the exteriority involved in hearing oneself speak be conceived as anonymous in a way which suppresses the difference among and within "individuals." By the same logic which insists that difference is always already involved in the "purity" of the speaking voice, one must as well conceive the possibility of a difference involved in *listening* which cannot be suppressed by anonymity. Rather than a simple juxtaposition of "interior," individual speech and "exterior" and anonymous language, one recognizes auto-affection as a speaking and a listening "prior to" the opposition of "interior" and "exterior."

Thus, paradoxically, Derrida's "astonishment" circumscribes the movement of "differance" within language as *the Other* to the exclusion of *others:* "The statement 'I am alive' is accompanied by my being dead, and its possibility requires the possibility that I be dead; and conversely" (*SP,* 96–97). There is *no difference* possible to this inscription. I cannot be "dead" *in this way,* the self-relation of the "I" constituted in and through this self-difference with this other, but only insofar as the "I" passes into the anonymity of the Other, of language. Thus later, in the conclusion, when Derrida writes that *"differance,* which does not occur outside this relation, becomes the finitude of life as an essential relation with oneself and one's death" (*SP*, 102), there is, again, no more at stake than an entry into language conceived as the Other. The movement of differance in the anomymity of language is the repression of differences—within the "subject" and among "subjects"—as auto-affection, as the producing of "self-relation within self-difference." There never has been any Other, only others.

An entry into anonymity, on the other hand, returns without complication to the repression of history through the contradictory constitution of the past as "of a piece." The theme of the Other and the theme of the past as monolith are interchangeable: "The history of being as presence, as self-presence in absolute knowledge, as consciousness of self in the infinity of *parousia*—this history is closed. This history of presence is closed, for 'history' has never meant anything but the presentation (*Gegenwärtignung*) of Being, the production and recollection of beings in presence, as knowledge and mastery" (*SP*, 102). To dispel this contradiction, this ahistorical historicity, auto-affection would have to be conceived *other than* on the basis of an anonymous Other as language. Then there could be no certain reading and no "mastery" of Husserl by predicating in advance "the theme of full 'presence'" (*SP*, 97), by the inscription of this other voice within the Other. For such is the move which limits the fineness of Derrida's thinking at exactly the point—of intrusion, of "astonishment"—when it should be capable of doubling back on itself, *making itself heard* only in and through the other voice of Husserl. This difference, this doubling of speech and hearing within and between each other in a way that is not an immediate identity—this remains excluded.

4

Charles Tomlinson: The Poetry of Experience

I

I have heard often enough in conversation my interest in Tomlinson's poetry dismissed as an interest in an anachronism, in a poet who has settled into a comfortable verse based on an outmoded conception of the self and an uncritical acceptance of sensory detail as the only basis for concrete poetic experience. Before we turn more directly to the poems, it is worth considering the implications of such a dismissal. For I find myself at odds with the historical paradigm which conceives "modernism" in literature as a crisis born from an increasing self-consciousness about the operation of language, with its corollary of an increasingly complex manner of doubling language back across itself. It is in direct relation to this paradigm that Tomlinson's poetry is thought to be "anachronistic," written as if the crisis had never occurred, or at least as if it portended no permanent value compared to the "realistic" norms of literature which it dispossesses. Now there might well be a sense in which one could call much of Tomlinson's poetry anachronistic, but there is also a context in which the charge becomes less dismissive than disturbing, less a reason for ignoring even Tomlinson's earliest work than a reason for exploring more closely the development of thought which allows the charge to be lodged. Rather than indicating a genuinely historical awareness, the label of "anachronistic" depends upon a presupposition which realizes the process of understanding a poem as a movement of escape from its particular valence and density. These mechanisms of escape are then projected onto literature itself, as if the only truly "modern" literature could be those works which incorporate within themselves the "crisis" that results when, through an awareness of language, the relation between understanding and distance becomes problematical.

The attempt to identify understanding with escape, with distance, has had itself a long and tenacious history. But for critical theory perhaps the classic example is Northrop Frye's image in *Anatomy* of the critic who must "back up" from the text in order to see more clearly its archetypal organization. The "closer" one is to the work, the more he is haunted by the contradiction of its language operating at once as "signs" pointing beyond the text into the fabric of lived experience and as "motifs" articulated within a coherent structure of the work as a whole. Recognition at this level is impossible; the critic must "back up," he must escape from the contradiction if he is to understand. The spatial metaphor is as much cause as effect, for what Frye is concerned to achieve is an escape which opens a new space, a new "ground" from which to turn and see the shape of what had appeared an insoluble knot.

The most powerfully evocative rendering in recent theory of this linking of escape and understanding is Harold Bloom's *The Anxiety of Influence*. For while Bloom accepts without reservation—in ways I shall discuss—the necessity of escape, he recognizes at the same time that the distance achieved is never synonymous with understanding. It is rather a misunderstanding, a "misprision." Bloom's theory is elaborated in the context of the poet's relation to his "precursor," but it has implications for criticism as well. (Bloom in fact recognizes no difference between poetry and criticism: "There are no interpretations but only misinterpretations, and so all criticism is prose poetry" [*AI*, 95].)* And in his review of the book, Paul De Man argues that

> underneath, the book deals with the difficulty or, rather, the impossibility of reading and, by inference, with the indeterminacy of literary meaning. If we are willing to set aside the trappings of psychology, Bloom's essay has much to say on the encounter between latecomer and precursor as a displaced version of the paradigmatic encounter between reader and text. [PDM, 273]

---

*See below, pp. 241–42, for a list of the works cited in this chapter and the abbreviations I have employed.

However, rather than a "displacement," I would suggest that Bloom provides in effect two alternative means of describing what is in fact conceived as a single movement: an escape that is always already a taking amiss, a misprision. Psychologically, this movement represents a problematic of *priority:* "But what is the Primal Scene, for a poet as poet? It is his Poetic Father's coitus with the Muse. There was he begotten? No—there they failed to beget him. He must be self-begotten, he must engender himself upon the Muse his mother" (*AI,* 36–37). To create at all, the latecomer must imagine an originative space whose existence proves the escape from his precursor's temporal priority with the Muse. The anxiety of this necessary illusion finds expression as the poem itself, which is thus always a usurpation, a mis-taking of his own origins as poet. Structurally, the Scene is understood as a play of substitutions, where the precursor's text contains the spiritual authority of the Word which the latecomer or reader must subvert by a sequence of revisionary ratios designed to substitute his own authority for that of the text. Substitution neutralizes by allowing the latecomer an escape into the freeplay of signification. However, these substitutions form as well a structure of anxiety to the extent that they both deviate from a primal authority and yet, as *deviations,* call into being the very authority from which they attempt to escape. And Bloom insists that these two codes, the psychological and the structural, are for the "strong poet" one and the same: "A Wordsworthian critic, even one as loyal as Geoffrey Hartman, can insist upon clearly distinguishing between *priority,* as a concept from the natural order [with its emphasis on time, on diachrony], and *authority,* from the spiritual order [with its emphasis on timelessness and synchrony], but Wordsworth's ode declines to make this distinction" (*AI,* 9).

Bloom's theory suggests a particularly devastating analysis of Frye's metaphor of escape. For surely the "Polemical Introduction" to *Anatomy* displays a great deal of anxiety about the critic's role in relation to the author's, a need to assert that the priority of the creative act does not relegate the critic to the role of "parasite," having to wait upon the origination of the text by the poet. Thus the critic's move of "backing up" is a means of neutralizing his status as inevitable latecomer, escaping the temporal priority of the

text by allowing him to swing into his vision an original pattern of
archetypal organization which the critic alone possesses, stretching
both forward and backward in time from the new space where he
stands. Yet this escape is of course a swerve, a deviation which
forever excludes from criticism the "direct experience" of literature. Hence the anxiety typically manifest at the end of a Frye
essay, where we are reminded in countless different ways that
the divisions by which the argument has developed really aren't
divisions and that our goal is of course not really an "anatomy" but
a power of possession. Structurally, on the other hand, the movement of backing up is represented as a play of substitution which
replaces Falstaff, for example, with the vegetation god or Moby
Dick with leviathan. Here, the goal is to neutralize the spiritual and
creative authority of the particular text by one's escape into the
freedom of archetypal similitude. And Frye's "explanation" of this
escape in "The Archetypes of Literature" offers a trenchant example
of that anxiety Bloom calls *tessera,* the denial of substitution as a
mis-taking by the completion or totalization of a whole from a part:
"One essential principle of archetypal criticism is that the individual
and the universal form of an image are identical, the reasons being
too complicated for us just now" ("AL," 19).

Yet despite the acuteness of his demythologizing of distance,
Bloom dogmatically insists that there is no escape for escaping, no
truthful understanding of misunderstanding. Quoting a letter from
Wallace Stevens in which Stevens says, "'I am not conscious of
having been influenced by anybody,'" Bloom adds that this "is
itself an illustration of one way in which poetic influence is a variety
of melancholy or an anxiety-principle" (*AI,* 7). The affinity with
catch-22 may be deliberate, but there is also an essential equivocation here insofar as one "proves" the anxiety of *misunderstanding*
to be inevitable only by assuming the inevitability of attempting
to identify *understanding* and distance. Every form of escape can
be realized as reductive or evasive, a form of misunderstanding.
However, it does not follow that genuine understanding is impossible
because it must be an escape and thereby a misunderstanding. The
connection is established only by accepting uncritically the evasion
Frye offers to criticism in *Anatomy,* of escaping to a new ground
where one no longer has to deal with such tortuous problems as the

relation between what a poem says and what it means or the relation between literature and those muddy sublimations of desire which are thought to constitute our daily existence: "Rhetorical, Aristotelian, phenomenological, and structuralist criticism all reduce, whether to images, ideas, given things, or phonemes. Moral and other blatant philosophical or psychological criticisms reduce to rival conceptualizations. We reduce—if at all—to another poem. The meaning of a poem can only be another poem" (*AI*, 94).

For this sense of thinking as "inevitably" reductive or evasive is itself the result of a specific historical development and not at all a necessary component of human understanding. Indeed, Bloom's own exposition offers a suggestive hint concerning the origination of an identity between understanding and distance: "Poetic misprision, historically a health, is individually a sin against continuity, against the only authority that matters, property or the priority of having named something first. Poetry is property, as politics is property" (*AI*, 78). The poet's only concern is said to be for commodities, for things already safely within the carefully closed boundaries of conscious tradition. Yet once one acknowledges that the literary work as palimpsest is analogous to the economic function of private property as a commodity, the obvious step should be to question the "inevitability" of misunderstanding or "misprision" in the same way one questions private property as a "natural law" of the species.

The lack of historical awareness in *The Anxiety of Influence* is evidenced in other ways as well (the appropriateness of the word "paradigm" to describe Bloom's sense of literary history is a telling symptom that something else is going on), for example, as the distinctive features of the "modern" suddenly begin to appear almost everywhere one looks in literature.[1] However, what is ultimately more damaging is the tacit constellation of these terms— "modern," "self-conscious," "complex," and their synonyms— such that their disentanglement comes to seem impossible. To be sure, it is a constellation which has a long history of development in aesthetics; one thinks immediately of Schiller's distinction between simple and sentimental poetry. But what is new as a result of the emphasis on language and intertextuality is the rendering of the equivalence as precisely a *tacit* one, such that it remains disguised within apparently unrelated directions of inquiry. Bloom's attempt to reveal an anxiety of influence operative throughout 300 years of English and American poetry must assume their linkage as a fait accompli during the very period of history in which it was being conceived and developed. Thus what begins as a historical insight assumes instead the character of a radically ahistorical structuration which can proceed without taking into account the actual historical development of the terms themselves, without realizing how they mean in quite different ways depending upon the specificity of context, and without trying to think through the connections between this elaboration of terminology and the social history within which it exists.

Now there are two convictions powerfully operative in much of Charles Tomlinson's poetry which pose as a resolution to a much less extreme form than Bloom's of the paradoxical coincidence of understanding and escape. There is the belief, ostensibly worked out in opposition to a neoromantic slush like that of Dylan Thomas, that poetic perception escapes from the confines of one's ego, forges out of the cleansed contact with the objects of sensation a new freedom from the all too common and banal interstices of subjective, psychic experience. At the same time, this escape is thereby a *return,* to things as they are, to the plenitude of natural objects available to a perception no longer decimated by the will to power over them. What makes this "resolution" seem almost anachronistic is precisely that it does betray something very like an anxiety of influence, born from a misreading of a genuinely strong precursor—not Dylan Thomas but Wallace Stevens:

> I first read "Thirteen Ways of Looking at a Blackbird" in Oscar Williams' anthology late in '49. It was a case of being haunted rather than of cold imitation. I was also a painter and this meant that I had gone far more into the particulars of a landscape or an object than Stevens. Stevens rarely makes one *see* anything in detail for all his talk about a physical universe. ["FC," 83]

Here, for example, is a much "stronger" poem than anything in *The Necklace,* Tomlinson's first published book. It is "Clouds" from *The Way of a World.*[2]

How should the dreamer, on those slow
  Solidities, fix his wandering adagio,
Seizing, bone-frail, blown
  Through the diaphanous air of their patrols,
Shadows of fanfares, grails of melting snow?
  How can he hope to hold that white
Opacity as it endures, advances,
  At a dream's length? Its strength
Confounds him with detail, his glance falls
  From ridge to ridge down the soft canyon walls,
And, fleece as it may seem, its tones
  And touch are not the fleece of dream,
But light and body, spaced accumulation
  The mind can take its purchase on:
Cloudshapes are destinies, and they
  Charging the atmosphere of a common day,
Make it the place of confrontation where
  The dreamer wakes to the categorical call
And clear cerulean trumpet of the air.

And is it not possible to think of the "meaning" of this poem as a
"swerve" from an early Stevens poem in *Harmonium*, "On the Manner of Addressing Clouds" (*CP*, 55–56)?

Gloomy grammarians in golden gowns,
Meekly you keep the mortal rendezvous,
Eliciting the still sustaining pomps
Of speech which are like music so profound
They seem an exaltation without sound.
Funest philosophers and ponderers,
Their evocations are the speech of clouds.
So speech of your processionals returns
In the casual evocations of your tread
Across the stale, mysterious seasons. These
Are the music of meet resignation; these
The responsive, still sustaining pomps for you
To magnify, if in that drifting waste
You are to be accompanied by more
Than mute bare splendors of the sun and moon.

Against Stevens's dreamy, muffled cloud-speech, its seeming "exaltation without sound," Tomlinson opposes his tense visual imagery and his marshaling of a sensory world fronting the poetic self. Thus, if we read the two poems together, Tomlinson is speaking not to but *as* a "Funest philosopher"; and one whose "spaced accumulation/The mind can take its purchase on" has less to do with clouds than with the deathy, anxious claim for having owned the properties of sensory precision and clarity which Stevens sought but never found. And by its very nature in Tomlinson's poetry, such a claim must be blind to the way it itself originates what the poet "sees." As Bloom's theory foretells, it is the critic-analyst who discovers "the accent of deviation" (*AI*, 93), the swerve of Tomlinson's misreading. Yet if we then attempt a genuinely "antithetical criticism," one whose task is to apply this "accent" to a "reading of the first"—that is, to Stevens—"and not to the second poet" (*AI*, 93), there are two immediate difficulties.

Most obviously, Bloom is convinced that in order to discover what a poem means we must ignore what it says; we must drive straight through its mere surface texture and uncover another poem whose perversion constitutes the "real" meaning of the poem at hand. And such an escape from surface, from "mere" saying, is just what Stevens's poem warns against. Unless one is to be content with the barest abstractions, it is necessary to attend to the transient, shifting sinuosities which are the subject of those "Gloomy grammarians," those obscure, mild drudges who labor in the "drifting waste." Our philosophers' meanings should glorify their work with "golden gowns," catch up their act within the shaping act of thinking. For it is the grammarians' humble attentiveness which, like the clouds, accompanies and sustains the "mute bare splendors" of sun and moon.

The more serious difficulty is that Bloom's poetics makes impossible any attention to the most striking quality of "On the Manner of Addressing Clouds," its generous and dramatic inclusiveness.[3] Poems like this one include within their movement both what they affirm and what they question, what they shape and what they are shaped by. Everything Bloom would think of as occurring after the poem, in the anxious critic's search for the poem's structure of anxiety, Stevens manifests within the dramatic development of the poem itself. Thus there is no way to approach this poem as a piece of property, wrested from another poem and held in abeyance until the advent of Tomlinson's "Clouds." Its openness is as beneficient as those poems Bloom imagines as happening only "before the Flood." Bloom's theory provides a way—and it is certainly not the only way—to approach "Clouds" just because, unlike "On the Manner of Addressing Clouds," all the drama of Tomlinson's poem does occur before and after the poem itself, where one imagines Tomlinson really thinking through his opposition to someone else—rather than amusing himself by the kind of specious questions with which the actual poem opens—and as the critic leaves the poem buzzing with questions about its firm tread.

However, unlike many of his contemporaries, Tomlinson has had the benefit of fine, generous criticism which can suggest the barrenness of Bloom's poetics even to deal with a poem like "Clouds." Calvin Bedient's eassy in *Eight Contemporary Poets* and a recent dissertation by William Saunders, "Reaching beyond Desire: Charles Tomlinson's Poetry of Otherness," are examples, and I must refer the reader to them for a full discussion of Tomlinson's development as a poet.[4] My concern will be with a few poems from two late volumes, *The Way of a World,* published in 1969, and most recently, *The Way In,* 1974. The importance for me of these poems of Tomlinson's is the way in which his dual conviction has been pushed to the point that it represents no longer a belief, and even less a source of anxiety, but rather the kind of inner impulse whose forward thrust suffuses the starkness of ideas. Thus there is the effect of being returned to the simplicity of asking without irony, without condescension, and without evasiveness or distance of any sort what the poet does in his work. And simultaneously, one finds in them the immeasurably complex realization that this is not an innocent question, asked in a way freed from a history of attempts to forge a role for the artist in the modern world. To take on this complexity is to assume not only the burden of historical community but also the present, immediate provenance of any human community. By itself, to work through such complex questions poetically would be a major achievement; to do so with the radical simplicity Tomlinson's poems at their best achieve is the miracle of generosity which Bloom's free-enterprise poetics with its interiorization of a thoroughly bourgeois struggle to "make it new" would forever preclude from "postlapsarian" poetry.

II

Now the two poems from *The Way of a World* I wish to discuss, "In the Fullness of Time" and "Prometheus," present an intricate problem for the critic. In simple opposition to the attempt at assimilating them into the structures of escape which would ignore their surface of meaning, it perhaps might be enough to demonstrate their uniqueness, the particularity of their poetic realizations. If distance is equivalent to misunderstanding, then the alternative would seem to be a criticism which stays as much as possible "inside" the poem, which feels its way along the contours and surfaces of the poem's advance. Yet this gives rise to another difficulty, involved less with the theoretical appropriateness of such a procedure than with the fact that in these poems the "surface" itself is deliberately insistent on a context beyond the construction of an individual aesthetic object. Thus, whatever direction one takes, it becomes necessary to come to terms not only with the assumed primacy of a con-text of other texts instituted by the mechanisms of escape but also with the historical paradigm these mechanisms project.

Indeed, "In the Fullness of Time" (subtitled "a letter to Octavio Paz") can be understood initially as an argument, directed against any such attempt to escape the slow unfolding of the movement of time by crushing together its moments into a kind of pure immediacy, an "imminent" space: "The time you tell us is the century and the day/Of Shiva and Parvati: imminent innocence,/Moment without movement." Against Paz, there is Tomlinson's argument for "the way/Time, in its fullness, fills us/As it flows," for the necessity to acquiesce to those slow, careful discriminations which arise from the temporal succession of moments. However, the striking quality about the poem is the way in which its own movement does not immediately sanction the rightness of Tomlinson's argument. The opening lines, for example, seem in their very rhythm to catch up the peculiarly minatory excitement of Paz's poetry. Then there is the period break, followed by Tomlinson's presentation. In this reading, the first line would scan as two iambs

swelling into the anapests which close the line. Yet the insistence
of Tomlinson's voice, the actively present "yes, but . . ." one senses
throughout, breaks up this simple succession of moments. By
forcing an accent on "you," it suggests that this is not only Paz's
argument but that argument as heard by and given us by Charles
Tomlinson. Thus it comes as no real surprise to discover Paz's
presence within Tomlinson's speech—"the day goes/Down"—as
the emphasis gained by placing "Down" at the beginning of the
line. Rather than a temporal succession of one argument followed
by another, there is an interpenetration of the two voices, each
speaking within the other.

The effect is to qualify subtly the point of both ideas, to dispel the
sense of two sharply delimited selves fronting each other in argument or agreeing like gentlemen "To negotiate a truce in time."
Thus what follows is Tomlinson's sudden, sharp reaction against
such messiness: "We met/Sweating in Rome and in a place/Of
confusions, cases and telephones," the chaos of the physical scene
paralleling the poet's feeling of being suffocated by a disordered
immediacy. The next lines indeed offer a clean break: a colon, "and
then," and a line break to "It was evening over Umbria," where the
passage of time can enforce rather than disrupt the point Tomlinson
wants to make:

> It was evening over Umbria, the train
> Arriving, the light leaving the dry fields
> And next the approaching roofs.

However, for all this relaxed imagery and the pleasure obtained
from the flow of moments, it is too easy, gained at the expense of
abandoning the kind of experiential doubleness which charged the
first part of the poem:

> As we slowed
> Curving towards the station, the windows ahead swung
> Back into our line of vision and flung at us
> A flash of pausing lights: the future
> That had invited, waited for us there
> Where the first carriages were.

The succession of tranquil images is transformed by a syntax which

curves the lines of the poem back across each other, and the allitera-
tion of "flung" and "flash" emphasizes this sudden resonance. It is
precisely the awareness of finalty, of arrival, which makes each
passing moment precious, which redeems temporal flux from being
merely passive accumulations of sense impressions. Rather than an
end in itself, such doubleness means that Tomlinson has curved
Paz's argument back into his own, the intimacy of their shared
experience suggesting, not "Paz is right in his way to emphasize
the finality of time, but don't forget its succession as well," but
instead "Paz is right, and *therefore* each moment must be treasured
before it ends."

The poem's final lines are again argumentative, but in a way which
reveals how much Tomlinson has learned from the experience:
"That hesitant arc/We must complete by our consent to time—/Seg-
ment to circle, chance into event." This is no longer the passive
beauty of succession, one experience passing into the next or one
argument succeeded by another, each to be appreciated in itself.
Even passive appreciation depends on the ability to shape creatively
the scene which one appreciates. The overconscious elaboration of
"To negotiate a truce in time" has given way to "our consent to
time" in this simultaneously active and passive sense, to the fullness
of an experience which blurs those sharp, polemical debates between
fixed positions. Thus the question, "And how should we not consent?" is less a question than a statement of wonder at the way such
differences as exist between himself and Paz can be so quietly and
joyfully dissolved. For both presences in the poem, Paz's as well as
Tomlinson's, blend a kind of consent which the poem has rendered
so well by its indirection. The whole experience is one which develops from Tomlinson's sensitively realized doubleness of feeling
for edge and mergence, for the spanning awareness of an alternation
of experience that explores the beauty and pain of every facet.

Yet Tomlinson recognizes as well that even this mutual consent,
this achieved harmony which touches both himself and Paz, is itself
momentary: "For time/Putting its terrors by, it was as if/The
unhurried sunset were itself a courtesy." The pleasure of indirect
and mutual balance can be enjoyed because of that from which it
has emerged, the sharpness which opens the poem in the terror of
a time torn between Shiva and Beauty. And this is almost a courtesy

beyond courtesy, one which will not abandon even painful disagreement for the flush of immediate friendship. Tomlinson will treasure his own poetic voice because he can listen to Paz's quite different one, and he can value their intimacy of shared experience because he knows how different their responses can be. "The fullness of time" is here identical with the fullness of poetic experience, the kind of quiet spaciousness so inclusive that it can admit even those cramped feelings of opposition and those indeterminate moments when all seems confusion and disorder.

To call such an achievement "anachronistic" betrays a failure to accomplish precisely what gives this poem its strength, the capacity to hear and include a voice and an experience that is not one's own, to realize that what the fullness of time involves is the development of just such a community, denied as effectively by the reduction to "texts" as by the insistence on the carefully limited notion of "subjectivity" the proponents of textuality are so insistent on repudiating. Thus it is not so much the ideas within the poem as it is the development of the poem itself which achieves the breakup of that constellation of "modern" with "self-consciousness" and "complexity" of language turned back on itself as language. For here is a self- and other-conscious attention to the experience unfolded in the poem which has as a result that escape from escaping which Bloom finds so impossible, a vibrant simplicity of language whose resonances extend as far beyond the prison-house of linguistic complexity as the critic is willing to follow.

Nevertheless, as one turns from "In the Fullness of Time" to "Prometheus," the problems of invoking Tomlinson's poetry as any kind of alternative to an ahistorical conception of literary influence become all too obvious. For "Prometheus" would seem to offer an almost paradigmatic example of a poet who has gone under, who no longer possesses even the strength to claim his "misunderstanding" as a creative necessity and who in fact affirms the only value to be a kind of nerveless refusal to possess any power over events or actions. The situation in the poem is this: The protagonist, having escaped from an electric storm outside, at least momentarily escapes from the banal, uniform life of English suburbia by turning the radio to a broadcast of Scriabin's *Prometheus,* punctuated by static from the storm. Safely enclosed by

the space of his own room, he begins to meditate on the pyro-
technics of music and storm together, fancifully equating the
disturbance in nature with the "disturbance" Scriabin hoped his
music would engender in the lives of men. Then, with elegant
sarcasm, he can pit the actual events of the Russian Revolution
against the dissonant harmonies of Scriabin's tone poem, mob
violence against the "mob of instruments." Out of these contrasts,
he begins to evolve what seems to pass for him as an inevitable
historical sequence: the unbridled passion surfacing in Scriabin's
music becomes Lenin's grim determination to revolutionize Russia,
but events take over and the naive conciliations of a Trotsky are no
match for their brutal progression. Everywhere "partitions" are
down, the world is "a single town of warring suburbs." At last, in
disgust, the "storm" over, he glances outside at the ice-cream van
playing "Greensleeves" and reflects that the result of such upheaval
is after all no more exciting than this ugly, conglomerate housing
development. True aesthetic virtue is anaesthetically ironic perception; Scriabin's "hope of transforming the world through music and
rite" becomes the most facile of illusions, a struggle in marmalade.

Now obviously, to make a case for the poem, I must demonstrate
the falseness of this characterization of its development. But the
task is not so simple. To argue that I have misunderstood my own
distance from the poem—sitting in the cool of my study in an
empty house, revising these last drafts of a manuscript—merely
confirms and perpetuates how I have described the poem. Distance
begets distance—what could be "truer to" the poem than that the
critic respond in kind? Nor will it do to say that what I have recognized "in" the poem is only part of what is "there," forgetting
for example the intricate ambiguities of lines like "You dreamed
an end/Where the rose of the world would go out like a close in
music." For while the poem indeed may be ambiguous and "paradoxical," its paradoxes hardly can be located in the control of
verbal context. Nothing would be more preciously ironic than to
contrast the elegant verbal ingenuity of paradoxical poetry to the
situation Tomlinson's protagonist delineates. Finally, and most
elaborately, one could split poet and protagonist, claiming that the
disgust felt at the end of the poem is Tomlinson's for the speaker
content to inhabit a world made safe by his removal from events.

This would at least have the virtue of making "Prometheus" after all into a "strong" poem, an anxiety of influence in unconscious Promethean struggle with its own origins. But it would also eliminate what in fact seems to me the poem's real strength, the birth of Tomlinson's awareness of himself as both poet and protagonist at the same time.

It is this form of poetic awareness which Bloom's theory most directly excludes from poetry. For like Frye—and despite Frye's denial—Bloom believes that one is either "a detached spectator or a preoccupied actor." In the midst of creation, the poet can be only an actor caught up in the "successful" struggle to break free from his predecessors. The critic, of course, as spectator-analyst, reveals that creative action as in fact a "misprision," a wholly unsuccessful attempt at liberation. Thus Bloom must characterize the conflict within a poem as an illusion, an escape which misunderstands itself as a creative origination. What I have to argue instead is that the struggle in "Prometheus" is against the very forms of escape themselves, realized in an act that is both creative and critical, in Tomlinson as simultaneously poet and protagonist.

In his analysis of Tomlinson's poetic development up to *The Way of a World*, William Saunders has demonstrated the extent to which Tomlinson's poetry relies on a number of fundamentally empirical presuppositions, the most important for Saunders being the belief "that there is a distinct division between the ego and the world; on the one hand there are human beings defined by their limited point of view, their determined, substantial identities, on the other hand there is the 'outside' realm of objects and places" ("CT," 1). These lines from the sixth part of "Antecedents" in *Seeing Is Believing* are exemplary: "Sun is, because it is not you; you are/Since you are self, and self delimited/Regarding sun." But the matter can be stated more closely, for this division is not unique to British empiricism. It belongs equally in Kant and Husserl, however much it may be qualified by their quite different epistemologies. What is more strictly an indigenous feature of empirical thought can be found succinctly stated by Bertrand Russell at the beginning of his logical atomism lectures: "When I say that my logic is atomistic, I mean that I share the common-sense belief that there are many separate things; I do not regard the apparent multiplicity of the world as consisting merely in phases and unreal divisions of a single indivisible Reality" (*LK*, 178). Thus the difficulty for classical empiricism in Locke and Hume was to account for the human intervention which constructs a unity from the plurality of existing things. How does the mind remain faithful to discrete particulars as the only source of knowledge and yet find it possible to describe coherent wholes?

The dark side of this anxiety has less to do with Hume's skepticism about the possibility for genuine knowledge than with the desire it awakens for a world untouched by human desires. By itself, the assumption that there is a division between subject and world does not imply necessarily this consequence, for the emphasis is on the means and the reliability of access to an objective world. But for empiricism, access is never a problem; sensation is a constant. The difficulty inheres in the persistence of those human feelings which forever goad us into *making something* of this access, which will not let be the world as it is, in its multiple and ever-changing plenitude that we try to circumscribe continually with our peculiar notions such as causality. (Russell, it will be remembered, reserved a special place in hell for those who could not accept Hume's argument about causality.) Paradoxically, the special strength of human intelligence at its greatest stretch becomes a capacity to deny what is human, to sense the presence of an objective world as it is.

"Variation on Paz," a short poem in *Written on Water*, expresses cleanly and forcefully this impatience with the overreaching of human feelings and desires:

> We must dream inwards, and we must dream
>   Outwards too, until—the dream's ground
> Bound no longer by the dream—we feel
>   Behind us the sea's force, and the blind
> Keel strikes gravel, grinding
>   Towards a beach where, eye by eye,
> The incorruptible stones are our witnesses
>   And we wake to what is dream and what is real
> Judged by the sun and the impartial sky.

There is little in the poem to qualify the sharpness of its description—"The blind/Keel strikes gravel, grinding . . . incorruptible stones . . . Judged . . . impartial sky"—and nothing of the doubleness of "In the Fullness of Time." The only excuse for the outward stretch of desire is the moment of its *cessation,* the waking force of having one's dreamy blindness judged by the stony, sunlit multiplicity of the world. There is little possibility within this conception for the kind of awareness I find in "Prometheus," but it provides an ideal scene or ground for the blind, psychic struggle which characterizes Bloom's theory of influence. And as such a ground, it offers as well a rationale for the witty mime with which "Prometheus" opens.

The poet, like his protagonist, knows a storm is only a storm, a "*Summer* thunder," as much a transient and recurrent phenomenon as the movement of the seasons. But it amuses him to take the fortuitous circumstance of the "stormy" music and drown its dissonance with the crackling electricity of the storm. The last line of the stanza, of course, gives the game away, just in case we missed the point: "Of this *mock* last-day of nature and of art." Nature is so easily corrupted by the fierce singleness of human desire and thus becomes a mock, a sham. The stunned, electrified imagery of the poem is to be contained by a scene remarkable only for its ordinariness. The curious quality about the stanza, however, is precisely the overemphasis of its last two lines, as the alliterative crescendo— "The radio simmers with static to the strains"—suddenly has the bottom fall out on the word "mock." And the first line of the next stanza is arresting just because with it comes the realization that this man, of all things, takes his emphasis, his cynical "wisdom" quite seriously: "We have lived through apocalypse too long"; *we* will not be mocked any longer by "Scriabin's dinosaurs!" This music—and surely there is an implicit inclusion of those poets among Tomlinson's contemporaries who persist in conjuring "new" apocalyptic fantasies with each succeeding volume—is like a huge beast periodically trundled out from the museum to stand blinking in the harsh glare of historical events. Whatever else is happening here, it would be difficult to argue that any distance separates poet and protagonist.

Thus the personal address which closes stanza 2 is condescending in its very judiciousness: "Let's don't blame Scriabin; his intent was merciful after all." Nevertheless, it's as if by this point the poet has been carried away with his own momentum, having unwittingly allowed the safety of the room to be invaded by a host of sounds and voices registered by the oddly disjointed sequence carrying through the third stanza:

> Alexander Nikolayevitch, the events
> Were less merciful than your mob of instruments.
>
> Too many drowning voices cram this waveband.
>   I set Lenin's face by yours—
> Yours, the fanatic ego of eccentricity against
>   The systematic son of a schools inspector
> Tyutchev on desk—for the strong man reads
>   Poets as the antisemite pleads: "A Jew was my friend."

What are the terms of the contrast here? Scriabin and Lenin, to be sure, but equally the balanced "saneness" of Tomlinson's judgments—"I set Lenin's face by yours"—set against "the strong man," the man who systematically carries through his intent and doesn't bother to fuss with the poet's "scrupulousness" or, for that matter, his self-pity, "persecuted" by the "drowning voices" which clog his radio, destroy his aloof pleasure at mingling storm and music.

Thus it is with a sudden, sharp access of awareness that Tomlinson must implicate not only his own poetic act but also Scriabin's music with the voice of his protagonist, as music and event are being wrapped into one texture within the poem: "Prometheus came down/In more than orchestral flame and Kérensky fled/Before it." The hymning *m*'s and *n*'s swell to a climax in the slide from the last syllable of "orchestral" into "flame" and then are suddenly minced by the chopping, segregated iambs which follow. Dissonant voices crowd the music everywhere, become a part of its chorus: "The babel of continents gnaws now/And tears at the silk of those harmonies that seemed/So dangerous once." The insertion of "now" and the line break causes a stunning, lingered accent on both "gnaws" and "tears," in a way that is more painful than brutal. What Kérensky had fled, the alarming transformation of dreamed musical ecstasy into an even more dissonant reality, has become a daily event. The effect of the lines which close the stanza—"You dreamed an end/Where the rose of the world would go out like a close in music"—is hauntingly antiphonal: from the very center

of his imagined protagonist Tomlinson ventriloquizes the ecstatic
hope of Scriabin's music, only to discover that the "dummy" is
speaking back to him in an accent which mimes his own desire
for release from this "babel of continents" in which he feels immersed. From within the security of his inward and private meditation on public events, Tomlinson imagines the theater of the
Russian Revolution as a drama played out to the music of Scriabin's
tone poem, but with the result that that external and public world
reappears in the mask of his own desire for a "white world," a
poetic "in-the-beginning," such that he can no longer avoid realizing
his most intimate desires and feelings as caught up in the turmoil
he would characterize from without.

   This is dangerous stuff, neither judicious nor sane, and the fifth
stanza opens with a thunder of deep brass intent on drowning out
what is drowning him:

> Population drags the partitions down
> And we are a single town of warring suburbs:
> I cannot hear such music for its consequence:

The fierceness of Tomlinson's attack in the next three stanzas
perpetuates this brassy, thudding weight of judgment: Lenin was
no more guilty than Blok for the butcheries of Stalin's reign; Trotsky was ultimately responsible for his own assassination. Here if
anywhere is the place to make an argument for the poem as an
anxiety of influence. For the more Tomlinson thunders, the more
Promethean the poem becomes in its attack on the unbalanced
ecstasies of Scriabin's Promethean aesthetic, culminating in the
blind assertion that idealistic fools like Trotsky and Scriabin aren't
really capable of influencing anything: "Chromatic Prometheus,
myth of fire,/It is history topples you in the zenith."

   Yet the breakdown in these stanzas is less awesome than I have
suggested, for after all, how Promethean is it to declaim against
a chorus of dummies, how much the "strong poet" could Tomlinson
be if he were faced with the real presence of a Scriabin, a Trotsky,
or a Lenin rather than the shadows which flit along the edges of
the names that throng the poem? Confined to psychic struggle and
misunderstanding, the "anxiety of influence" is no more an evidence
of strength than this absurdly clipped English voice baying at the

radio. What saves the poem is the remarkable drama taking place in
the last two stanzas, engendered out of a force of recognition so
devastating that the conclusion to the poem is in effect no ending
at all. The first part of stanza 8 sums up the indictment of Scriabin,
Blok, and those like them with absolutely no ironic distance separating Tomlinson as poet from his own protagonist, speaking now in
the most balanced, sane, judicious way possible:

> Scriabin, Blok, men of extremes,
>> History treads out the music of your dreams
> Through blood, and cannot close like this
>> In the perfection of anabasis.

These men understood art as a physician who cures by pushing the
fever to a crisis, and what they forgot is that every perfecting desire,
by whatever obscure means and hidden connections, is mediated by
a history of suffering by real poeple in real situations, no matter
how merciful the intention. The empirical evidence is all around
him; the music has ended, the houses remain "and refuse to burn."
Could it have been worth it, after all?

Amazingly, however, this same voice continues, pressing out with
sibilant contempt at the end of the eighth stanza and on into the
ninth the reciprocal judgment by Scriabin on Tomlinson and his
world, on the poet who as the poem began felt the peaceful vacuum
of this English scene as a genuine basis for the elegant cynicism he
had turned on Scriabin's tone poem. The horror of Tomlinson's
world is that it represents not just a "coda"—another possible
ending to counter the brutality of Stalin's violence—but "incessant
codas," endless changes rung on the same theme, a perpetually
judicious voice condemning all the stuff and fury of the foreigners
as one listens to the repetitions of "Greensleeves" played by an
ice-cream van. Mercifully left "alone" in his room to mouth moral-
isms at the radio, conduct his arguments, marshal his logic, the very
solidity of his sense of person and place has become a cruel dic-
tator: "and at the city's/Stale new frontier even ugliness/Rules
with the cruel mercy of solidities."

Tomlinson remains identical with his protagonist in the poem, for
beyond what that protagonist has said already, at the beginning of
stanza 8, Tomlinson cannot talk back to this judgment. Scriabin

remains as well, refusing to die with the music. Whatever queer transmutation of history has made the Russians responsible for English suburbia, Tomlinson now stands condemned by the lunacy of his own logic. Yet it is of course Tomlinson himself who has evoked the judgment, who has made Scriabin's presence felt in the poem, as the composer himself and as the force of a desire for poetic transformation which Tomlinson must recognize as belonging to his own activity as well. Thus the poem does indeed represent an "anxiety of influence," but in a far more potent sense than Bloom would have us imagine. It is no blind, Promethean struggle by a preoccupied poet, left as a piece of property for the critic-analyst to reveal what the poet fails to realize. The dramatic force of the poem inheres precisely in that realization.

III

The success of "Prometheus" is the quality of dramatic immediacy which thrills to the extent that one feels he is attending to an almost impossible birth of a living awareness from a poet-protagonist who seems to glory in his own obtuseness. And as I have suggested, the poem thus represents an anxiety of influence at its most difficult, at the point where one realizes that what "influence" names is that influx of force or power that seems to come from beyond the poet, from that which is other than himself, and to which it is preeminently the reader who attends as it is the poet of "Prometheus" who is buffeted. On the other hand, to restrict the context of influence to precursor and latecomer is to construe by critical fiat every poem as necessarily anachronistic at birth, placed in a way which condemns the poem to be only an illusion of creative origination at the same time that it locks both precursor and latecomer into a spatial frame possessed by the critic. Surely influence can be recognized as the work of another poet, but it can be as well something as sudden as the taut, minatory awareness of perceptible difference in the somatic processes or as massive and static as Eliot's understanding of "tradition" in "Tradition and the Individual Talent," as simple as the irritating gesture of a friend or as complex as Bloom's theory of influence itself. Whatever the particular case— and it is no evidence of critical strength to legislate its occurrence—the ambiguous power of influence inheres in its being born within the poem and yet beyond it. And influence becomes an anxiety when, as in "Prometheus," the force of recognition stuns the poet into silence.

I hardly intend to ignore the impact of "Prometheus"; in fact, as one turns from the experience of the poem to those poems which make up the first section of *The Way In,* there seems a kind of inevitable *loss* of force, a grim grisaille livened only by the most impossibly stretched-out rhymes: "All that a grimy care from wastage gleans,/From scrap-iron down to heaps of magazines." By the standard of immediate, dramatic power set in "Prometheus," this title poem of the new volume would have to be judged a failure. For Tomlinson is fully and attentively present from the poem's first lines: "The needle-point's swaying reminder/Teeters at thirty, and the flexed foot/Keeps it there." Rather than overturning literally everything which has come before, the final line of "The Way In"—"This is a daily discontent. This is the way in"—merely reiterates what was expressed at the beginning.

Yet the moral, of course, is that it is blinkering to judge by past perfections. Not only is it impossible to expect that the meaning of a poem will be a perversion of a poem by another author, but also one cannot expect even that the poems of a single author, taken together, will display a firmly delineated corpus open to the analyst's probe. It is such assumptions which make Bloom's insistence that all criticism is solipsistic a grim reality. One indeed hears within "The Way In," directly and indirectly, echoes of many previous poems, not merely as a field for source hunting but as caught up in the most intimate flux of the poem's meaning. However, the reason is that this poem is written by a poet who has listened to his own voice—and the voices that have touched it—long and attentively, who in the present moment of thinking can include his memory's echo as palpably immediate and thus hear not only his voice but that voice as his ears hear it, a sense beyond sense as it were.

There is no struggle to contact or internalize a realm of felt otherness, either of nature as in a poem like "Swimming Chenango Lake" or of other men as in "Prometheus." Everything in the poem is at once other and internal. It is only within his own arc of thinking that this grim, ugly scene can be realized in its distinctness from remembered places. Yet the very movement of his thought remains strangely unfamiliar, as Tomlinson listens to the way in which past feelings have been articulated in such different ways: "I thought I knew this place, this face/A little worn, a little homely." The hard echo of the internal rhyme grips the feeling of strangeness within the tight, coiled movement of thinking. But because it is rhyme and not a repetition, the echo is slightly skewed; the scene manifests its strangeness out of the poet's very closeness to what it has been as well as what it is. Even the clarity of the poet's vision is complicated by the drifting indeterminacy of past and future—"But the look that shadows *softened*/And the light *could grace*, keeps flowing away from me/In daily change"—and by the equivocal reference of "look," either what is seen or that which sees.

Thus "The Way In" cannot possibly possess the charged immediacy and excitement of "Prometheus," the struggle to accommodate feelings which break free from the limitations of Tomlinson's poetic self fronting the radically different ecstasies of Scriabin. The discovery of "The Way In," on the other hand, is that such feelings not only result from a response to an alien world but also, and equally important, well up from within the assumed seamless interior of the self, in its fragile, labile shiftings of memory, desire, and perception: "I thought I knew this place, this face," where both "place" and "face" are both his own and the streets of the city through which he drives. What is lost of the breathtaking achievement of "Prometheus" is more than made up for by Tomlinson's meditatively experiencing the thrust of feeling which cannot be delimited, even at the source.

The problem of response to such poetry is that it offers no specific challenge, no clearly defined "problem" which a critic-analyst can discern and reveal within the obfuscations of poetic surface texture. As a result, it is easy enough to be put off by the deliberately strained rhymes, perhaps, in the lines I quoted previously. But even this discontent should not freeze the poem into mere artifice if one attends to it as scrupulously as Tomlinson listens to what he does. In stanzas 5 and 6, for example, the echo one hears is from "Machiavelli in Exile:"

> butcher, publican
> Miller, and baker quarrel at their cards
> And heights and hill-roads all around are filled
> With voices of gods who do not know they're gods.
>
> Nor are they, save for a trick of light and sound

Yet the shadow of contempt which offends in this earlier poem is no longer present in "The Way In."

Like Machiavelli as Tomlinson imagines him, Tomlinson is himself forced into a kind of exile as he picks his way through what is for him the discards and waste of a demolished city. Yet his very act of driving is of course a way of contributing to that demolition he so despises. And he is not the only exile; it is a whole "race in transit." While the hard, graceless rhyme ("see/Mnemosyne") purges any trace of merely sentimental community with the particular pair, there is no self-congratulatory toughness on Tomlinson's part for facing up to, for seeing what they do not. Nor does he withdraw from them: "Perhaps those who have climbed into their towers/Will eye it all differently," but he will not. His Eve's body hordes what her eyes blink; her mindless memory births the muse Tomlinson invokes in the poem. Thus his strangely affecting apostrophe in the seventh stanza:

> She is our lady of the nameless metals, of things
> No hand has made, and no machine
> Has cut to a nicety that takes the mark
> Of clean intention—at best, the guardian
> Of all that our daily contact stales and fades,
> Rusty cages and lampless lampshades.

Tomlinson's articulation of his anger at the waste of human life transformed into junk goes far beyond his "Eve-Mnemosyne's" mindless unseeing, but with no condescension and no detached irony. This is the more remarkable to the extent that the poem offers nothing like "the fallacy of imitative form"; sympathetically watching the slow progress of the couple, our educated poet still talks a language of Eve and Mnemosyne. The temptation, here and throughout, would be to savage one's own language to accommodate the grainy textures of the experience, thereby reducing "common life" to the prison-shades of an Ulro world, poetry to the perfecting fires of apocalyptic hope. Tomlinson achieves the far more difficult task of inhabiting poetically a world of "nameless metals" and faces, while at the same time feeling as an absence all those qualities of poetic experience he values the most: "This is a daily discontent. This is the way in."

The reiteration of "will" in this last stanza, and its crucial placement in the stanza immediately preceding, again echo an earlier poem—"Eden"—one of the bleakest in *The Way of a World:*

> There is no
> Bridge but the thread of patience, no way
> But the will to wish back Eden, this leaning
> To stand against the persuasions of a wind
> That rings with its meaninglessness where it sang its meaning.

And again, the feeling of the earlier poem—this grim, angry toughness of "Eden"—has been subtly modified. Tomlinson has said he intended to write a third poem, "Eve," to complete the "Eden" and "Adam" sequence of *The Way of a World,* and perhaps in its own way this poem is it.[5] For the half jocular reminder that "It will need more than talk and trees/To coax a style from these disparities" threads the supple awareness which characterizes a poet whose voice is capable of recognizing and including the most disparate forms of influence.

Now I have suggested that the locus of influence in much of Tomlinson's poetry was conceived as natural objects of perception, that multiple world which is "Sun" and not "Self," which provides the standard of comparison whereby Scriabin's music is found wanting at the beginning of "Prometheus" and which is conspicuous by its very absence in "The Way In." For the latter poem is dominated by Tomlinson's realization that it is not the magnificence of a natural world whose influence shapes his poetic perception (significantly, the title of the section which "The Way In" introduces is "Manscapes"). Rather, he has turned to that world only insofar as he is haunted by a city like Bristol whose "worn" and "homely" face he thought he knew so well and whose very commonness would seem to make it inappropriate as any kind of influence. This is the awareness which frees Tomlinson for the achievement of the four poems that make up the second section of *The Way In:* "Under the Moon's Reign" (the title poem of the sequence), "Foxes' Moon, "The Dream," and "After a Death." Together, they represent Tomlinson's most sustained exploration of "influence" in the broadest possible sense, realized in the uniqueness of a poetic act which shapes the dramatic inclusion of both self and other to the extent that even the buffeting force of a poem like "Prometheus" can become an integral element in these poems.

Surprisingly, however, the most striking quality of the title poem to the sequence is Tomlinson's initial refusal to accept a world which is thoroughly human, which is "social" or "political" right down to the tiniest detail of perception. Indeed, Tomlinson never has had much patience with the notion that everything outside the realm of human interchange is dead, a material to be labored on or a mere screen for the mythy projections of our fears and desires. And the poem begins with an impatient flick, clearing away the debris of such self-aggrandizement: "Twilight was a going of the gods: the air/Hung weightlessly now—its own/Inviolable sign." After the colon, the lines then can appear a hushed sweep of expectancy, the air brushed and cleansed of all human interference, weightless in its pristine integrity. This scene holds no spirit, no humanized center, even though habit keeps us peering into the obscurity:

> From habit, we
> Were looking still for what we could not see—
> The inside of the outside, for some spirit flung
> From the burning of that Götterdämerung
> And suffused in the obscurity.

The arch abstractness of "*The* inside of *the* outside" and the tolling rhyme of "flung/Götterdämerung" mock the very possibility.

Yet angling his vision off the pools, "scraps" of images float "Scattered across scraps of water"; he has willed the breakup of those conceptual myths which would dominate a "dead" nature, and now what he sees is that breakup, nothing more. If he looks directly at the scene, trying to suppress his desire for relief, for what he expects to find, he discovers instead only a "thronging shade," seeming almost maliciously to beckon him to let go, let go, project what you will for each man is his own sun. His only response is a petulant "None of which belonged there": I shall see what I want to see which is what I would see if I didn't want to see anything in particular except what is actually there to see. The palpable contradiction of "Variation on Paz," for example—that poem which so forcefully and actively lionizes passive acquiescence—is here being brought to the surface and resolved.

For the speaker must recognize nature as an "outside," as that which is other than himself, to be in fact a fundamental law of *his* nature. He can see things as they are, as distinct from himself, only to the extent that he actively feels their distinctness within the movement of his own creative vision. The problem with projection is not that it denies the reality of things but rather that it denies the reality of his own self-nature which insists on the real "outness" of objects in the natural world.[6] The most deceptive form of projection is precisely that desire for nature as purely and wholly Other which cannot recognize itself as desire and which thereby results in nothing more than an electric frieze of a dead world.[7]

> And then the moon
> Drawing all into more than daylight height
> Had taken the zenith, the summit branches
> Caught as by steady lightning

The interior movement of the poem can then sweep to its triumphant conclusion, one which celebrates the outness, the otherness of nature as always and everywhere realized through *this* inside of *an* outside, this "momentary perfection" whose sovereign and self-conscious reality doubles a self and a world as joyously at one in their distinctness, each figuring forth the other "Under transfigured heavens, under the moon's reign."

The disturbing and almost unnoticed limitation felt in this conclusion is its pastness—"the eye that *saw* it/*Gathered*"—the sense that this is memory's rendering of poetic discovery, tinged with the thrusting forward of a new and painful discontent left unresolved even by this poem's working through of the relation between eye and world. For what Tomlinson must realize as well is that the natural world as understood in "Under the Moon's Reign" can offer no clean freedom with which to chasten the stale, too-much-handled contacts of human affairs. As long as he could accept something like Russell's belief in the multiplicity and plenitude of a nature undisguised by human intervention, his own acts of perception, without disturbing conflicts or questions, could be thought of as moral acts: "The dreamer wakens to the categorical call/And clear cerulean trumpet of the air" ("Clouds"). The very success of "Under the Moon's Reign"—that lucid joy of accepting another world as his world, of knowing things as they are to be suffused with the warmth of his own feeling—makes it already a memory, disrupting in its most intimate and vital center the easy equations which mark the progress of "Clouds."

"Foxes' Moon," the second poem in the sequence, arises from the harrowing cleavage between two sources, giving it the clenched and almost inhuman edge felt throughout its movement: "Night over England's interrupted pastoral,/And moonlight on the frigid lattices/Of pylons." England's "pastoral," like "Clouds," is an equivalence of idyll and sermon, pastoral and pastor, percept and precept, but now interrupted by "Under the Moon's Reign" and realized in its full, present horror. It is a secondhand world, merged and mingled into one common denominator, perception a "desolation of grisaille," morality a "babbling undertow." Nothing can be primary, nothing felt spontaneously, not even clouds. Dreams are but shadows of other dreams, sunrise a headlight, the last plowed farm row becoming insensibly the first row of houses. Those within the fold touch almost nothing of a world beyond themselves:

> Warm sleepers turn,
> Catch the thin volpine bark between
> Dream on dream, then lose it
> To the babbling undertow they swim.

And Tomlinson fronts their world in disgust and anger, under the sign of the foxes who "bring/Flint hearts and sharpened senses to/This desolation of grisaille in which the dew/Grows clearer, colder."

"Foxes' Moon" evokes more directly than *The Anxiety of Influence* what has become indeed a pervasive anxiety for the contemporary author, the awareness, as Tomlinson has it in "At Stoke," of everything "Too handled to be primary." (John Barth tells us that

after having written *The Sot-Weed Factor,* he discovered Lord Rag-
lan's schematic of "heroic" characteristics, scored Ebenezer on
eighteen out of twenty, and determined that Giles would qualify on
all counts.) The anxiety Tomlinson understands so well in "Foxes'
Moon" is not a question of what do do that Joyce or Stevens or
Wordsworth or Shelley or Milton hasn't already laid first claim
to. Rather, it is how to live in the face of what has happened to
these authors' efforts, the way in which they have been so assimilated and reduced by everything from a critical museum such as
Anatomy to the concoctions of television and the advertising world.
No wonder Tomlinson's poetry has so often occupied itself with
"landscapes," for this is a situation in which one longs for a heart
of flint, for the possibility of inhabiting an utterly inhuman world
if by that means one can erase the bloated countenance of a human
god gorged with its own commodities, decorated by its most illus-
trious artifacts.

However, the second source of the poem is Tomlinson's uneasiness
with these "fox hours"; while the foxes can "move through/The
white displacement of a daily view/Uninterrupted," he cannot. As
fox, he may draw the very lines of the poem into a ghostly clarity
against the "daily view," refining them to a piercing edge, a "thin
volpine bark." But as the poet capable of making "Under the Moon's
Reign," he must sense as well the "ravenous quiet" of the foxes on
their rounds, uninterrupted either by the "babbling undertow" or
by his own drying voice. Their world is as indifferent to his as it is
to the world of the sleepers:

These
Are the fox hours, cleansed
Of all the meanings we can use
And so refuse them.

Tomlinson can evoke this cold, cleansed, and inhuman realm only
by the shock of a kind of double cleavage, as he opposes it to the
"daily view" and to his own meaningful, angered disgust at that
waste. Thus the poem represents no facile antihumanism which
imagines one can simply conjure up a new space beyond the name
of "man." Although penetrated by their chill touch, he has no
choice but to let the foxes go and return to the "desolation of

grisaille," haunted by the need to renew a contact with that faintly kindled world almost dissolved by the acids of "Foxes' Moon."

"The Dream" is at once the most surprising and the most spacious of Tomlinson's poems in *The Way In,* the triumphant, creative surmounting of the burden of influence etched with such finality in "Foxes' Moon." Its spaciousness inheres in Tomlinson's attentiveness to the way in which an interior world—"Shaped by a need that was greed no longer"—spills into and suffuses a community whose very nature enacts the fragile, shifting life of each of its members, each both "Strange and familiar" to each other and to themselves, each animated by the spanning awareness of the poet's act. It is an action which breaks down every distinction between self and other, poet and dreamer, only to shimmer them into a new and replenished palpability where they draw from each other's distinctness the source of their own being.

As the poem opens, the drying voice of "Foxes' Moon" has given way to a long, soft susurrus which overflows the discretely edged elements in their opaqueness to each other, in a way that eye alone cannot:

> Under that benign calm eye that sees
>   Nothing of the vista of land and sky
> It brings to light; under the interminably
>   Branching night, of street and city,
> Vein and artery, a dream
>   Held down his mind that blinded him
> To all except the glimmering, closed-in warmth
>   Of his own present being.

It is only the poet who sees; yet it is as if his eyes were learning the very flex and stress of their musculature as they swarm with branching vein and artery reflecting city street, rush to meet moon and night sustained by the animate pressure of the voice which curls its almost physical softness around each word drifted into being. In their very distinctness (and this from the author of "Variation on Paz"), poet and dreamer are one: the dreamer's dream blinds him to what the poet sees and closes him in the "glimmering . . . warmth" of his physical being; the poet's vision opens for him as a warm, familiar treasure the physical copresence of body and world. And like the poet, the dreamer is "Alone/And yet aware within that loneliness/Of what he shared with others—a sense/Of scope and pleasure in mere warmth."

Thus, within his dream, the dreamer begins to experience the kind of fullness granted to the poet's vision:

> He seemed the measure of some constricted hope
> That asked a place in which it might pursue
> Its fulness, and so grew away from him,
> Swayed into palpability like a wall:
> He knew that he must follow out its confine
> To his freedom, and be taught this tense fluidity
> Always a thought beyond him.

If the other half of vision's clarity is the swarming fullness of physical presence, the other half of such blind dreaming is the transformation of a hope becoming palpable wall becoming fluid thought, forever opening into new spaces the equal of what the poet sees as "interminably/Branching night":

> now
> The transitions of the dream, the steps and streets,
> The passageways that branched beneath
> Haphazard accumulation of moon on moon,
> Spurned at each turn a reality
> Merely given—an inert threat
> To be met with and accommodated.

His dreamy fantasma proves his resurrection from the "inert threat," from his dream-struck blindness, as the poet's vision at the beginning has effected *his* resurrection from the eye's registering of sensations as "Merely given." Each is both "Strange and familiar": the "Haphazard accumulation of moon on moon" different from the poet's vision of "that benign calm eye," yet in a way he finds himself able to sense and approve; the dreamer's very hope "Always a thought beyond him," yet palpable to his touch.

The poem's conclusion is a paean to these intricate transformations of self and world, waking and sleeping, poet and dreamer, present and past, as the dreamer wakes into the poet who would read

now "with opened eyes/The intricacies of the imagined spaces"
he has dreamed, and as the waking poet finds the familiar vision
of "the lines that map a hand" as strangely wonderful as if he
dreamed it. It is this imagined wholeness, this haunting, dream-lit
"dream of a city under the city's dream" and not the inhuman
"white displacement" of "Foxes' Moon," which can provide the
only genuine measure of the city's spreading ugliness. Tomlinson's
way in culminates in the transformation and inclusion of influence,
the capacity to realize that one sees the city as it is only insofar
as one feels it as it might be, "Always a thought beyond," from
within the pressure of dream-sustained dream as it flowers into
this fragile contact of a fully human world.

The question which dominates my sense of "After a Death,"
the last poem in the sequence, is whether death is being understood
as the final and inalterable arbiter of influence, a common denominator which registers for all in the same way, or whether even
this influence is various, whether in fact each death is unique because felt within *this* community in *this* way. Now ordinarily one
does not have to work too hard at Tomlinson's titles. They call
attention to themselves only to the degree that they seem so deliberately inconspicuous, a "simple description" of the poem's
subject matter—for example, "Clouds," "Swimming Chenango
Lake," even "The Dream"—or a phrase lifted from the poem:
"The Way In," "Under the Moon's Reign." "After a Death," on
the other hand, shows Tomlinson embattled from the beginning.
Is it "after a death" read with slight, dry irony, or does one refuse
even here the comfort of such anonymity, gritting one's teeth on
"*a* death?"

Destroying at a touch the expansiveness of "The Dream," the
opening line will not entertain even the equivocation of the title:
"A little ash, a painted rose, a name." But then, with equally sudden
directness, the second line of the poem begins a sweep through an
expanse of space which echoes both the elastic stretch of "The
Dream" and the conclusion to "Under the Moon's Reign" (as well
as an earlier, ambitious poem from *Written on Water* entitled
"Movements"), only to come rounding back to the reminder of
Tomlinson's dread antagonist:

> A moonshell that the blinding sky
> Puts out with winter blue, hangs
> Fragile at the edge of visibility. That space
> Drawing the eye up to its sudden frontier
> Asks for a sense to read the whole
> Reverted side of things. I wanted
> That height and prospect such as music brings—
> Music or memory. Neither brought me here.

The sky which had brought such comfort under the moony warmth of "Under the Moon's Reign" becomes itself a pale reminder of blue indifference, blending into insignificance the patches of color, the vague elevations of human effort:

> This burial place straddles a green hill,
> Chimneys and steeples plot the distances
> Spread vague below: only the sky
> In its upper reaches keeps
> An untarnished January colour.

Moons rise, are buried, and rise again: "We buried / A little ash."

Yet it is with a blaze of verse that the poem parades such grim facticity, the very certainty "that / Whatever can make bearable or bridge / The waste of air, a poem cannot," realizing not the equivalence of an "untarnished" January sky but rather the embattled strain of the poet's refusal to accept this intransigent influence which will not be conjured or annealed:

> Time so broke you down,
> Your lost eyes, dry beneath
> Their matted lashes, a painted rose
> Seems both to memorialize and mock
> What you became. It picks your name out
> Written on the roll beside a verse—
> Obstinate words: measured against the blue,
> They cannot conjure with the dead.

Sentiment touched by irony is only sentimentality, "Your lost eyes" and "a painted rose," the fallacy of a poetics of words which seeks escape from feeling by the coruscations of ironic distance. For words used like this invoke their own closure; "measured against the blue" space they conjure up, "They cannot conjure with the dead."

Working in a way which is genuinely poetic, however, language performs another task entirely:

> Words,
> Bringing that space to bear, that air
> Into each syllable we speak, bringing
> An earnest to us of the portion
> We must inherit, what thought of that would give
> The greater share of comfort, greater fear—
> To live forever, or to cease to live?

To face either the presence or absence of death as an inalterable finality is itself the final form of escape, a swerve toward the fear which engenders irony or the comfort which induces sentimentality, both a projection of desire into the void. If all come to the same end, all reduce to the same common denominator, would that be comforting, would it be fearful, would it offer sentimental community or ironic protection? If all stretch time into perpetuity, would that? To choose either is to escape into the solipsistic possession of generalizing life as property, as if it were something one owned rather than one's very nature. Death as it really is comes variously incarnated in each word we speak, in each life beyond our own which we inhabit, in those whose loss we mourn and in those who will mourn us. Every living act inherits its "earnest" of the particular "portion," the particular death that is ours or those we love. And Tomlinson remains embattled through the poem's conclusion:

> The imageless unnaming upper blue
> Defines a world, all images
> Of endeavors uncompleted. Torn levels
> Of the land drop, street by street,
> Pitted and pooled, its wounds
> Cleansed by a light, dealt out
> With such impartiality you'd call it kindness,
> Blindly assuaging where assuagement goes unfelt.

To think such an "imageless unnaming upper blue," such impartial
light, would be like the finality of death for the community of all
men is perhaps a kindness, a way of submerging one's particular
grief for the person loved, a false calm of surrender to an omni-
potent force. But the "assuagement goes unfelt" by this poet who
knows what it is to feel within the living act of the poem the death
of one who means this much. Tomlinson's insistence is so aggressive
that he will not even name for us the person who died; there is no
possibility of dissolving the poem into a misty region of loss with
which we can all empathize, substituting our names for his and
thereby refining all these mere names back into an "unnaming
upper blue." Can more be asked of a poet than that such spaciousness as is realized in *Under the Moon's Reign* be inclusive even of
this death's grief, hold shimmering in its span even this influx, this
earnest of what it is to live and die with another?

Appendix

IN THE FULLNESS OF TIME
A LETTER TO OCTAVIO PAZ

The time you tell us is the century and the day
   Of Shiva and Parvati: imminent innocence,
Moment without movement. Tell us, too, the way
   Time, in its fullness, fills us
As it flows: tell us the beauty of succession
   That Breton denied: the day goes
Down, but there is time before it goes
   To negotiate a truce in time. We met
Sweating in Rome and in a place
   Of confusions, cases and telephones: and then
It was evening over Umbria, the train
   Arriving, the light leaving the dry fields
And next the approaching roofs. As we slowed
   Curving towards the station, the windows ahead swung
Back into our line of vision and flung at us
   A flash of pausing lights: the future
That had invited, waited for us there
   Where the first carriages were. That hesitant arc
We must complete by our consent to time—
   Segment to circle, chance into event:
And how should we not consent? For time
   Putting its terrors by, it was as if
The unhurried sunset were itself a courtesy.

PROMETHEUS

Summer thunder darkens, and its climbing
   Cumulae, disowning our scale in the zenith,
Electrify this music: the evening is falling apart.
   Castles-in-air; on earth: green, livid fire.

The radio simmers with static to the strains
Of this mock last-day of nature and of art.

We have lived through apocalypse too long:
   Scriabin's dinosaurs! Trombones for the transformation
That arrived by train at the Finland Station,
   To bury its hatchet after thirty years in the brain
Of Trotsky. Alexander Nikolayevitch, the events
   Were less merciful than your mob of instruments.

Too many drowning voices cram this waveband.
   I set Lenin's face by yours—
Yours, the fanatic ego of eccentricity against
   The systematic son of a schools inspector
Tyutchev on desk—for the strong man reads
   Poets as the antisemite pleads: "A Jew was my friend."

Cymballed firesweeps. Prometheus came down
   In more than orchestral flame and Kérensky fled
Before it. The babel of continents gnaws now
   And tears at the silk of those harmonies that seemed
So dangerous once. You dreamed an end
   Where the rose of the world would go out like a close in music.

Population drags the partitions down
   And we are a single town of warring suburbs:
I cannot hear such music for its consequence:
   Each sense was to have been reborn
Out of a storm of perfumes and light
   To a white world, an in-the-beginning.

In the beginning, the strong man reigns:
   Trotsky, was it not then you brought yourself
To judgement and to execution, when you forgot
   Where terror rules, justice turns arbitrary?
Chromatic Prometheus, myth of fire,
   It is history topples you in the zenith.

Blok, too, wrote The Scythians
   Who should have known: he who howls
With the whirlwind, with the whirlwind goes down.

In this, was Lenin guiltier than you
When, out of a merciless patience grew
   The daily prose such poetry prepares for?

Scriabin, Blok, men of extremes,
   History treads out the music of your dreams
Through blood, and cannot close like this
   In the perfection of anabasis. It stops. The trees
Continue raining though the rain has ceased
   In a cooled world of incessant codas:

Hard edges of the houses press
   On the after-music senses, and refuse to burn,
Where an ice-cream van circulates the estate
   Playing Greensleeves, and at the city's
Stale new frontier even ugliness
   Rules with the cruel mercy of solidities.

Note: Tomlinson's note to this poem: "'Prometheus' (p. 4) refers to the tone-poem by Scriabin and to his hope of transforming the world by music and rite."

THE WAY IN

The needle-point's swaying reminder
   Teeters at thirty, and the flexed foot
Keeps it there. Kerb-side signs
   For demolitions and new detours,
A propped pub, a corner lopped, all
   Bridle the pressures that guide the needle.

I thought I knew this place, this face
   A little worn, a little homely.
But the look that shadows softened
   And the light could grace, keeps flowing away from me
In daily change; its features, rendered down,
   Collapse expressionless, and the entire town

Sways in the fume of the pyre. Even the new
   And mannerless high risers tilt and wobble

Behind the deformations of acrid heat—
  A century's lath and rafters. Bulldozers
Gobble a street up, but already a future seethes
  As if it had waited in the crevices:

A race in transit, a nomad hierarchy:
  Cargoes of debris out of these ruins fill
Their buckled prams; their trucks and hand-carts wait
  To claim the dismantlings of a neighborhood—
All that a grimy care from wastage gleans,
  From scrap-iron down to heaps of magazines.

Slowing, I see the faces of a pair
  Behind their load: he shoves and she
Trails after him, a sexagenarian Eve,
  Their punishment to number every hair
Of what remains. Their clothes comes of their trade—
  They wear the cast-offs of a lost decade.

The place had failed them anyhow, and their pale
  Absorption staring past this time
And dusty space we occupy together,
  Gazes the new blocks down—not built for them;
But what they are looking at they do not see.
  No Eve, but mindless Mnemosyne,

She is our lady of the nameless metals, of things
  No hand has made, and no machine
Has cut to a nicety that takes the mark
  Of clean intention—at best, the guardian
Of all that our daily contact stales and fades,
  Rusty cages and lampless lampshades.

Perhaps those who have climbed into their towers
  Will eye it all differently, the city spread
In unforeseen configurations, and living with this,
  Will find that civility I can only miss—and yet
It will need more than talk and trees
  To coax a style from these disparities.

The needle-point's swaying reminder
  Teeters: I go with uncongealing traffic now
Out onto the cantilevered road, window on window
  Sucked backwards at the level of my wheels.
Is it patience or anger most renders the will keen?
  This is a daily discontent. This is the way in.

Under the Moon's Reign

UNDER THE MOON'S REIGN

Twilight was a going of the gods: the air
  Hung weightlessly now—its own
Inviolable sign. From habit, we
  Were looking still for what we could not see—
The inside of the outside, for some spirit flung
  From the burning of that Götterdämmerung
And suffused in the obscurity. Scraps
  Of the bare-twigged scene were floating
Scattered across scraps of water—mirrors
  Shivered and stuck into a landscape
That drifted visibly to darkness. The pools
  Restrained the disappearing shapes, as all around
The dusk was gaining: too many images
  Beckoned from that thronging shade
None of which belonged there. And then the moon
  Drawing all into more than daylight height
Had taken the zenith, the summit branches
  Caught as by steady lightning, and each sign
Transformed, but by no more miracle than the place
  It occupied and the eye that saw it
Gathered into the momentary perfection of the scene
  Under transfigured heavens, under the moon's reign.

FOXES' MOON

Night over England's interrupted pastoral,
    And moonlight on the frigid lattices
Of pylons. The shapes of dusk
    Take on an edge, refined
By a drying wind and foxes bring
    Flint hearts and sharpened senses to
This desolation of grisaille in which the dew
    Grows clearer, colder. Foxes go
In their ravenous quiet to where
    The last farm meets the first
Row from the approaching town: they nose
    The garbage of the yards, move through
The white displacement of a daily view
    Uninterrupted. Warm sleepers turn,
Catch the thin volpine bark between
    Dream on dream, then lose it
To the babbling undertow they swim. These
    Are the fox hours, cleansed
Of all the meanings we can use
    And so refuse them. Foxes glow,
Ghosts unacknowledged in the moonlight
    Of the suburb, and like ghosts they flow
Back, racing the coming red, the beams
    Of early cars, a world not theirs
Gleaming from kindled windows, asphalt, wires.

THE DREAM

Under that benign calm eye that sees
    Nothing of the vista of land and sky
It brings to light; under the interminably
    Branching night, of street and city,
Vein and artery, a dream
    Held down his mind that blinded him
To all except the glimmering, closed-in warmth
    Of his own present being. Alone
And yet aware within that loneliness

Of what he shared with others—a sense
Of scope and pleasure in mere warmth—
   He seemed the measure of some constricted hope
That asked a place in which it might pursue
   Its fulness, and so grew away from him,
Swayed into palpability like a wall:
   He knew that he must follow out its confine
To his freedom, and be taught this tense fluidity
   Always a thought beyond him. His hand
Still feeling for that flank of stone,
   The space that opened round him might have grown there
For the resurrection of a being buried
   By the reality that too much defined it: now
The transitions of the dream, the steps and streets,
   The passageways that branched beneath
Haphazard accumulation of moon on moon,
   Spurned at each turn a reality
Merely given—an inert threat
   To be met with and accommodated. The ways
He walked seemed variants on a theme
   Shaped by a need that was greed no longer,
The dream of a city under the city's dream,
   Proportioned to the man whom sleep replenishes
To stand reading with opened eyes
   The intricacies of the imagined spaces there
Strange and familiar as the lines that map a hand.

AFTER A DEATH

A little ash, a painted rose, a name.
   A moonshell that the blinding sky
Puts out with winter blue, hangs
   Fragile at the edge of visibility. That space
Drawing the eye up to its sudden frontier
   Asks for a sense to read the whole
Reverted side of things. I wanted
   That height and prospect such as music brings—
Music or memory. Neither brought me here.
   This burial place straddles a green hill,

Chimneys and steeples plot the distances
  Spread vague below: only the sky
In its upper reaches keeps
  An untarnished January colour. Verse
Fronting that blaze, that blade,
  Turns to retrace the path of its dissatisfactions,
Thought coiled on thought, and only certain that
  Whatever can make bearable or bridge
The waste of air, a poem cannot.
  The husk of moon, risking the whole of space,
Seemingly sails it, fraily launched
  To its own death and fulness. We buried
A little ash. Time so broke you down,
  Your lost eyes, dry beneath
Their matted lashes, a painted rose
  Seems both to memorialize and mock
What you became. It picks your name out
  Written on the roll beside a verse—
Obstinate words: measured against the blue,
  They cannot conjure with the dead. Words,
Bringing that space to bear, that air
  Into each syllable we speak, bringing
An earnest to us of the portion
  We must inherit, what thought of that would give
The greater share of comfort, greater fear—
  To live forever, or to cease to live?
The imageless unnaming upper blue
  Defines a world, all images
Of endeavors uncompleted. Torn levels
  Of the land drop, street by street,
Pitted and pooled, its wounds
  Cleansed by a light, dealt out
With such impartiality you'd call it kindness,
  Blindly assuaging where assuagement goes unfelt.

II. Dialectic as Creation and Critique

5

Raymond Williams and Marxist Criticism

I

It is hard to realize Raymond Williams's recent study, *The Country and the City*, as critical theory in any generally accepted sense of that term. For Williams seems at once too immersed in the analysis of historical detail—so much space devoted to the Enclosure Acts, after all—and too immediately personal, in his response to George Eliot and Hardy for example. Even the sense of schematic coherence glimpsed at the beginning becomes so burred over with digressions and qualifications that it almost disappears. Certainly, given as a standard the theoretical texts I discussed in part I, *The Country and the City* is deeply flawed. Like Tomlinson's poetry, it reveals that peculiarly English absorption in geographical discrimination and even in more generally empirical habits of perception which are so out of key with recent critical thinking. But where Tomlinson's public image—fastidious, aloof, conservative—can support the "idiosyncracies" often attributed to his poetry, Williams has been recognized for some time as perhaps England's most influential Marxist thinker. No other English voice at least has been at once so scrupulous about and yet so critical of the merely personal and private, of that "modern" preoccupation with individual and creative self-realization.

Rather than being contradictory, however, I would suggest that these extremes in Williams's criticism are inherent in the very nature of dialectical thinking. And it is by way of insisting on them that I want to argue dialectical criticism as something other than an alternative method to the critical methods discussed in part I. To this point I have exploited a traditionally recognized function of dialectic as a weapon of critique, as a means of revealing the presuppositions and limitations of other forms of thought. With

Williams's criticism, and with the criticism of Fredric Jameson I shall discuss in the next chapter, I think it necessary to emphasize the way in which dialectical thinking can be itself creative as well as critical. It is as a synthesis of creation and critique that dialectical criticism opposes the very idea of a critical methodology.

The thread of Williams's discussion in *The Country and the City* which I wish to follow can be understood as a single crucial problem. And so it is that my emphasis risks an inevitable abstraction from the intricacy of his argument in a way that would not be the case if I were to concentrate more directly on an attempt to win recognition for Williams's achievement as, precisely, critical theory of the highest order. Yet the nature of the problem is suggested both by his involvement with specific historical circumstances and by the way he attends to individual literary works, by, that is, a certain convergence of those traditional antagonists, Marxist and New Criticism. Thus, if I am right about the importance of this nexus within *The Country and the City,* then the larger question of the book's opposition to other and typically methodological exercises of theoretical thinking at least can be recognized as a necessary one.

There are of course many forms of both Marxist and New Critical understanding of literature, and as many ways of distinguishing between them. It would negate Williams's own sensitivity to critical differences to offer his work as a means of integrating this multiplicity into a single synthesis. Yet I think a general distinction can be made that is important to *The Country and the City.* For a New Critic such as Cleanth Brooks, each individual work of literature represents a *sui generis* context. That is, it must be understood through its own internal relations. Fredric Jameson, in *Marxism and Form,* underscores the profound antipathy of Marxist thought toward such a conclusion: "That Flaubert is *sui generis* is to say nothing; but that he is no longer Balzac, that he is not yet Zola, and this in a host of determinate ways, is to articulate the structures inherent in and constitutive of the novel of Flaubert" (*MF,* 314–15).* Jameson finds such differential perception at least implicit

---

*See below, pp. 242–43, for a list of the works cited in this chapter and the abbreviations I have employed.

in all criticism. Marxism simply carries it through to a logical conclusion, to a study of the actual social and historical conditions from which the work emerges. But his immediate assimilation is too easy; the response from New Critics has been always that one has to understand the individual nature of the poem, what in fact it is, before it can be related to anything else. The initial difficulty in understanding *The Country and the City* is to get beyond this antithetical way of posing the problem without, however, refusing its importance altogether.

I can suggest the following as a tentative formulation: the New Critics were concerned in their different ways with an idea of literary creation that could integrate a holistic conception of literature with the particular forms and techniques of individual works; Marxist critics on the whole have been preoccupied less with the specific character of literature than with the means of developing a dialectic of critical response to it. Pushed to an extreme, these positions yield the antinomy I have described, with the New Critics arguing for an understanding of each individual work as sui generis and Marxist critics arguing for a dialectical awareness of the individual work in relation to a social context. But what must be realized instead are the pressures which originate these positions.

The Marxist concern with critical response rather than with the interior constitution of literature can be related directly to the powerful critique of "rationalist" or "contemplative" philosophy, most notably achieved by Georg Lukács. In *History and Class Consciousness,* he argues that this most essential form of bourgeois thought develops through a duality. On the one hand, there is a belief in the power of *systemization,* of introducing a principle of inclusiveness by means of which any given phenomena attain significance insofar as they conform to theoretically determinant rules of constitution. Thus,

> the correct positing of a principle implies—at least in its general tendency—the positing of a whole system determined by it; the consequences are entailed in the principle, they can be deduced from it, they are predictable and calculable. The real evolution of the totality of postulates may appear as an "infinite process," but this limitation means only that we cannot survey the whole

system at once; it does not detract from the principle of systemization in the least. [*HCC*, 117]

On the other hand, there is the correlative postulate of an ultimately inaccessible matter such as the Kantian "thing-in-itself," an "irrational" content forever excluded from the system. Thus the principle of inclusion operates at the same time as a limit, a means of exclusion. Everything that we know can be accounted for systematically; that which cannot be systematic cannot be known.

Once this duality is grasped, that any principle of systemization is simultaneously inclusive and exclusive, the attempt to construct a totality of the knowable is abandoned. There is a "rejection of every 'metaphysics' (in the sense of ontology) and also ... [the] positing as the aim of philosophy the understanding of the phenomena of isolated, highly specialized areas by means of abstract rational special systems, perfectly adapted to them and without making the attempt to achieve a unified mastery of the whole realm of the knowable" (*HCC*, 120). For literary criticism, this specialization means an attempt to define literature as an intrinsic system of literary norms in opposition to a set of extrinsic structures—typically social or historical—that are felt to be outside the proper domain of literary study.

Thus, in this critical mode, Marxist thought is itself essentially a response to the antinomies of bourgeois ideology and social structure. A Marxist critic will be concerned primarily, not with the unique features of the individual work or with the set of literary norms that connect it to other works of literature, but rather with the kind of response that can escape the dualism of intrinsic and extrinsic. Social content does not exist "outside" the structure of literature but "inside" as well; critical response incorporates the work of literature into a dialectical action, where social structure is to literary form as a latent content which becomes manifest in the work through the deformation of a system of norms thereafter to be recognized as the negative pole of an actual, social tension.

The danger here is the temptation to deply this interior deformation of the systematic into a new positivity, a new system of the same sort Marxist criticism is intended to rectify. In the more tendentious theories of social realism, for example, the conception of "social content" ceases to operate as a dialectical means of signification, as a content which is actual only in relation to the forms of the systematic it opposes. Instead, this content becomes itself a system, the ultimate explanatory code which underlies all literary phenomena. Thus the emphasis on critical response in Marxist thought is doubly necessary. For a genuinely Marxist criticism must resist any attempt to assimilate the work of literature into an intrinsic system of the exclusively "literary." And it must operate also as a self-critical response, as a corrective to the elevation of previously "extrinsic" elements into a new form of the systematic.

Now the special importance of Raymond Williams's criticism has been his refusal from the outset to recognize any division of intrinsic and extrinsic in the study of literature. Such divisions propagate a false consciousness, although they are of course symptomatic of an important history of twentieth-century thought. Thus Williams is especially sensitive to the need for Marxism to act in direct and critical relation to normative systems of literature. In his first major study, *Culture and Society,* he makes his defense of the great English realistic novelists on the basis of an argument ranged against any attempt at assimilating their work into a notion of an autonomous culture, not by erecting a prescriptive system of social realism as a norm for literature. In the essays which make up *The Long Revolution,* he begins, not by a systematic equation of creativity with revolutionary change, but rather with a critical account of the way in which creativity has been detached from the actual perception of social relationships and placed in the realm of the purely aesthetic. *Modern Tragedy,* in part, is a critique of the notion of tragedy as embodied in a long literary tradition where change is registered merely as the displacement of certain central norms in a way that can be systematically—and ahistorically—analyzed. In each case, Williams's own conception of literature is made to emerge from within a dialectical engagement among the forms of critical response.

Once these reasons for a concern with critical response to literature have been understood, it is possible to suggest some similarities to the work of the New Critics, as well as an essential difference. For despite the polemics between their proponents in the United States during the thirties and forties, the best New Criticism hardly

could be said to ignore the social content of literature. It should not
have been really surprising that *Seven Types of Ambiguity* and
Milton's God were written by the same man. And as Perry Anderson
has argued in *New Left Review,* it is likewise no accident that
Williams as one of England's leading Marxists should be, of all
things, a literary critic.[1] It was his predecessor at Cambridge, F. R.
Leavis, and not the English Marxists of the thirties who provided
in his actual work with literature the most sustained and penetrating critique of English culture.

Perhaps more importantly, the New Critics were equally concerned
in their own way to avoid any systematic division between intrinsic
and extrinsic. Even R. P. Blackmur's early emphasis on "technical"
criticism can be understood in this way. For Blackmur, an approach
through "technique" recommends itself over other approaches
because it can be inclusive; it does not have to be blinkered by
the demands of a systematic doctrine, and as a consequence it is
free to explore the most complex implications of literary form. And
in his later essays, when he fears that a technical approach has itself
become a methodology, his interest in the relations between literature and the sociocultural becomes an explicit and overriding
problem. In the quite different work of Eliseo Vivas—a profoundly
conservative critic—there is still the emphasis that nothing is to
be conceived as extrinsic or external to the creation of literature,
certainly not historical or social substance. Rather than a system
of uniquely literary norms, Vivas's conception of the specifically
literary refers to a creative inclusiveness that cannot be reduced to
any form of systematic description or explanation. And although
Vivas hardly would choose to call his own thinking dialectical, he
nevertheless attempts continually to reconcile the universal and the
particular, an essential and holistic nature of literature with the particular conditions and problems in the individual work.

However, the motive for these ways of refusing a division between
extrinsic and intrinsic was fundamentally different, inhering in a
need to provide a positive being for literature. The "heresy of
paraphrase" formula was less a statement about what the critic
should not do than a statement about what literature does, a constitutive and not a regulative formula.[2] Literature was to be defended
at all costs from being assimilated into the abstract and discursive

modes of the social sciences on the one hand and of liberal political rhetoric on the other. The New Critics of course developed a whole array of specific "techniques" for talking about works of literature, but insofar as these were made explicit, they were conceived as a propaedeutic to response and not response itself. Thus it was perhaps inevitable as the energy of the New Criticism hardened that it should become a means of alienation rather than a force which liberated one from the tendentiousness of doctrine, as Blackmur had imagined. The result was the kind of pedagogical elitism with which we are all familiar, where literature becomes a Holy Temple of creative mystery and the critic a high priest, one who had remembered the ritual techniques for sensitive discernment but who had forgotten the real possibility of inclusive order which sustained them. The point, however, is that this is no more a fair representation of the best New Critical work than a naive projection of social realism fairly characterizes the best Marxist criticism.

Now *The Country and the City* suggests as a means of integrating these divergent forms of criticism an understanding of dialectic as *both* creation and response, both creative and critical such that it can take up the New Critical concern for the autonomous nature of individual poems and yet realize within their creative activity a necessary critical relation to other works of literature and to a social world. The necessity for such integration arises from Williams's reaction to the pressure from archetypal and structuralist methodologies which currently dominate critical theory. For poised against the New Criticism, Marxist criticism could afford to maintain its critical stance, its insistence on elaborating just those connections which an extreme New Critical concept of a poem as a sui generis context ignored or suppressed. However, these new methodologies elevate the distinction between creation and response into a systematic division which Williams has understood to be a far greater danger.

And such methodological formalism is itself ambiguous. On the one hand, it is a deep-felt response to a disorder within the field of criticism that has transformed what should be an exemplary and inclusive human community into a town of warring suburbs. E. D. Hirsch's plea for a methodological purity that would not confuse the meaning of a text with its significance has as its basis a desire to mediate the kind of internecine quarrels that arose in France, for example, between Roland Barthes and Raymond Picard over the interpretation of Racine. Frye is even more explicitly evangelical: "A society in which the president of the United States can be changed by one psychotic with a rifle is not sufficiently real for any thoughtful person to want to live wholly within it. What real society is, is indicated by the structure of arts and sciences in the university" ("IMP," 7). What Frye develops is an essentially mythic vision of human community within which literary criticism will play a central role.

On the other hand, these forms of criticism participate in a profound change within the human sciences that would direct their effort from a new "center" provided by the model of language. Understood in this way, language promises a basic code to permit the very process of interpretation, but it generates at the same time a mechanism of discontinuity which refuses an ultimate identity between signifier and signified, between any given system and its object. Thus, not only does such formalism suggest a new and radically different concern with critical response to literature, but also it eludes Marxist arguments against the attempt to systematize the essential and intrinsic qualities of literature. The ambiguous relation between signifier and signified includes within the formal model itself the discontinuity Lukács had argued would lead to increased specialization, to a plurality of unrelated systems. Yet at the same time it does not make the equation between system and object, between the principle of systemization and the knowable which Lukács had rejected.

However, the important point for Williams is that the consequence of this twofold impulse remains paradoxical. Even in Frye, the embodiment of human community in myth never quite coincides with the radical formalization of knowledge promised through the model of language. The total, mythic form of literature as the city of human desire is always potential and never actual. As I argued in chapter 3, for a structuralist critic like Roland Barthes, the very presence of discourse at once builds the city and yet walls in its inhabitants: "human knowledge can participate in the becoming of the world only through a series of successive metalanguages, each one of which is alienated in the very moment that determines it. . . .

the semiologist is he who expresses his future death in the very terms by which he has named and understood the world" (*SM*, 293). As for the suicide sculptor in the way Barthes reads Balzac's "Sarrasine," every signifying system has as its signified a *lost* object of desire. Only the process itself continues, and "this infinite construction is not sophisticated" (*SM*, 293); it can never return on itself in any concrete actuality.

Thus, in *The Country and the City*, Williams has understood that this methodological formalism introduces within literary criticism another form of the division between intrinsic and extrinsic, a problem of whether literature actually can enter into critical discourse, of what rights a "creative work" is to be accorded within the suddenly rigorous boundaries of the city of criticism. For the shift from a concern with the nature of literature in the New Critics to a concern with the substance of critical method not only employs the concepts of "privilege" and "displacement" but also enacts them in its own constitution. Literature can enter, not as itself a system, but only through the privilege of critical systemization, as an infinite repetition of the Same, while the power to create is then displaced into a wholly autonomous Other, ranged just beyond the city limits in silent and perhaps even menacing attendance for who knows what secret and underground passage to open up. Even Frye, that most consummate city dweller, must turn occasionally an oblique glance toward the outskirts: "The presence of incommunicable experience in the center of criticism will always keep criticism an art, as long as the critic recognizes that criticism comes out of it but cannot be built on it" (*AC*, 8). Here, the mechanism of alienation is no longer an elitist awareness of the special nature of literature but an apotheosis of "inside" and "outside" which relegates creativity itself, in either artist or critic, to the silent, the incommunicable, the hopelessly private and subjective expanse of wilderness that fronts the city community at every point.

It is against this mythic and infinitely deferred form of community that Williams will posit in *The Country and the City* the Marxist revolutionary community: "Out of the cities, in fact, came these two great and transforming modern ideas: myth, in its variable forms; revolution, in its variable forms. Each, under pressure, offers to convert the other to its terms. But they are better seen as alternative responses, for in a thousand cities, if in confused forms, they are in sharp, direct, and necessary conflict" (*CC*, 247). Yet Williams's argument registers an important change in emphasis. For what he must develop is not only a negative rebellion against the exclusiveness of systematic thought but also, and like the New Critics, some positive being for literary creation which can overcome the discontinuity that stalks a theory of critical systemization such as Frye's.

II

In a late interview with a member of the Yugoslav Communist party, Lukács expressed a number of reservations about "the increasingly polyphonic character of Marxism" ("TC," 325). But Williams's thinking makes it clear why in fact such a "polyphony" now exists. It arises from the stress of transforming an essentially critical response to bourgeois social structure and ideology into a positive and dialectical theory of social change. Marx was well aware that in devoting the major effort of his later years to *Capital*, he had in no way accomplished that transformation. In his preface to the second edition, he insists that the value of his work as a dialectical understanding "is in its essence critical and revolutionary" (*Cap*, 26). And the preface to the first edition underscores the awareness that such critical understanding does "not signify that to-morrow a miracle will happen" (*Cap*, 16). For "even when a society has got upon the right track for the discovery of the natural laws of its movement—and it is the ultimate aim of this work, to lay bare the economic law of motion of modern society—it can neither clear by bold leaps, nor remove by legal enactments, the obstacles offered by the successive phases of its normal development. But it can shorten and lessen the birth-pangs" (*Cap*, 14–15), the signs of which Lukács finds so disconcerting.

In his concern for "totality" in *History and Class Consciousness*, Lukács had struggled with the problem of transforming a fragmented and specialized bourgeois relationship to social and material environment into a dialectic. What bourgeois ideology views as a systematic product or commodity, proletarian consciousness understands as merely one aspect of a continuous process. Yet this identification of dialectical process with the consciousness of the proletariat led

Lukács to his conception of the proletariat as "the identical subject-object of history," a conclusion he repudiates sharply in a preface to *History and Class Consciousness* published in 1967:

> But is the identical subject-object here anything more in truth than a purely metaphysical construct? Can a genuinely identical subject-object be created by self-knowledge, however adequate, and however truly based on an adequate knowledge of society, i.e. however perfect that self-knowledge is? We need only formulate the question precisely to see that it must be answered in the negative. [*HCC*, xxiii]

As Lukács seems to realize, idealism inheres precisely in the immediate identification of conscious reason with the becoming of the world.

Nevertheless, this self-criticism still glosses the central problem. Even if one assumes, as Lukács does in the 1967 preface, that beyond self-conscious awareness totality is implicity in the "objective" historical situation, it is impossible to make praxis contingent upon such an assumption, any more than it can be contingent upon the assumption that the proletariat represents "the identical subject-object of history." For the real difficulty in Lukács's argument is not, as he seems to think, the identification of "subject" and "object" *in proletarian consciousness* but rather the presupposition of totality as a fait accompli, whether in proletarian consciousness or in the "historical situation." The very nature of praxis as dialectical must involve the refusal of *any* immediate identification.

Despite his caution throughout *Capital,* this essential point is often far from clear in Marx himself. There is the belief in *The Communist Manifesto,* for example, that an awareness of the infrastructure of society can become not only a dialectical means of social change but also a total and fundamental truth. When recognized in its transparency, freed from the encumbrances of cultural resistance, it would immediately obligate the individual to revolutionary praxis. Once granted access to the ugly truths of urban and industrial capitalism, the urban proletariat would be in a special position to shape revolutionary change, at whatever expense to those rural populations whose consciousness had not yet been raised to this inclusive point of awareness.

For Williams, it was this ambiguity that helped produce a terrible distortion within the history of communism:

> The exposed urban proletariat would learn and create new and higher forms of society: if that was all that had been said it would have been very different. But if the forms of bourgeois development contained, with whatever contradiction, values higher than "rural idiocy" or "barbarism" [these are direct quotations from *The Communist Manifesto*] then almost any programme, in the name of the urban proletariat, could be justified and imposed. . . . To see exposure creating revolution was one thing; to see more of the same producing something quite different was at best an apocalyptic hope. [*CC,* 303]

There is no reason to assume that, even if in the course of capitalistic development the infrastructure of socioeconomic truth were to be laid bare, a new and revolutionary society would emerge as a necessary consequence. A perception of the infrastructure can bring to a crisis the very possibility of human community, but crisis and resolution are not identical, nor do they come from the same source. To assume that they are again reduces a conception of totality to a fait accompli, an idealization which has more in common with "rationalism" than with dialectic. In Sartre's memorable formulation: "The heuristic principle—'to search for the whole in its parts'—has become the terrorist practice of liquidating the particularity" (*SMeth,* 28). Out of a crisis, genuine praxis must create the the means of forging a new community through a realization of the multiple activities of all its members. Pluralism tolerates differences by cleanly separating them into discrete realms; "totality" as an *activity,* as praxis, develops only in and through the particular ways it can be manifested.

These considerations are not as remote from critical theory as they may seem. For what is involved in a critical theory of systemization is precisely the "liquidation" of the individual, creative effort which shapes a work of literature. The point is simple but essential. As long as we protect ourselves by that ideological reflex which determines a poem as an "object" or a "product," there is no perceived violence in coercing that poem into one's own critical structures. But once a poem is allowed to assume its full nature as an actual human effort, such practice can be recognized for what it is. The deepest objection to a book like *S/Z* addresses, finally, not its self-deceptive methodology but rather its inherent arrogance, its almost casual reduction of "Sarrasine" to an impersonal event to be manipulated.

The strength of Williams's argument in *The Country and the City* is his recognition that the intensely subjective nature of creativity and the communal forms of response are intimately related; neither can exist as an isolated activity. The creative voice of the artist comes into being only as that voice is heard critically. Thus Williams argues that Joyce in *Ulysses* shapes the novel's development only as he hears his own voice in the context of other and different voices and individuals—rather than offering a single, universal language "to speak for everyone and everything" as in *Finnegans Wake*.[3] Likewise, critical response is never a simple matter of exposure to the anatomy of creative literature in hopes that some new and dramatic fusion will occur. It requires the same kind of personal and creative act as the author's, and not by any mystical insight or incommunicable experience. The critic can hear the author's speech because the author has heard it; his voice comes into existence in the act of realizing itself as one voice among many. Each work and each critical response is thus a form of community in and through the very action by which it comes into being.

Thus this act to which Williams would attend is a continual creation and inclusion of individual differences rather than a totality defined as the absence of existent differences and distinctions. Even as modified by that 1967 preface, Lukács's argument in *History and Class Consciousness* remains an essentially two-term mechanism: the stasis of the systematic, in whatever form, is broken up by a radical perception of the infrastructure of society which gathers up the fragments of a specialized knowledge into a totality. Williams's thinking introduces a third term in a way which transforms this ambivalence into a dialectical action involving three distinct, though integrally related moments: the creative act of the individual; the critical and revolutionary awareness of the actual, shifting social relationships through which that act comes into existence; and a realization of a new form of community made possible. For Williams, literature can be creative only to the extent that it is also in critical relation to a social world, and the response to literature is possible only insofar as it is personally creative as well.

Now the explicit problem Williams has set himself in *The Country and the City* is to analyze the real historical development of "country" and "city" in English life in sharp contrast to the powerful multiplicity of ideological meaning that has accrued to these as terms, as concepts, as "structures of feeling." And it is necessary to ask about the relationship between this overriding problem and the theme I have been elaborating. For however simple Williams's argument may seem in its origination, it very quickly becomes more complex than a matter of separating actual history from its ideological disguise. He has recognized, convincingly and in detail, the truth hinted at by Engels in his letter to Joseph Bloch in 1890:

> The economic situation is the basis, but the various elements of the superstructure—political forms of the class struggle and its results, to wit: constitutions established by the victorious class after a successful battle, etc., juridical forms, and even the reflexes of all these actual struggles in the brains of the participants, political, juristic, philosophical theories, religious views and their further development into systems of dogmas—also exercise their influence upon the course of the historical struggles and in many cases preponderate in determining their *form*. [Engels, 294]

Williams makes clear his commitment in the last chapter, that "capitalism, as a mode of production, is the basic process of most of what we know as the history of country and city" (*CC*, 302). Later, he restates in more detail this fundamental contention:

> The division and opposition of city and country, industry and agriculture, in their modern forms, are the critical culmination of the division and specialization of labour which, though it did not begin with capitalism, was developed under it to an extraordinary and transforming degree. Other forms of the same fundamental division are the separation between mental and manual labour, between administration and operation, between politics and social life. The symptoms of this division can be

found at every point in what is now our common life: in the idea and practice of social classes; in conventional definitions of work and of education; in the physical distribution of settlements; and in temporal organization of the day, the week, the year, the lifetime. [*CC,* 304–05]

But the point to be made is that this history has been the result of a complex interaction of economic forces and ideology, of infrastructure and superstructure. For the possibility of praxis depends upon the recognition not only that revolutionary change in the modes of production can be effected now but also that the infrastructure of society, through and through and from the beginning, has been "contaminated" by the pressure from the history of ideology, that, more exactly, it is one history and not two which has to be understood. Thus the relatively static and ahistorical analysis of appearance and reality—of ideological content in the terms "country" and "city" and the underlying economic development of actual cities—becomes transformed into a dialectical awareness of interaction at every step of the way.

This means, to begin with, that a discussion of the Enclosure Acts, for example, is not a translation of purely literary experience back into some more fundamental perception of social reality but rather one way of articulating critically a process already at work *in* the literature at hand. This is what must be implied by the refusal of any division between "intrinsic" and "extrinsic" in the study of literature. Conversely, discussions of literary archetypes or other methodological programs go beyond a status as elements of the superstructure. They participate in and articulate a specific social and political commitment, even an economic mode of consumption. Such "mythic" forms of community are to be resisted, not because, as ideological appearance, they falsify by not telling the whole story, but rather because of what they do enact, what they do entail at every point.

Williams's insistence on "making the connections," on understanding literature within a single, complex historical development suggests the relationship between his concern for "country" and "city" and the conception of a literary work as a community which I argued to be Williams's way of resolving the antinomy of creation and response. They come together in the refusal of literature as a reflection of an existent social reality, a "known community" which would then provide a "larger context" for the individual work of literature. Instead, they offer the genuinely creative aspect of literature as the shaping of a "knowable community" that goes beyond the existing class divisions and carefully circumscribed distinctions that make up a "known" social world and to which the author's creative integrity in his work puts him always in direct and critical relation.[4] At the same time, the conjunction of these powerful ideas in Williams's argument engenders another and equally difficult problem of defining the nature of that "knowable community."

The implication I have drawn from the conception of a work of literature as a dialectic of creation and response is that it opens the work toward the future in a way that recognizes and includes the uniqueness of each individual voice. "Community" thus assumes a positive definition of inclusiveness or "totality" as an activity, where to love one's neighbor means simultaneously to realize that such love is possible only because that neighbor is not and never can be oneself. It is a creative and not a mimetic love. But such an action involves an inevitable risk, an openness to a future that is *unknown,* an otherness which never achieves even potential visibility within the interstices of a "knowable community." Literature is frightening, not because it is a monument, or even because its origin may be in a past beyond recovery, but rather because each work at the moment of "completion" has almost its whole life ahead of it. It *may* live into a knowable community, and it may not.

The major thrust of *The Country and the City,* on the other hand, is directed toward the refusal of "divisions" and "the conviction that the system which generates and is composed by them is intolerable and will not survive" (*CC,* 305). The effect is twofold. For the complexity of the dialectical relationship between creation and response is again reduced to a static mechanism, where the critical recognition and refusal of divisions in the "known community" become immediately identical with the creation of a new and inclusive "knowable community." And correlatively, the risk involved in a creative openness to the future is thereby both minimized and devalued. It is minimized to the extent that the future is felt as wholly immanent within the present—the system of divisions "will not survive"—and consequently the present loses its opaqueness for us. We know the future, and so we can work with what we know will work. Thus any risk is devalued as well, for the widest implications of a "knowable community" become nothing more than a "known community" deferred into the conceivable future.

What is missing in Williams's argument here is the awareness that "totality" or "inclusiveness" has not one but two critical antagonists. As he realizes—perhaps more profoundly than any other contemporary theorist—it must be posited against every kind of systematic division, whether that takes the more familiar form of a division of labor in all its various aspects or the equally intransigent, though less obvious, division between infrastructure and superstructure such that a single, complex historical development is broken into an ideological appearance and an underlying reality. The second antagonist, however, is the reduction of all individual uniqueness to the order of the Same, the "knowable," the future wholly immanent within the present moment. The opposition to this reduction involves that conception of autonomy I argued for in chapter 2, which now can be called upon to enforce an awareness that the most important distinction to be made is that between distinctiveness—or autonomy—and division. Without this second and indispensable realization, there remains no inherent means of preventing a rapid slide from "totality" to "totalitarian," the more painful because it originates in a diametrically opposed impulse. It is not really that we ask too much of literature when we insist that it provide the apocalyptic hope to sustain the possibility of overcoming all division in our human community. As the best work of the New Critics—and Williams himself—testifies again and again, we ask too little if we do not expect each work of literature to develop in ways that are impossible to calculate in advance, into futures of such infinite richness and diversity that they pale into a shadow world any conceivable completion.

6

Dialectic and Form

I

My title is an allusion to Fredric Jameson's *Marxism and Form*, for the problem I wish to pose is in part his as well: the means of developing a dialectical understanding of literary form. The charge most often and explicitly laid against Marxist criticism is that it fails to deal with those aspects of literary technique, of style, of tone; in short, precisely the *formal* qualities of literature for which modern criticism has realized such an elaborate vocabulary. Lukács's bias toward the novel, and specifically the nineteenth-century novel of Balzac and Tolstoi, can be cited as evidence of an inability to comprehend poetry as that inclusive literary genre where such formal qualities are most important. Yet this states as a conclusion what in fact should be a premise. It is true that Lukács—as well as Raymond Williams and other Marxist critics—has devoted significantly more critical attention to novels than to poetry. But any further elaboration at least must take into account the powerful arguments these critics have mounted against the ideological commitment which they find betrays itself in an exaggerated concern for "form" and "technique." Thus a serious consideration of the question very quickly becomes involved in a meditation on the nature of "ideology" and "class." For Jameson, it is not a matter of relating these social forces to the intricacies of literary form; they are already and intrinsically related, and the task of criticism is to articulate those relationships.

Nevertheless, the very idea of "class" initially seems to promise only the most alien and disturbing way of understanding literature. For in the most explicit Marxist formulations, class names the relationship between population and the modes of economic production. So it is that rather than beginning from the activity of the imagination—or the individual text, or the conjunction of texts, or the premise that literature is one among many uses of language, and so forth—one's actual starting point would be the *publication* of texts, the production and consumption of literature as a commodity, and the way in which groups of the population are related to this process and to each other through it. The distinction between what might be called a "sociology of literature" and a genuinely Marxist analysis inheres in how this economic ground is understood. For the former, literary form operates as so much "advertising," rhetorically seductive ways of encouraging further consumption and of creating a whole group of people whose primary function is to "interpret," that is, merchandise, the product. Yet as salutary as these "reductions" may be to an audience which imagines itself de facto removed from the marketplace, the easy cynicism they invite actually blocks rather than heightens critical awareness.

Marxist thought could understand the privilege accorded to "formalist" interpretation of literature as a kind of optical illusion of substance, a typical and thoroughly bourgeois hypostasis of one stage in a whole process, a whole action. Literature becomes a commodity precisely to the extent that the finished poem or novel is treated as if it had a life of its own, independent of the author's effort of making the poem, of the social and historical context in which he lived and worked, and ultimately, of course, independent of the relations of production and distribution by which a poem is printed in a book to be sold to and read by others. The real distinction is between literary form as an independent object of analysis and form as part of a continual process, a socioeconomic reality. From this larger perspective, a "sociology of literature" amounts to a fetishism of the economic comparable to the very illusion it was intended to rectify.

And already, in the very terms of such analysis, the idea of "class" has realized still another and equally powerful meaning. As Jameson argues, "*class* is problematical precisely because it is the mediator between these two different notational systems: for class is population articulated according to economic function, but it is also that which permits us to translate data about machinery and the operations of production back into human and interpersonal terms" (*MF*, 297).* Thus an understanding of the reification of literary form involves not one but two related conceptual operations. Its history can be described in linear relation to the development and expansion of "publication," where the appearance of the idea of a separate and autonomous realm of the "aesthetic" in late eighteenth- and early nineteenth-century thought corresponds to a whole complex of phenomena, ranging from the individual "ownership" of creative work given ultimate expression by the copyright laws to the growing possibility of "public education" as a marketplace for texts and textual interpretation.

But it also involves an intricate and less immediately obvious development of *class consciousness and class conflict,* where the "aesthetic" is often understood to operate, paradoxically, as a criticism rather than a ratification of an existent social structure. Thus even the attempt to determine literature as an independent object, in a specific historical context, can take on quite different meaning, as a way of refusing the assimilation of literature into a ruling ideology. This second conceptual operation makes possible the kind of criticism associated with Lukács, and before him with Marx and Engels themselves. In their analysis of Balzac, for example, the argument is that in Balzac's novels the techniques and forms of cultural awareness are turned against that culture, with the result that, almost despite himself, Balzac succeeded in laying bare the latent content of socioeconomic reality and class struggle in the very terms of the culture that was designed to obscure that reality. Rather than ideological falsification, literary form becomes the means of expressing the dynamics of a social situation as it can be made available to conscious understanding. Here, the distinction I drew between literary form as an independent object of analysis and form as part of a continual process is complicated still further by an awareness of "form" as in a sense already a dialectical interaction of form and content.

This is also the point where the importance of Sartre's *Critique de la raison dialectique* makes itself felt, for Jameson's argument in

*See below, p. 244, for a list of the works cited in this chapter and the abbreviations I have employed.

Marxism and Form but also for the very possibility of Marxist criticism. Indeed, one way to understand the *Critique* is as an effort to realize, since *History and Class Consciousness* at least, what has remained only an implicit promise of Marxist thought: the development and history of class consciousness *from the inside,* or perhaps more exactly, as it represents actual, lived experience in continuous interaction with a material reality. For surely to the extent that a work of literature can be said not only to express but also to criticize an existent social structure—even to articulate the possibility of a new human community—then the analysis of literary form in direct relation to economic production is not so much false as it is incomplete. One need only remember the statement from Engels in a letter to Margaret Harkness, that he had learned more from Balzac about actual French society "than from all the professed historians, economists and statisticians of the period together" (Engels, 115), to understand something of the importance of Sartre's effort for Marxist criticism.

In *Search for a Method,* which prefaces the *Critique,* Sartre must try to show the relationship between an obvious and explicit Marxist understanding of action as a whole process based within an economic infrastructure and his own earlier and "existentialist" insistence on every human action as establishing a primary relation to Being. For, in *Being and Nothingness,* Sartre had described the essentially human and immediate quality of lived experience as a lack, a void or hollow in the plenitude of Being. Standing over against man is the world of objects, its very facticity radically and irreducibly alien to human thought and existence. Man defines himself as a "project," an action directed toward the future in which one freely takes responsibility for his relation to Being. Rather than the ideological mystification of superstructure, existentialist criticism thus focuses on the subtle and intricate devices of consciousness that obscure the responsibility inherent in the project, what Sartre had termed *bad faith.* The great work of literature, again, is a kind of laying bare, but of consciousness; it is an action which turns the intricacies of consciousness against themselves in order to reveal a more primary content, a more primary relation.

The argument of *Search for a Method* refuses to suggest that the real problem is one of reconciling these apparently contradictory ways of thinking, these two conceptions of what a "whole action" entails. Nor does Sartre attempt to explain one on the basis of the other. Either alternative would focus attention on the object of action, on Marxism as concerned with a special kind of economic content or on existentialism as concerned with another kind of content, with the phenomenology of individual, lived experience. And thus they would be ways of reifying thought, comparable to the priority of substance over action rejected by Marxism and existentialism. Rather, Sartre wishes to pose the problem of *mediation* as central to both, the means through which one aspect of experience can be related to any other, from the most intimately personal to the most sweeping development of historical change. What Jameson will call "translation," the mediating movement from one kind of experience to another, is for Sartre the place of the genuinely concrete, where the antinomies of logical analysis dissolve into the process of dialectic and where both a Marxist and an existentialist sense of "the whole action" can be realized at the very moment of their coming into being within a development that implicates every dimension of a human world.

Jameson argues that the advantage for literary criticism in this sense of action as *translation* is that it does not elevate a special object of analysis to supreme importance, neither economic institutions nor the "authenticity" of consciousness. Rather, it provides the means for a technical analysis of formal unity to be translated without loss of meaning into the full, lived reality of history. Criticism thus opens the work to the movement of time, preserving its density, its unique nature, its formal qualities of expression, while at the same time allowing it to speak to a future as well as a past and a present.

Yet Jameson's sense of "translation" or "mediation" as the only concrete reality poses a difficult problem: "For a genuinely dialectical criticism, indeed, there can be no preestablished categories of analysis" (*MF,* 333). Nothing exists outside the mediate act itself, neither category nor substance; there is no "larger context" in which mediation can be placed and understood. And isn't "class" in either way Jameson uses the term precisely just such a category?

Thus here is what happens to the idea of "symbolism" through Jameson's reading of Lukács:

> Thus symbolism results not from the properties of the things themselves but from the will of the creator, who imposes a meaning on them by fiat: it represents the vain attempt of subjectivity to evolve a human world completely out of itself. In this, it is much like the earlier middle-class ethic of the moral imperative, the ideal of the *Sollen,* which Lukács criticizes in *Theory of the Novel.* [*MF,* 198]

That is, symbolism comes to be *understood* at the point when it can be resolved into a distinctively middle-class relation to material objects. And this understanding is then turned back on works of literature, such that "the furniture in *The Spoils of Poynton,* the brooding cities of Dickens and Dostoyevsky, the morally expressive landscapes of a Gide or a D. H. Lawrence, exist in the work of art as self-sufficient elements, carrying their meaning built into them" (*MF,* 197), as symbols, as indicative of certain class relationship to the world.

What is missing here is that "heightened self-consciousness" Jameson ascribes to dialectical thought, the turning back *on itself* which would recognize in the very terms of this analysis a "symbolic" mode of *criticism.* Like unfamiliar, alien objects, the novels of Dickens and Lawrence are assimilated into the known, familiar context of class structure. Just as the author, through the process of symbolizing, is said to imply "that some original, objective meaning in objects is henceforth inaccessible to him" (*MF,* 197), so it is that the critic treats these novels as objects which possess no such "original, objective meaning" until reintegrated within the context of class analysis by which he approaches them. It is as if we first had to accept the reification of literary form as a given and then show how this quantum of alien matter loses its opaqueness for us at the point when it can be reinvested with the intellectual configuration of class structure which we carry in our heads.

Yet there is of course another way to understand Jameson's argument. In *Women in Love,* after the death of Gerald, Birkin searches out the spot where Gerald had died:

He went over the snow slopes, to see where the death had been. At last he came to the great shallow among the precipices and slopes, near the summit of the pass. It was a grey day, the third day of greyness and stillness. All was white, icy, pallid, save for the scoring of black rocks that jutted like roots sometimes, and sometimes were in naked faces. In the distance a slope sheered down from a peak, with many black rock-slides. [*WL*, 544]

What Birkin comes to realize as his eyes scan up from the hollow where Gerald had died is the sense in which this cannot be a neutral "landscape," or more exactly, that its meaning has been altered fundamentally, less by the imposition of his (or Lawrence's) subjective will upon it than insofar as it has now been touched and handled by the look through which Gerald encompassed it as he marched away through the snow from Gudrun and Loerke, and as it bears the imprint of his death. Birkin almost intuitively makes the connections to what he has known and realized about Gerald, from his relationship with Gudrun to the death at the water party to the scene with the horse at the railroad crossing to Gerald's class position as "Industrial Magnate." Birkin is "defeated," not by having to fall back upon the imposition of a "symbolic" meaning to this "landscape," but rather as he feels the shock of meaning imparted to him *by* the landscape.[1]

This second argument suggests that the relation between literary form and class structure, between symbolism and a determinate relation to a material environment, does not come after the fact, in a critical translation of the opaqueness of the novel back into the terms of what one already knows about class structure. Rather, the critical act is a continuation in a new form of the process of "translation" or "mediation" already at work in the novel, where now one is no longer "talking about" the novel, imposing upon its shifting and intricate relationships a structure of meaning, "symbolizing" the novel in Jameson's sense of "symbolizing." Like the shock of self-judgment which comes to Birkin as he continues to meditate on the landscape of Gerald's death ("Gerald might have found this rope. . . . He might! And what then? The Imperial road! The south? Italy? What then? Was it a way out? It was only a way in again" [*WL*, 545]), the novel talks back to the critic through that constitutive shock of realization when one is forced to understand that as he begins to speak he already has an audience in the novel itself, just as Birkin's thoughts are brought up short by that responsive landscape at which he gazes.

I think it is some such dialectical interaction which must be implied by Jameson's statement "that each work is the end result of a kind of inner logic or development in its own content, it evolves its own categories and dictates the terms of its own interpretation" (*MF*, 333). The difficulty in *Marxism and Form*—and, I shall argue, in Sartre's *Critique* as well—is to reconcile this idea with the argument that comes two pages earlier:

> But for Marxism the adequation of object to subject or of form to content can exist as an imaginative possibility only where in some way or another it has been concretely realized in social life itself, so that formal realizations, as well as formal defects, are taken as the signs of some deeper corresponding social and historical configuration which it is the task of criticism to explore. [*MF,* 331]

This passage explains a great deal about why Marxist criticism typically has valued the novel over poetry, a point I shall return to in my conclusion. In its very length, elaboration, narrative, and developed "world" of characters, the density of the novel more obviously and directly "corresponds" to a "deeper" social reality as Marxism understands it. Yet insofar as this "configuration" is indeed "deeper," the critical act is once again transformed into the excavation of an underlying reality which then can be turned back on the opaqueness of literary works as a way of reinvesting them with a meaning already known and comprehended. That is, such a procedure corresponds to the first and not the second way I have characterized Jameson's argument about "symbolism."

Nevertheless, I do not want to suggest that, if class structure *as a set of known relationships* is inadequate for the criticism of literature, it is because there is something in the very nature of literary form alone that transcends such analysis. This merely reaffirms a specious independence to the work of literature that is but one more step in the process of making literature over into a negotiable commodity. Instead, I think it possible to read the *Critique,* and

Jameson's discussion of it, as the heuristic means of realizing "class" to be less known strata of the population than a way one becomes known in continuous relation to others and to a material environment. For criticism, it is never a question of how class consciousness or class conflict *gets into* literature—as if they were aliens waiting in a smuggler's night—but how literary creation realizes a complex world of human relationships. There is no "deeper . . . social and historical configuration" to which the work of literature corresponds. It is itself, through and through, a social reality. Thus, in conclusion, I shall try to show that an understanding of "class" is not merely a long digression but rather an appropriate means of coming to terms with what is implied by literary form.

II

Despite the difference in language, perhaps the immediate difficulty in understanding the *Critique* is the temptation to assimilate it backward into *Being and Nothingness*. In an otherwise sympathetic analysis, Wilfred Desan for example understands both to be avatars of that extreme subjectivity which by its very nature covertly elevates the Cartesian cogito as the central core of human identity. I shall argue later that such assimilations are themselves ideologically symptomatic. The point, in any case, is that we can know in advance what happens if the *Critique* is determined as merely a further elaboration of the argument in *Being and Nothingness*. Jameson's idea is sounder, that in effect the appearance of the *Critique* once more renders *Being and Nothingness* an *open* problem to be reread as something infinitely more suggestive than a moment in a past we know already how to criticize.

It is the analysis of interpersonal relationships which provides the most concrete manifestation of the difficulties involved in *Being and Nothingness*. The relation of self and other, of *two* projects, is conceived in terms of an initial and inescapable recognition: even as I look at the other, suspending him as an object at the end of my gaze, his eyes are doing the same to me. What I am forced to see is no longer an object at which I can stare or pass by as I choose. Rather, there is an "object" who has the unique capacity to make me into an object through his gaze exactly in the way

I am transforming him into an object. As it was for Hegel, the brute existence of the Other proves a necessary scandal to my subjectivity. Thus the description of human relations that follow from this mutual look is a history of attempts at domination. Two freedoms, two projects, conflict inevitably. Alienation thereby becomes the most constant feature of interpersonal relations, as both the loss of self which results insofar as I realize myself as an object through the "look" of another, and as the distance my own look imposes *between* myself and others. Not only does social existence become a riddle, as Lukács argued in his critique of existentialism, but one's own experience has a perpetually dissolving effect. Merely to open the eyes is to enter a world of hard, predatory surfaces that mock and distort every contact.

Yet the *Critique* reminds us how facile it is to assume, as Desan and others have, that these difficulties arise from the ontological priority Sartre accords to subjectivity. For the subject is said to be an ontological *lack*, a kind of "nothingness" which comes into existence only as it realizes itself in the action of the project, or "pro-ject," as it claims a relationship to Being. Sartre's argument has an initially dialectical thrust in precisely this refusal of an essential category of subjectivity out of which all else is engendered. The analysis of *scarcity* in the *Critique* indicates that the real problem in *Being and Nothingness* develops from the nature of the antithetical moment in its incipient dialectic. It is conceived not as scarcity but as a plenitude of *Being,* a fullness of possession "in-itself," where there can be no possibility for the equivocal freedom of the project to penetrate such a massive and alien facticity. So it is that the "in-itself" in some sense "projects" the action of the project back onto that project, and it is in fact this *redoubling* which seems to operate in *Being and Nothingness* like the more familiar idea of a substantial "subject." And such redoubling is as well the paradigm for the antagonistic mutual "look" which governs interpersonal relationships. Thus I am tempted to reverse entirely the usual criticism of *Being and Nothingness* and argue that it stands as a warning less to those who would continue to "privilege" the subject than to any hope of escaping subjectivity that is not rigorously critical of a presupposition such as Sartre's "in-itself" which paralyzes the dialectic of *Being and Nothingness,* whether that "in-itself" is conceived as a plenitude of Being or, for example, as a system of binary oppositions such as exists in structuralist thought.

Thus what Sartre must accomplish in the *Critique* is not a simple and schematic refusal of a Cartesian cogito, but rather the actual priority of mediation over *any* idea of an immediate given such as the "in-itself." In the *Critique,* the almost purely ontological and ahistorical concept of "lack" becomes instead what Sartre now calls "need"; as the inner, driving force of his new dialectic, need is already a "totalizing relation" (*C,* 166). It comes into existence only through the relation to its very opposite, a world of *scarcity*. And obviously, scarcity can "be" scarcity only in relation to need. Hence the duality of for-itself/in-itself is at once relativized and yet in another sense made more absolute and inclusive. Where the for-itself only could be *limited* by the in-itself, the "totalizing" or mediating relation between need and scarcity has no limits beyond the actual, historical situation which is its own coming-into-being.

Further, the relationship of need and scarcity implicates not only the material world but also the Other at the very core of subjectivity: "Scarcity realizes the passive totality of the individuals in a collective as the impossibility of coexistence" (*C,* 205). Here, the conflict is no longer between an isolated individual and a massive, recalcitrant world. Compared to *Being and Nothingness,* the most immediately important characteristic of the *Critique* is that the antithetical moment of its dialectic is itself in ferment. In a world of scarcity, no man is "left alone" with his work. Even a positive action can result in a kind of *dialectical* return of matter onto man, something quite different from what I have called the "redoubling" of the project. The Chinese peasant who removes a tree in order to cultivate his land is eventually faced with destruction by flood, without protection from a land that has been deforested by himself *and others.*

In less catastrophic circumstances, the result is what Sartre terms "seriality," a multiplicity of people related to each other solely through their mutual domination by the "practico-inert," by material which has been shaped by human labor but which now operates as if by its own laws. Sartre's example to explain this new terminology is a bus stop on St.-Germain-des-Prés. Each person is waiting alone, isolated from the others. Yet not only does each respond in the same way to an external stimulus, there is also a definite order among them—who is to board first, second, third, and so forth. How many people will ride is contingent on the size of the bus, who will ride on the serial order of arrival at the stop by the potential riders. It is an extreme and yet a common version of alienation, for the success at gaining a seat depends upon having become wholly Other, exactly as everyone else has been doing. Thus the center of the collective is Other, determined by the material nature of the bus.

Even within this antithetical moment, however, the scandal is not the brute existence of the Other as in *Being and Nothingness:* "Rather, I do not discover this constant risk of annihilation of myself and of everyone only in *Others,* but *I myself am* that risk insofar as I am Other, that is, insofar as I am designated *with the Others* as a possible expendable by the material reality of the environment" (*C*, 206). Alienation is thus neither the loss of self nor the inevitable distance imposed by the subject's gaze on an external and alien reality. The recognition of need in a world of scarcity leads to alienation through a process of abstraction, by *suppressing* the awareness of objectification, the awareness that "I myself am that risk" in a way which can only result in a vicious circle of coercion and domination. If this awareness is not suppressed, on the other hand, the very process of objectification contains at the same time the seeds of overcoming alienation, an indissoluable need for genuine *group* autonomy as the negation of seriality. To recognize fully one's own alienation is simultaneously to recognize the alienation of others as well. Thus it becomes impossible merely to lift oneself into an authentic relationship with Being through the freedom of the project, for the self-as-other is already intrinsic in individual praxis. While it seems paradoxical to think of alienation as a comfortable concept, Jameson points out in one of the most striking passages in *Marxism and Form* that once it is allowed to conceal the abstraction which inheres in it, alienation can become comfortable indeed to the extent that it does not demand "of the mind any reciprocal attempt to imagine a state in which man is no longer alienated" (*MF*, 164).

In the example of group formation Sartre chooses, the storming of

the Bastille, the group comes into existence through an inner movement of need, a force of "autodetermination" against the material
object: "The third, structurally, is the human mediation through
which *directly* the multiplicity of epicenters and ends (identical
and separated) *makes itself organized* [my italics here] as determined by a synthetic object" (*C*, 398). Dialectically, this "third"
is the coming-into-being of the individual as he realizes that his
individuality is an action which creates himself as subject negating
himself as object, as a member of a serial order. He is not locked
into a project whose action inevitably must conflict with every
other project, nor is he, as object, a product of a material situation
which determines a certain action on his part. His genuine individuality is collective, a synthetic totalization which comes into
existence as one-among-many.

The formation of the group is at its height when even the threat
posed by the external object becomes internalized by the group in
the form of the *oath* which binds them together. "This is the beginning of humanity" (*C*, 453), the point at which man assumes
the freedom of full autodetermination. It represents a complete
negation of seriality, which Sartre calls, following Malraux, the
Apocalypse. Rather than *elsewhere,* as in the case of the approaching
bus or in the ominous threat of the Bastille, the center of the collective is *everywhere.* Each member of the group is an observing
"third" to himself and others. Group unity no longer depends
upon the look of the outsider, for that look has been internalized
as necessary to one's existence in freedom. Thus the concept of
totalization in the *Critique* may be understood as an extension
and a completion of the project of *Being and Nothingness.* It is
the freedom of dialectical interchange in which each individual
simultaneously plays all the roles, of subject, object, and the third
which unites them.

However, although perhaps unavoidably, I have simplified Sartre's
forbidding and complex terminology that describes this operation
by which praxis as "totalization" is realized through the mediation
of the "third," through the possibility of acting and being aware
of one's action at the same time. And the question posed by this
terminology is crucial, since one way to understand the ahistoricity

of *Being and Nothingness* is to sense its invention of new terms as a refusal of the drag of history and tradition, as if thought could live and create in a vacuum. Certainly in both the idealist and the Marxist tradition, there exists already a conceptual terminology that is at once simpler and more familiar than that of the *Critique*. I find the idea of the "practico-inert" and the idea of "seriality," for example, both implied within Marx's analysis of commodity-structure. And as I have suggested, the very concept of praxis as a dialectical identifying of thought and action comprehends everything which Sartre is at such pains to elaborate with his enormously complex system of "revolving thirds."

Yet once *Being and Nothingness* is allowed to have a history—that is, once the *Critique* again opens up *Being and Nothingness* to the movement of time—then it is possible to realize the new terminology of the *Critique* as at least intended to be resolutely historical. It is made necessary by Sartre's awareness of how the language of *Being and Nothingness* and of Marx's own work, *historically,* has been hardened into a rigidity of definition which precludes or at least disguises the most crucial insight the *Critique* has to offer: rather than two distinct realms of human activity to be explored—the phenomenology of individual lived experience opposed to social existence—these are to be understood as dialectically one and the same. So it is that the terminology of the *Critique* is intended to come as a kind of conceptual shock which reopens an older language to the movement of time and history, just as I have suggested that the first act necessitated by the *Critique* is a rereading of *Being and Nothingness,* to which I would now add a rereading of Marx as well.

Thus it is in the first place the very language of the *Critique* wherein the concern articulated in *Search for a Method* is to be realized. This is language which stubbornly refuses to be assimilated into known relationships, which in its complexity and ambiguity recognizes the historical difficulty of coming to terms with the central argument of the *Critique*. For that argument implies that, even at the most extreme point of personal identity, what one discovers is not the transparence of the Self, the immediate self-presence Husserl posited, but instead a necessary otherness, a degree of indissoluable difference. The "individual" is to be conceived as already a kind of interior community through which those larger communities of group and social class come into existence. Even isolation and loneliness are social in this sense; the pain of being truly alone requires the continual imaginative awareness of the others who are not present. The intensity of this change in Sartre's own thinking is what Desan's criticism of Sartre as "the last of the Cartesians" (*M*, 279) ignores. Desan's most telling argument, the continuing emphasis on conflict in the *Critique,* resolves itself as well into the terms of a new understanding. Conflict occurs not only between two projects, between self and other, but also and more importantly *within* the self as other.

Nevertheless, having insisted on the importance of the language of the *Critique,* it is necessary to recognize a second crucial problem engendered by that terminology. For Sartre's protestations that the group as he conceives it is not merely an ideal concept, that it comes into being "through sweat and blood" (*C*, 434), only serve to highlight the curiously timeless and almost antiseptic quality of his analysis of group formation. The objection can be understood initially by way of contrast to a more traditionally Marxist history with its elaborate terminological means of characterizing the temporal development of economic institutions. Sartre's group, on the other hand, experiences time only as a dissolution, a "fall" from the moment of intensity in the "Apocalypse," an obvious and telling choice of words. Thus the group-in-fusion settles into a group organized around a personal authority, a "sovereign," and then into an even more rigid organization governed indirectly by institutionalized structures whose impersonal power heralds the return of seriality. As Jameson notes, there is "an almost Viconian recurrence of the fixed stages of seriality, group-in-fusion, institutionalization, and the ultimate fall back into seriality itself" (*MF*, 289). If instead of "seriality" and "practico-inert," Sartre had employed and developed Marx's intricate set of terms for relating commodity-structures to the economic modes of production, he could have realized that changes in the latter inevitably result through a complex interaction with changes in social organization. Hence "seriality" at one point in a specific historical development cannot be identified so casually with "seriality" at a later stage of that development.

Further, it would be possible to realize how the "cyclical" nature of Sartre's group formation and dissolution in fact corresponds to an increasingly familiar phenomenon in developed Western economies, at the point where the network of commodity relationships seems almost capable of a kind of self-reproduction or autogenesis, where even work is in a sense "produced" by the demand for commodities whose use value was never existent. Once the reality of labor is no longer disguised, but systematically discounted and absorbed in advance, as that which in effect has *always already happened,* then the experience of temporality as an inevitable dissolution becomes a fundamental category of everyday reality. Indeed, it helps to understand the increased dominance of intellectual models of recurrence and repetition as less the application of supposedly "scientific paradigms" than as distorted reflections of this more basic and contemporary situation. What must be remembered, of course, is that such a phenomenon is a specific and local "history," neither indicative of a general "human condition" nor even by any means global in its implications.

In another sense, as Jameson points out, Sartre's emphasis on "dissolution" is precisely a way of countering an overestimation of group Apocalypse, of insisting that it is not an achievement of stasis, a plenitude of Being once and for all. Yet insofar as it is within Apocalypse that the quality of both social and individual existence is said to be realized, this defense will not work. It is one thing to argue the impossibility of achieving a plenitude of Being and quite another to understand time as the inevitable loss and dissolution of the unity of individual and social life. This is merely to posit such unity as an ideal and not an actual, dialectical development. It is to think of Apocalypse as a transcendent *telos* of human "totalization" and not the continual activity of totalization itself.

Now, for Jameson, Sartre's analysis really can lose its abstract and atemporal character only in the concluding section of the *Critique,* when the level of the truly social is reached through the integration of the group into a conception of social class. The

mystique of Apocalypse is thereby doubly dispelled, as it is continually thrown back into the reality of class struggle and as even
its dissolution provides the objective possibility for new groups to
arise within the class. It is on this basis that Jameson will suggest
Sartre's argument is genuinely Marxist:

> This is to say that Marxism, owing to the peculiar reality of its
> object of study, has at its disposal two alternate languages (or
> codes, to use the structuralist term) in which any given phe-
> nomenon can be described. Thus history can be written either
> subjectively, as the history of class struggle, or objectively,
> as the development of the economic modes of production and
> their evolution from their own internal contradictions: these
> two formulae are the same, and any statement in one can with-
> out loss of meaning be translated into the other. The notion of
> class is problematical precisely because it is the mediator be-
> tween these two different notational systems; for class is popula-
> tion articulated according to economic function, but it is also
> that which permits us to translate data about machinery and
> the operations of production back into human and interpersonal
> terms. It now becomes clear in what way the *Critique,* as differ-
> ent as it is from the traditional Marxist descriptions, is nonethe-
> less profoundly consistent with the model of society proposed
> by Marx in *Das Kapital:* it is simply the reverse of that mod-
> el. . . . This accounts, for one thing, for the apparent discrepancy
> between linear historical development and the more cyclical one
> implied by the theory of groups. It is easier to write a history
> of matter than of consciousness, and the changes in the type of
> commodities produced and in the systems that produce them has
> somehow a tangible linear content that is lacking in the story
> of the productive power of labor and the ferocity of human
> antagonisms at every point of the way. [*MF,* 297-98]

This is of course the full context of the passage from which I quoted
earlier, and the question now can be raised in detail: to what extent
is "class" being posited as a genuinely dialectical reality, to what
extent a set of known relationships whose presence in the *Critique*
signals a simple and unambiguous return to the "concrete"?

III

The immediate difficulty is that "class," *even as a term of critical analysis,* must perform two apparently antithetical operations. On the one hand, it describes an underlying or "unconscious" reality which conditions the very quality of personal experience. Thus, for example, the almost instantaneous focus created by the appearance of a black in a room full of whites seems on the level of conscious experience to be the attraction of the alien, the mixture of guilty apprehension and aggressive curiosity occasioned by the fascination for what is immediately and visibly *different.* But class analysis would reveal that fascination itself as an illusion of privilege, as if one were granted an impartial dispensation to collect and categorize sensations registered by a purely private sphere cushioned from the shock of external contact. That is, only within the security of class position, through the relatively unconscious and hidden basis of *not* being different, of belonging to a ruling class, is one free to meditate the complex of experience created by such an "intrusion."

On the other hand, the distinctively Marxist insistence on praxis, on the ultimate identifying of thought and action, means the impossibility of understanding class only in this way. The goal of class analysis remains the capacity to *change* and not merely interpret a situation such as the one I suggested above. And this is only to say that class becomes a genuinely dialectical reality at the point when it becomes personal experience, in the constitutive shock of self-judgment and the corresponding impulse to engender a new set of possibilities. Thus, rather than a hidden bias of class privilege in personal experience, the critical antagonist now becomes a very complex ideology. The various constructions of analysis in the competing disciplines—of sociology, psychology, ethnology, as well as literary criticism itself—conspire to remind us again and again that such self-judgment, and with it the unifying action of praxis, remains impossible to achieve. One lives one's life immediately and intuitively, so the argument runs, and through the massive assimilation of analytic techniques at times is permitted *to see* the full dimensions of that experience, as conditioned by a given set of social controls, as pathological or as the recurrence of mythic patterns, and so forth. But these are separated by an almost onto-logical gap: there is a level of actual, lived experience and a situation where that experience, as it were, is suspended and made visible through the mediation of conceptual methodologies. The difficulty, of course, is that class analysis in the first sense seems to operate in a way that is almost identical with what becomes, in this second sense, the ideological illusion such analysis is called upon to rectify.

For Jameson, the conceptual link between these two ways of using class analysis is the dialectic of "appearance" and "reality" which Marx inherited from Hegel and stood "right side up," reversing the emphasis from the Ideal to the complex of the socioeconomic. So, in *Capital*,

> the appearance is that of commodities and of the "objective" network of relationships which they entertain with each other and which ultimately include within themselves the whole legal and property system itself, as well as the economic modes of distribution and production: yet paradoxically, this illusion of objectivity forms the very existential fabric of our lives, which are characterized by *belief* in this reified appearance (fetishism is a form of belief) and which are wholly absorbed with the acquisition and consumption of commodities in general. The reality of social life, on the other hand, lies in the labor process itself, in the transparency of human work and action which is ultimately responsible both for the commodities produced and for the very social mode in which commodities form the principal category of production. [*MF*, 296]

Thus the unconscious bias toward a purely private density of experience in my first example, and the hypostasis of an immediate, intuitive life to be studied objectively in my second, can both stand resolved into an illusion or an "appearance" generated out of the network of commodity relationships. In the former, "experience" is treated as if it were private property, a commodity one owned. And in the latter, one "believes" this to the extent that "experience" becomes merely a flux of data, of "raw material" to be made intelligible. Class analysis in both cases operates to reveal the underlying social reality "of human work and action" which has produced this appearance and at the same time of course suggests the direction of necessary change.

Nevertheless, this dialectical assimilation cannot be understood as if it were a direct and unmediated development. There is nothing inherently dialectical about an operation which merely dissolves an illusory appearance into a more basic reality, revealed in its transparency. Indeed, this defines the essential characteristic of what Sartre in the *Critique* calls "analytic thought," the breaking down of a complex surface into its simple, basic elements. Thus the visual metaphor of "transparency" is a telling one, suggesting not dialectical interaction but rather the priority of a contemplative gaze that would clarify the "facts" as they are by brushing aside all merely "extraneous" concerns:

> content does not need to be treated or interpreted, precisely because *it is essentially and immediately meaningful in itself.* . . . Content is already concrete, in that it is essentially social and historical experience, and we may say of our own interpretive or hermeneutic work what the sculptor said of his stone, that it sufficed to remove all extraneous portions for the statue to appear, already latent in the marble block. [*MF,* 403-04; my italics]

The genuinely *dialectical* conclusion to be drawn from the premise that the "content" of social reality "does not need to be treated or interpreted" would understand that this is because such "content" is already a dialectical action, whose meaning is developing through a process of *mediation* within which the critic participates and which he continues in his own activity. To argue, on the contrary, that social reality "is essentially and immediately meaningful in itself" merely reduces it to a datum, a given reality not unlike the presupposition of the "in-itself" that paralyzes the dialectic of *Being and Nothingness.*

Thus, to the extent that one understands the movement in the *Critique* from group formation and dissolution to class struggle as the passage from a still illusory appearance to an immediately meaningful reality, class retains only an analytic and not a dialectical force. Indeed, Jameson's own argument goes on to suggest a similar conclusion:

> For the class struggle, in history, recapitulates the basic moments of the earlier interpersonal dialectic: each class passing from object to subject in succession, through its own look objectifying the other class, conferring on the latter an exterior, a face. The other class reacts in its turn in an attempt to recuperate this being which is beyond its reach, outside it, in the eyes and judgment of its adversary: and just as I learn myself through the mediation of other people, both from their judgments and from an attempt to parry their judgments, so each class learns to see itself because it is seen from the outside. It comes to define itself against the other, by interiorizing the other's look, and transforming what initially was experienced in shame into a sense of pride or identity (what on the level of class is known as class consciousness). [*MF*, 301]

Just as the individual within the group learns his identity through the mediate development of "revolving thirds," as he plays all the roles of subject, object, and the "third," so it is that class consciousness or class identity comes into being through this complex interaction of mediating relationships. "Class" no more than "individual" or "group" represents an "in-itself," a given content.

Further, it is the reality of class that provides a necessary temporal and historical realization of these mediating relationships for Jameson, justifying his contention that the concluding section of the *Critique* achieves a level of concreteness impossible to the discussion of group formation and dissolution. For "in my individual daily relations with other people, it would seem that there is no built-in priority of subject to object, and that I am both in succession" (*MF*, 301), precisely as in Sartre's description of Apocalypse.

> In history, however, each rising class is initially an object for the dominant one, and learns itself in shame before it arrives at the stage of becoming a subject in turn. Thus, the bourgeoisie initially defined itself through its humiliations before the nobility; the proletariat through those suffered at the hands of the bourgeoisie. Only then does the proletariat begin to see the

bourgeoisie in its turn, and to furnish the latter with yet a new image of self to live in guilt and fear. [*MF*, 301-02]

This is indeed a second and quite different answer to the question of whether "class" represents merely a set of known relationships as a more fundamental and basic reality. For now the atemporality of Sartre's Apocalypse, the mystique of group fusion, is an "appearance" only because it remains abstract and nondialectical, to be resolved into a genuine dialectic realized as historical change and development.

But if such logic is followed through to a conclusion, then it is not enough to argue with Jameson that there is "a basic dissymetry between the personal and the class experience" (*MF*, 301), between the mystique of unity in the Apocalypse and the reality of class struggle. Not only does the goal posited in *Search for a Method* refuse an ineluctable division between "personal" and "class" experience, but more importantly, as I have suggested, it is just such a gap—fueled by the methodologies of the social sciences—that class analysis should correct. Thus it is necessary to return to Sartre's discussion of group formation, to discover a sense in which "a basic dissymetry" can be realized within personal experience itself, but now transformed into the dialectical opposition through which praxis is born.

Jameson understands Sartre's triadic structure of revolving thirds to be the means of dispelling that hypostasis of personal experience which would comprise the data for an "objective" study of social relationships. The difficulty, both in the *Critique* and in Jameson's reading of it, inheres in the very description of what it is such triadic structure would negate: a commonsense view of interpersonal relationships is said to be "secretly abstract" because it assumes two people "cannot share a common world since each one sees it from the other end, since each is an object in the other's perceptual field" (*MF*, 242). Rather, "every confrontation" of this sort "always takes place against the background of what is a little hastily called society, or at least against the background of swarms of human relationships" (*MF*, 242). The idea of the "third" simply describes this role of "outside observer or witness" (*MF*, 242) as the medium of exchange, the "principle of identity which puts the two freedoms, the two totalizations, in equivalence with each other" (*MF*, 243).

The face-to-face "look" always already takes place within the larger context of the "look" of the third which mediates the contact, which establishes a common world between the two.

However, the real abstraction in any notion of a fundamental and dyadic interpersonal relationship is the privilege accorded to the "look" itself, to the priority of that vision by which another becomes an object in my "perceptual field." After *History and Class Consciousness* at least, there should be no question that such constitution of a "perceptual field" at a distance imposed by the contemplative gaze is not a general and inescapable human condition but part of that whole complex of experience associated with the rise of the bourgeois class and its distinctive way of relating to others and to a material world. Thus class analysis must continue to function as a critical demystification as long as our descriptions of "personal experience" conform to the constitutive bias of bourgeois consciousness.

Already in *Being and Nothingness,* of course, the serenity of the contemplative gaze is complicated by Sartre's insistence on the reciprocity of that "look," the fact that not only does one see others, but he is seen by others as well. The argument of the *Critique* goes still further, recognizing in the role of the "third," whether exercised by an outside observer or by objects themselves, a doubleness which transcends the abstractness of the isolated observer contemplating a perceptual field. Eventually, in the group at its most intense fusion, every member becomes both an actor in the situation and the "third" who observes the action of himself and others. The externality of the observing witness or third party becomes interiorized within each member of the group. Yet these remain complications of a basic and abstract model, and Jameson's comparison to "the rotation of Ptolemaic epicycles" (*MF,* 252) is apt to the extent that no matter how reciprocally complex this "look" becomes in Sartre's argument, it remains at the center, much as did the earth for the Ptolemaic astronomers. Against the dominant methodologies of the social sciences, Sartre affirms the possibility that at least in the Apocalypse of the group-in-fusion, one can act and observe his own action at the same time. But however much one wants to sympathize with this affirmation, its underlying abstractness first must be realized and overcome.

Much earlier in the *Critique,* Sartre offers a tantalizing insight which remains undeveloped through the context of what follows: "Everything is discoverable in need: this is the first totalizing relation between that material being, a man, and the material group to which he belongs. This relation is *unilateral,* a relation of *interiority.* Through need, as a matter of fact, there appears in matter the first negation of negation and the first totalization" (*C,* 166). What this suggests is not some fundamental ontological gap opening between what one is and what one perceives others to be, a distance imposed between two people by the "look." Rather, it is as if the vague, almost prehensive awareness of need realizes a basic alterity within its own movement—"a relation of *interiority*"—an obscure sense that what one *is* is already an object to what one is becoming. Read thus, the passage seems almost an echo of this from Marx's Paris manuscripts:

> neither is *human sense* as it immediately *is*—as it is objectively— *human* sensibility, human objectivity. Neither nature objectively nor nature subjectively is directly given in a form adequate to the *human* being. And as everything natural has to have its *beginning, man* too has his act of origin—*history*—which, however, is for him a known history, and hence as an act of origin it is a conscious self-transcending act of origin. [*EP,* 182]

Marx's language is still very Hegelian, but the idea is not. For rather than beginning from a concept of Being as Hegel attempts, Marx asserts the priority of Becoming as the mediate relation whereby "the essential force of man energetically bent on its object" (*EP,* 182) is actualized in the making of that object. Man thus becomes both subject and object in the act of "conscious self-transcending." Only by the imposition of a fundamentally different awareness does the object come to seem an alien reality standing over against the subject which "looks" at it. In the former operation subject and object become a genuine opposition. In the latter, the "look" reduces this opposition, in effect, to a contradiction.[2]

Thus "personal experience" itself has a history developed through a triadic relationship, a mediate act of thinking which realizes its immediate subjectivity only in the act of becoming its opposite and objective reality. Or, as I suggested in chapter 2, the self as mediate subject is so completely the producer of history that one recognizes himself as immediate subject only in relation to what is not his self, to the product of that history. The individual is not a "mind," a subject or a "feeling" which has an outside, an exterior, conferred upon it by the "look" of another. Nor is the act of "conscious self-transcending" an operation performed by a subject, a thinking substance, on an inert matter. Indeed, I find Sartre's term "need" to be accurate only if one understands it to name the necessary alterity of personal experience as a ceaseless becoming of itself. Need cannot be, as Jameson describes, "a lack of being, an emptiness striving toward some stasis and plenitude, toward *being itself* . . . in effect . . . a definition of time" (*MF*, 274; my italics). For temporality and history, as Marx realizes, are the affirmation of becoming, of mediation, as the essential reality for which any and every vision of stasis or plenitude offers only a faded copy, a valorization of the past as completed object over the possibilities latent in the movement of time.

Once understood in this way, "class" *as the mechanism of social division* enters into experience through a clinging to the privilege of what has been achieved, of what is existent; it is the interpretation of the past for the purpose of *repeating* its essential moments. Marx's reference to our "history" as in fact a "prehistory" criticizes these attempts to repeat and thereby idealize and divide the movement of time into successive instants, successive realizations of some idea of plenitude. Thus the most difficult truth Marx asks us to accept is that such idealizations are always and everywhere a threat; their possibility is never transcended once and for all. The error in either the prophecy of an "authentic" personal experience or of a future and classless society *as such* inheres in the failure to realize that the very description of such plenitude merely repeats a moment of the past, but now shorn of its conflicts and contradictions. The liberation from economic oppression is the *beginning* and not the end of history.

The importance of bringing "personal experience" and "class experience" so closely together is twofold. On the one hand, it involves the recognition that the attitude which one takes toward that necessary otherness of the self realizes as well how one responds to other people. To suppress or deny the often painful reality of living at once inside and yet beyond oneself translates into the violence exerted against those who threaten to destroy the privilege of class or of personal identity. And conversely, class analysis reveals, in Jameson's terms, the "composition of those privilege-defending groups to which one is then bound to be hostile" (MF, 282), or perhaps more exactly, the elements within oneself, within each individual member of a group, and within each group which work to constitute a defense of privilege.

Indeed, as I suggested earlier, it is in the final analysis an awareness of class which demystifies the "look" of contemplative distance. For class conflict as Jameson describes it (MF, 304), as a fundamental feature of our modern world, comes into existence less as the rebounding of the "look" back on the bourgeoisie by the working class than as the result of that bourgeois "look" itself, the act of putting at a distance, of separating out a whole class of people. The sense of being looked at in return is nothing but the corollary of that initial violence, of trying to imagine "what they are doing out there" once the human connections have been severed. (Are they looking back? Perhaps, but one doesn't know. Maybe there is something else entirely.) Instead of others, of other people, the excluded class becomes the Other, a mute and antagonistic mass. And I am convinced that it is in these politically charged terms one should begin to understand the recent intellectual fascination with "the Other," whether as language in Lacan and Derrida or as the fetishism of the unconscious in more traditional psychology—so many complex ideological disguises following from an initial reification of the terms of human relationships.[3] In any case, and despite the obvious counterintention in Sartre's model of reciprocity, the "look" is at least in part the source and not the result of the ferocious class antagonism Jameson describes. And as Raymond Williams points out in another context, it is Apocalyptic indeed to expect something different to come from more of the same.

IV

It is possible to return here to the long-suspended discussion of what is involved in a dialectical understanding of literary form, with a heightened sense of the characteristic modes of thought it criticizes. Even before History and Class Consciousness, and indeed throughout his work, Lukács realized the ideological bias apparent in the idea that form acts as a way of organizing and controlling a mass of "raw material," a flux of sensation or experience which possesses no inherent intelligibility. His discussions seem to me to need no explanatory footnote, and I have argued at length in chapter 3 against the more contemporary and sophisticated versions of this "formalist" bias. However, Sartre's argument in the *Critique* goes further, suggesting in fact that formalist criticism is "secretly abstract" in much the same way as the presupposition of face-to-face contact as the primary interpersonal reality. Jameson makes the point succinctly, that "Sartre's triadic model is an implicit challenge to structuralism, whose binary oppositions fail to take into account precisely the movement of the exchange itself as a third element, as a mediation" (*MF*, 243).

Thus I am tempted to reverse the typical nomenclature entirely and argue that neither structuralist nor archetypal criticism is formalistic at all. Their operations posit a peculiar and static *content,* arranged as the terms of binary opposition or along a sliding scale of displacement. The idea that Milton's *Lycidas,* for example, develops through the recurrent patterns of pastoral elegy doesn't really explain what organizes *Lycidas* but merely names a particular selection of detail from a history of literary tradition. That is, it tells us something about a certain kind of content Milton makes use of in the poem, but more often than not in a way which suppresses the actual historicity of literary tradition. Williams's *Modern Tragedy* is exemplary of the conceptual reversal I have in mind. For he shows in convincing detail that the reduction of tragedy to a set of generic conventions is in fact a hypostasis of a certain kind of material, cut off from the actual historical development of quite different works of literature and brought into being to articulate a complex set of ideas. Similarly, I argued in my fourth chapter that Harold Bloom's consideration of literary form as a structure of anxiety—as a crisis which results from the realization that formal distance imposes a necessarily misdirected and thereby problematical relationship to a particular content—in reality names but another kind of content, an assumption that the effort of understanding is equivalent to the creation of distance.

So it is that the argument which would convict Marxist criticism of a conceptual inability to understand the formal qualities of literature often will prove to be only a charge that Marxism ignores the privilege accorded to a particular and determinate content which, in one way or another, has dominated so much twentieth-century critical theory. Thus if the almost instinctive bias of critics such as Lukács and Williams toward the "realistic" novel is to be accounted for in genuinely formal terms, it is necessary to develop some very different meaning to the idea of "form," perhaps best accomplished by returning for the moment to the passage from *Women in Love* I quoted at the beginning of this chapter.

As long as this passage is conceived as a process of symbolic meaning, then one is caught in an antinomy. Either the passage can be described as a technical device, a "formal" realization only in the sense I have suggested above, where "form" names the hypostasis of a particular content; or it can be understood as the disguised expression of a deeper and corresponding social reality, the failure of bourgeois consciousness to recover some original meaning in objects themselves.[4] I want to argue instead that the form of the passage is precisely the dialectical translation of personal into social experience and back again. It involves the articulation of Birkin's deepest, most intimate personal experience as it comes into being in relation to Gerald, to Gerald's death, and to the natural landscape where the death took place. Form is thus the mediate development— or, in Jameson's terms, the "translation"—wherein the actors and the situation which they inhabit come into existence. And even here, "form" is perhaps a misnomer, implying as it does an inevitably dualistic antithesis to "content." As I have argued throughout, such mediate development is always triadic and never dualistic. Only in this way can one preserve the force of Jameson's insistence that each work of literature "evolves its own categories and dictates the specific terms of its own interpretation" (*MF*, 333).

Further, it is a conception of form which does not predispose the critic toward a novel any more than toward a poem or a drama. Even the most ostensibly private and inwardly meditative poem, such as Eliot's "Prufrock," reveals itself as the activity of mediation between personal and social that I have called form. For what the epigraph to that poem suggests is that Prufrock's is a world dominated by the conviction that the impulse to *talk*, to self-dramatize one's frustrations and fears, is possible only if one imagines the presence of another voice that won't respond, a voice no longer living, condemned to its own inferno: "If I thought my answer were given/to anyone who would ever return to the world,/this flame would stand still without moving any further." Prufrock can talk because he can imagine no real response.[5] Eliot in making the poem, on the other hand, is forced to realize in Prufrock a voice which *does* respond to Eliot himself, which dramatizes the danger in self-dramatization to be that it is never impersonal, that it assumes a real and devastatingly critical response. One "drowns" not only in others but in the self as other, in the ineluctably social character of even one's most private meditations. And unlike Eliot as critic, who had only the kindest things to say about the process whereby a poem becomes "impersonal," "The Waste Land" at least transforms this profound horror of the social into a scrupulous integrity that by the end of the poem understands the failure inherent *in seeing other people that way,* in condemning others by the standards through which one has resisted the breakup of his purely internal and private space.

Obviously, form as dialectical mediation is not confined to works of literature. Indeed, as I argued in chapter 2, it becomes specifically *artistic* form when the moments of its dialectic are suffused and dominated by the immediacy of feeling, where even the self-critical judgment implied in the act of thinking is less an effort of analysis than a kind of reciprocal touch, a prehensive contact which senses the terms of relationship in the most intensely felt and dramatic way. And this suggests that the critical obligation imposed by such a conception of artistic form is twofold. On the one hand, genuine criticism begins only when the critic has worked himself through the painstaking analysis of technique, biography, the social reality the artist inhabits, the elements of literary tradition he embraces, rejects, and modifies, to the point where his own critical act seems to be the continuation of the author's act of translation. Thus it is when the critic's illusion of *private space,* of the freedom to walk around the work of literature as if it were a static object, dissolves itself into the reality of his intimate, personal experience born anew through the interaction with the work.

On the other hand, one has the responsibility *to be critical,* to resist being swept up into the intensity of the artist's activity to the extent that one's own experience and intelligence merely consecrate the existence of the work. The danger here is not only that one then ignores the awareness that as a human action a work of literature can be self-deceptive, limited, or biased in its own way. The more consequent failure engenders out of such identification a massive and forbidding solipsism, an abrogation of that most exacting process of realizing in the movement of one's critical thinking the difference between the artist as artist and oneself as critic which alone gives value to both and asserts the continuing existence of the work as distinct from and yet related to one's critical act. The critic's is a community where his every thought and word must speak for himself and for another, the artist whose poem he catches up in his critical performance. Criticism is the continuing life of the work in time, and while that restores the pressure of ambiguity and difference at the very heart of the critic's identification with the movement of the poem, it also realizes the only viable form of human community, where one learns to love his neighbor because of his difference and not in spite of it. It is thus a community where "privilege" itself becomes reciprocal, something impossible to gain at the expense of others. It can be achieved only to the extent that another is allowed a privilege that is different, and yet equally full. This, I take it, is what is meant by Blake's enigmatic aphorism about the wars of Eden, that opposition is true friendship.

7

The Fiction of Interpretation:
Faulkner's *Absalom, Absalom!*

In "Three Dimensions of Hermeneutics," E. D. Hirsch proposes a basic distinction between interpretation and criticism: the former is concerned with the meaning of a text and the latter with the significance of that meaning as it is heard in relation to a particular experiential context of any kind.[1] My distinction is no less simple, although the intent is quite different. Interpretation reconstructs language, character, and event in accordance with an underlying pattern or structure of meaning. Criticism recognizes an identity of meaning and significance immanent within language and within the actual relationships among characters. Where an interpretive procedure must fasten on the text as raw material to be "worked over," criticism understands it as an action to be continued in critical performance. Thus interpretation remains deeply solipsistic, while criticism is inevitably both personal and social.

My distinction has a particular relevance to *Absalom, Absalom!*, for the most serious objections to Faulkner's work involve neither quarrels about the validity of an interpretation nor disputes about the significance of his meanings. Rather, implicitly or explicitly, they raise the question of whether and how the novels mean at all, and thus they can be answered only by criticism. Far from being impressed by Faulkner's formal experimentation, Georg Lukács for example finds in his work a failure of intelligence, "the lack of a consistent view of human nature. Man is reduced to a sequence of unrelated experiential fragments; he is as inexplicable to others as to himself."[2] Now it is easy enough to dismiss Lukács's objection in this form for a number of reasons. He reads all of literature with definite political ideas of man in relation to history and a social

188

world—as if the rest of us didn't—and he has on more than one occasion proven himself actively hostile to "modern" literature. More consequentially, one could hardly expect Lukács, for whom "American English" was not even a second or third language, to be aware of the intricacies of Faulkner's usage.

Yet his objection is serious. On the one hand, it implies that a novel like *Absalom, Absalom!* ruthlessly demonstrates within its very nature what Faulkner assumes to be the impossibility of interpretation; none of the characters can "make real sense" of Sutpen's life, and Faulkner concurs. And on the other, the force of Lukács's argument can be felt within even the most single-minded interpretive effort. For with the attempt to construct a latent structure of meaning that can clarify the ambiguous, shifting multiplicity of narrative voices and actions in *Absalom, Absalom!* must go the generally unspoken assumption of serious deficiency in a work where so many layers of mystification need to be peeled away. Melvin Backman and C. Hugh Holman, for example, describe *Absalom, Absalom!* as a novel about history and the difficulty of arriving at historical truth, and Holman even goes so far as to suggest that the "foolishness" of Faulkner's rhetorical flights can be negated if we keep in front of us the formula for detective fiction. Backman candidly admits that "one might still question whether a novel whose pitch is too shrill, whose approach is emotional and poetic, whose perspective seems unclear and shifting—one might question whether such a work presents the best way of getting at historical truth." Cleanth Brooks and Olga Vickery have found the meaning within it as a pattern of great tragedy, but even Vickery allows that "the tortuous style" and unresolved ambiguities make the terms of the tragedy hard to reach.[3]

Thus, rather than being able to meet Lukács's objection squarely, these interpretive efforts result in a division between "depth" and "surface"—between an underlying, coherent pattern of meaning and a distracting, ambiguous texture of language—which in fact perpetuates Lukács's claim that Faulkner's work is in need of a consistent perspective lacking or obscured in the novels themselves. And of course the enormous variation in interpretive patterns "discovered in" the novel only lends more support to what I understand as the implicit suggestion in Lukács's critique, that Faulkner's novels are engines of destruction, calculated to frustrate any effort of interpretation.

I want to argue instead that *Absalom, Absalom!* possesses its own intimate order of intelligibility which cannot be fractured into a mystifying surface and a basic structure of coherence, and this requires that my distinction between interpretation and criticism be expanded in a way that realizes within it two very different conceptions of action in a novel. An interpretation such as that offered by Olga Vickery defines the meaning of Rosa Coldfield's narration as the pattern of action found in Gothic melodrama. That is, beneath Rosa's incalculably difficult rhetoric, a simple story emerges: characters are etched in superhuman black and white; conflict remains located on the level of abstract good versus abstract evil. Presumably Faulkner's point is that "eye-witness" perception is in fact the least accurate. Yet the very first section of the novel ends with the remarkable account of Ellen finding both Judith and Henry watching Thomas in hand-to-hand combat with one of his slaves, something Rosa herself has not seen but which she recounts in mercilessly "realistic" detail, almost as if Faulkner had told it. The final exchange between Sutpen and Ellen is marvelously rendered by Rosa, leaving no clear sense of who was really culpable or, indeed, what exactly he/she might be culpable for. If withdrawal into fantasy as Vickery defines it means a retreat into the simplistic world of Gothic melodrama, then the fact that Rosa comes to this ambiguous tangle of motives should indicate that the movement of her thinking is not toward fantasy at all.

However, the problem is not that Vickery is still baffled by the appearance, the disguise of events and narration, and just hasn't got her basic story right yet. For Faulkner is not content to let his own imagination rage and play against the mere shell of a character who occupies one limited place within the novel's total pattern of meaning. He must sense those characters' inner vitality and realize their action as the impulse of feeling at the point of articulation. Thus he does not reduce Rosa to a figure in the pattern of the tale she narrates; he creates her as in the act of creating the Sutpens. If it were only a product of her imaginative action, Rosa's narrative could be treated condescendingly, as an abstract formula of Gothic melodrama, or however else one might classify it. But considered as a vital act of self-translation, its meaning and value are incommensurable. And what is true of Rosa is true of *Absalom, Absalom!* as a whole. Its drama does not reside in an imaginative artifact, an objectified pattern or perspective or structure of action which provides the interpreter with his meaning. Rather, the drama is in the act of objectifying itself, of translating innermost feelings into the world of the novel. Criticism alone is capable of attending to this action.

Such a conception of action can suggest as well an answer to Lukács's objection that Faulkner's work represents merely a multiplicity of fragments, an "attentuation of reality" and a "dissolution of personality" within a subjective flux. Lukács is right, I think, to the extent that *Absalom, Absalom!* deliberately makes interpretive perspective impossible, but only because within the novel Faulkner opposes interpretation to a genuinely critical and creative activity which is of another order entirely. For the striking quality about Rosa's narrative, as well as Mr. Compson's and later Shreve and Quentin's, is that none of them can be construed as merely a subjective projection of the Sutpen story. There is no given "fact" to which each narrative offers an "approach." Like the lives of the Sutpens themselves, these narratives are in their origin and development profoundly social acts through and through. For example, Mr. Compson's account of Charles and Henry's visit to New Orleans bears all too obviously his *odi et amo* feeling for the dissolution of the Old South, his love of the exquisitely decadent, his valorization of the past against the present. Yet at the same time it is told with the purpose of freeing Quentin from his preoccupation with Henry's murder of Charles. However inadequate the means, his narration is told for love of his son, and his failures and distortions can be measured within *this* feeling which he struggles to make intelligible to himself and to Quentin. Compson is talking *to be heard,* and no norm of judgment or abstract and generic classification of his narrative can afford to ignore the intricate, personal relationships it shapes and is shaped by.

The sense in which the novel is both "historical" and "tragic" does not reside at a level beneath this "surface" of multiple narration, of cross-purposes and conflicts among the characters. Just as the social context of each character's speech is realized within the most intimate and internal movement of thought, so too it is here where the historical and the tragic are to be experienced. Faulkner's individuals are not placed against a background of history or against a background of tragic "forces." Their very individuality is traversed and animated by both. To focus through the interstices of their language and character onto something else is simply to abstract from the wholeness and density of Faulkner's creation. Far from being an intimidating weight of mystification, the novel's "surface" has a scrupulously imagined integrity; it is the realization of a creative force whose care articulates every shared detail of a human world with meaning and grace.

I

Interpretation of *Absalom, Absalom!* typically lays a great deal of stress on sections 6 through 8 of the novel, for it is in Shreve and Quentin's reconstruction that the most coherent and complete account of the Sutpens seems to emerge. Yet this distracts attention from the larger problem of Faulkner's own relation to their tale. And if it can be shown that his attitude toward the narratives of Rosa and Mr. Compson is at least as complex as it is toward Shreve and Quentin's, then the novel comes to be less a succession of relatively more complete patterns of understanding, more complete interpretations, than a whole action in which each of the parts realizes in its own way the fullness of Faulkner's creative activity. The first four sections of *Absalom, Absalom!* are not technical experiments in point of view. They represent a social drama of the highest order.

However, the truth registered by the search for an underlying pattern of coherent meaning in *Absalom, Absalom!* is the fact that the language of the novel, for all its interior complications and sheer abundance, somehow is never fully present, never finally and visibly complete: "From a little after two oclock until almost sundown of the long still hot weary September afternoon . . ." The single syllables emphasize their own discreteness, having the hard, flat impact of stones flung into mud. Yet the lack of punctuation between the five adjectives achieves at the same time a continual flux, a blurring of the edges which leaves a sense of dissatisfaction with each particular word as soon as it is pronounced. Quentin's reaction to Rosa both embodies and describes this tension felt everywhere in the novel, in Faulkner's language as well as Rosa's:

> It (the talking, the telling) seemed (to him, to Quentin) to partake of that logic- and reason-flouting quality of a dream which the sleeper knows must have occurred stillborn and complete, in a second, yet the very quality upon which it must depend to move the dreamer (verisimilitude) to credulity—horror or pleasure or amazement—depends as completely upon a formal recognition of and acceptance of elapsed and yet-elapsing time as music or a printed tale.[4]

Thus, in the first section of the novel, one is not presented with a single, flat curve, Rosa's idiosyncratic "version" of the Sutpen story. The Sutpens are like a "dream," suspended as it were within Rosa's grim, iron-gray narration to which the reader, like Quentin, is compelled to attend. Her fascination is less with herself than with her relationship to Sutpen, the feeling of incalculable loss which she can neither explain nor extenuate and which shadows every word she delivers to Quentin. Sutpen himself becomes a kind of "objective correlative" for that feeling, and so she invests him with all the vagueness and mystery attendant on her continual brooding. As she herself later recognizes, it is nothing so simple as having him and then losing him, because she never had him to begin with. Still, the feeling of loss remains as the ground and sustenance of her existence. She can neither forgive Sutpen nor take revenge upon him nor damn him completely, for to do anything at all would be to lose irrevocably the sense of loss itself, that shadowy and indefinite pain which can be kept alive only by not relinquishing it to the passage of time that has brought Sutpen's death or to the "realistic" canons of probability by which she has been able to eke out an existence for forty-three years. This is the heart of Rosa's "impotent frustration." She better than anyone knows the inadequacy of her tale. Her life, such as it is, depends upon the inability to resolve her personal history into a clear pattern, even as her frustration arises precisely because the inadequacy is necessary. The first section begins with her Gothic fantasy—Sutpen as demon—but it ends with the ambiguity of Sutpen's denial

that he has brought Judith to watch him fight and Rosa's statement
that she was not even there to see Judith in the loft.

Thus the tension Faulkner suggests is most obviously manifest in
Rosa's language, which seems almost woefully inadequate to her
feeling, spoken out of a furious and overwhelming desire to force
it into a fullness of being which the language, in its inevitable temporal sequence, cannot contain. However, Mr. Compson's narration
poses a very different problem, for his speech seems to move softly
and languorously from phrase to phrase, finding in some acciden-
tally unearthed word a treasure which spurs the development of
the next phrase:

> "But Sutpen wanted it. He wanted, not the anonymous wife and
> the anonymous children, but the two names, the stainless wife
> and the unimpeachable father-in-law, on the license, the patent.
> Yes, patent, with a gold seal and red ribbons too if that had been
> practicable. But not for himself. She (Miss Rosa) would have
> called the gold seal and the ribbons vanity. But then, so had
> vanity conceived that house and built it in a strange place and
> with little else but his bare hands and further handicapped by
> the chance and probability of meddling interference arising out
> of the disapprobation of all communities of men toward any
> situation which they do not understand. And pride: Miss Rosa
> had admitted that he was brave; perhaps she even allowed him
> pride: the same pride which wanted such a house, which would
> accept nothing less, and drove through to get it at whatever
> cost." [51]

The words pile up slowly until "patent" appears and shifts the
direction, bringing with it the gold seal and red ribbons which
eventually unearth "vanity" that, in turn, controls the slow, sensual
accumulation until "pride" arrives out of nowhere and again shifts
the flow.

In section 4, one is thus well prepared to hear Mr. Compson's
"dream" of the past in his careful, loving elaboration of Henry's
visit to New Orleans with Bon. While he may like to think of the
Sutpens as characters larger than life, "'simpler and therefore,
integer for integer, larger, more heroic'" (89), like characters in a
Greek tragedy, his way of telling the story is as different from a

Greek tragedy as Beardsley from Phidias. Nevertheless, it is through Mr. Compson's narration in section 3 that Rosa begins to emerge as a less forbidding figure, one far more immediately present in his language than the Sutpens. He finds in her what he does not find in them, a victim, as he imagines himself, of the dissolution of the past and its ideals. Created and trained as a Southern lady, she is forced to act in the equanimous squalor of the present without ever having had a chance to live what she was destined to have been. Against Quentin's impatience at having to endure the ramblings of a bitter, broken old woman, Mr. Compson would attempt at least to understand something of the pain and loss Rosa feels.

Likewise, in section 4 the most immediately present concern is not only Compson's dreamy story of Charles and Henry but also his realization of Quentin's desperate involvement in their relationship. As his words accumulate, almost overpowering the story by his fustian elegance, the entire narrative is shadowed by the terrible poignancy of his statement about Judith and Sutpen:

> "They were as two people become now and then, who seem to know one another so well or are so much alike that the power, the need, to communicate by speech atrophies from disuse and, comprehending without need of the medium of ear or intellect, they no longer understand one another's actual words." [122]

It is the worse because Quentin does understand without comprehending his father's plenitude of words, not as Judith had done, but because he doesn't particularly care; he is preoccupied with the very thing Mr. Compson would save him from and knows already that his father is impotent to relieve him. Later, when Quentin thinks that Shreve sounds like Mr. Compson, it is not only because Shreve has said something Mr. Compson might have said but also because Quenin recognizes that Shreve, too, is trying to "save" him.

Mr. Compson attempts to convince Quentin of his own sense of what happened to the Sutpens as a dream of the past, as something which cannot bear a living analogy to his present or to Quentin's. Yet the very presence of his father, for Quentin, is the imposition of the past which he finds so paralyzing. The more Mr. Compson attempts to persuade, the more oppressed Quentin must feel. As Mr. Compson persists, he realizes that he must give Quentin the

letter Judith had entrusted to Quentin's grandmother, but at the
same time he hopes to abrogate the profound connection between
past and present Judith gives as her reason for abandoning the
letter. For Mr. Compson, Judith's very act of releasing it proves
she must have been a different kind of person, with a different
strength and a different faith, from anyone alive in the present. And
he does not give Quentin the letter until he has done the best he
can. The contents of the letter surely are no more important than
the tenderness and pain with which, once more, it is passed on.
Like Rosa, Mr. Compson is haunted by loss, by the realization
of what he has lost in Quentin.

In its development, Faulkner's attitude toward his two narrators
is at least as complex as Rosa's attitude toward Sutpen or Mr.
Compson's toward Quentin. And this is something the very premises
of interpretation make impossible to understand. For once the novel
has been reduced to a completed action, a pattern of meaning, one
can never reason backward to recover a sense of the author's creative
action. Instead, either the critic is faced with a necessity to find
"latent" meaning over and above an author's explicit statement—
whatever *that* might mean—or he must displace his interpretive
effort back into the "psychology" of the author, attempting to find
whatever patterns of repression or deformation existed in the
author's "personality" and somehow "got themselves into" the text.
But if, on the other hand, the novel is understood from the beginning as itself a creative act of thinking, then it becomes possible
to realize how the author is at once shaping the novel and listening
to what he does, creating his characters and judging self-critically his
success or failure. That an author is thus most human in his work
seems to me much less demeaning than to imagine creation as an
inspired burst of energy and authors as almost mythical beasts who
provide us with the raw material for our interpretive discussions.

At the University of Virginia, Faulkner made the statement that
"there are very few people that have enough grandeur of soul to
be able to use people and not develop contempt for [them]," and
Absalom, Absalom! represents the concrete working out of that
proposition on Faulkner's part as well as by his characters.[5] For
within the novel, it is easy enough to sense Faulkner's genius at work
using both Rosa and Mr. Compson's weaknesses mercilessly, coercing

these characters into the pattern he desires for his novel. Thus the initial characterization of Rosa is as unequivocal as her initial characterization of Sutpen: she is a frustrated old maid, more dead than alive, a grimly ironic Persephone. I have already suggested that even in section 1 Rosa begins to escape this rigid frame, to the extent that her own feelings about Sutpen emerge as far more ambiguous than she had imagined. Thus the abrupt shift in section 2 comes as almost a contemptuous dismissal of Rosa when she steps beyond the pattern of the character Faulkner has determined. Likewise, at the end of Mr. Compson's narrative in section 3, when both he and Rosa are beginning to be realized as characters fully alive in their own right, Faulkner again dramatically shifts the focus of narration, forcing Mr. Compson's attention to that New Orleans trip in a way he must know will reveal Compson's preoccupations at their worst.

It is Faulkner's greatness as a writer which triumphs over these patterns he would impose upon his characters, integrating his "grandeur of soul" and his petty insistence on owning and controlling his novel as completely as Sutpen once owned and controlled his estate. Just as Rosa and Mr. Compson are made to explore more fully their own feelings about Sutpen, about Henry and Charles and Quentin, so Faulkner must about his narrators. (Or more exactly, the analogy is not as Rosa to Sutpen, so Faulkner to Rosa. Rather, Rosa is to Sutpen as Faulkner is to both Rosa and Sutpen.) Thus the dramatic development of *Absalom, Absalom!* is shaped by Faulkner's growing awareness of his own limitations as well as by his sense of the limitations of his characters. He does not indulge in the magisterial sweep of imagination which contemplatively examines each new perspective as it arises, ignoring his own involvement in what is presented. For it is a feeling of loss which impels not only Rosa and Mr. Compson's narratives but also the novel as a whole; the title, of course, is David's cry at the loss of Absalom. Faulkner's creation is realized only as he splits himself into two, three, and even more vital centers of activity, each of whom is allowed a fullness of presence in the novel which cannot be reduced to a mere hard edge of meaning.

The very experience of creating the novel is the experience of losing one's immense and godlike self-absorption to its necessary bodily expression and the resulting engagement with others, an act of life which is to lose one's soul in order to gain it, discovering in the petty, violent, sordid business of creating in time among the lives of others the grandeur that makes petty the monstrous egotism with which one began. The feeling is like Rosa's, but with the awareness of the essential loneliness of solipsism which she does not achieve until section 5. It is like Mr. Compson's fear of losing his son to what he sees as the irrevocable dissolution of history. As becomes apparent later, it is like Sutpen's desire for a son which never escapes the false grandeur of his "design" by recognizing its cruelty and pettiness, like the conflict between Henry and Charles through Judith which results in her loss of both husband-to-be and brother, like Wash Jones's loss of his grand sense of himself revealed to him through the cruelty of Sutpen, like the bitter defeat felt by those in the South who survive the war, like Shreve's attempt to sunder Quentin violently from his past in order to save it for him, like the kingdom of Jerusalem promised to David but arriving to him through the loss of Absalom.

Faulkner is not playing a game of technique, juxtaposing fictional perspectives with Rosa and Mr. Compson's narratives. (Do we still need our novelists to remind us that there is an element of fiction in every point of view? Surely they can be released for more important tasks.) For within their thoughts and feelings he patiently meditates on his own preoccupations as well, discovering through his characters the quality of his own feeling. Such activity is nothing one can hold up for display, as here a dazzling image, here a particularly stunning transition, here an unexpected use of generic convention. Yet unless this vital source is tapped, one's criticism remains a shell, fronted only by the chimera of finding what it has been decided upon in advance to find.

Thus it is no contradiction to realize that within the intensely personal and heightened rhetoric of section 5, a larger and more insistent problem is posed: the profound connection between the movement of time and the development of human relationships. It is in section 5 that the luminous presence of the Sutpens intrudes itself most forcefully within the present of the novel, no longer as shadow and fantasy, as the vehicle by which present relationships are articulated, but now in the blazing light of Rosa's vibrantly immediate account of her journey to Sutpen's Hundred. A central passage occurs early in her narrative when she echoes Faulkner's statement (22) which I quoted earlier:

> Or perhaps it is no lack of courage either: not cowardice which will not face that sickness somewhere at the prime foundation of this factual scheme from which the prisoner soul, miasmal-distillant, wroils ever upward sunward, tugs its tenuous prisoner arteries and veins and prisoning in its turn that spark, that dream which, as the globy and complete instant of its freedom mirrors and repeats (repeats? creates, reduces to a fragile evanescent irridescent sphere) all of space and time and massy earth, relicts the seething and anonymous miasmal mass which in all the years of time has taught itself no boon of death but only how to recreate, renew; and dies, is gone, vanished: nothing—but is that true wisdom which can comprehend that there is a might-have-been which is more true than truth, from which the dreamer, waking, says not "Did I but dream?" but rather says, indicts high heaven's very self with: "Why did I wake since waking I shall never sleep again?" [143]

Awake now, she remains haunted by that "dream" sense of herself as outside of time, comprehending in an instant "*all of space and time and massy earth,*" and her struggle in part is to re-create the "dream" as such; thus the long, long acount of the instant of passing Clytie on the stairs. At the same time, she knows that she can "*never sleep again,*" that her present sense of herself is of someone in the past because she is haunted by its loss, though the very fact of her still feeling the loss means that the "dream" is not just dream but physical, present reality:

> See how the sleeping outflung hand, touching the bedside candle, remembers pain, springs back and free while mind and brain sleep on and only make of this adjacent heat some trashy myth of reality's escape: or that same sleeping hand, in sensuous marriage with some dulcet surface, is transformed by that same sleeping brain and mind into that same figment-stuff

warped out of all experience. Ay, grief goes, fades: we know
that—but ask the tear ducts if they have forgotten how to
weep. [143]

She must recognize that her present journey to Sutpen's Hundred
with Quentin forces an admission of what she says she cannot
admit, that Sutpen is dead. She thinks of herself, too, as "dead"
at the instant of waking, although the knowledge that the waking
was a kind of death depends upon her present awareness. Thus she
struggles to integrate a sense of herself as both alive in the past
(journeying to Sutpen's Hundred with Wash Jones) and in a present
(making the same journey with Quentin) which depends upon both
Sutpen's death and the awareness that "something" is still living out
there which she must discover.

Vickery insists that Rosa never escapes her self-delusion: "With
the grim air of a vengeful Cassandra, she waits for all those who
have provoked her censure to 'prove not only to themselves but
to everybody else that she had been right.'"[6] However, the statement Vickery quotes is Shreve's judgment, which he later modifies:
"'But at last she did reconcile herself to it, for his sake, to save
him, to bring him into town where the doctors could save him, and
so she told it then, got the ambulance and the men and went out
there'" (374). Quentin, too, thinks at first that what he sees on
Rosa's face is triumph at what she's found at Sutpen's but later
realizes differently: "'Maybe my face looks like hers did, but it's
not triumph'" (371). Finally, Shreve's initial judgment which
Vickery quotes is based on Rosa's assessment of herself: *"only being*
right is not enough for women, who had rather be wrong than just
that; who want the man who was wrong to admit it. And that's
what she can't forgive him for: not for the insult, not even for
having jilted her: but for being dead" (170).

As long as she remains prisoned within her own dream, Sutpen's
death is an outrage. Her release is her acceptance of the movement
of time that brings Sutpen's death and her ultimate loss of him
while it also opens for her the possibility of a future embodied in
the goal of the journey to Sutpen's Hundred and Quentin: *"But I*
forgave him. They will tell you different, but I did. Why shouldn't
I? I had nothing to forgive: I had not lost him because I never

owned him" (171). Rosa's triumph—and it most emphatically *is* a triumph—makes it impossible to dismiss her characterization of Sutpen in section 5 as foolish self-delusion.

Sutpen remains a fantastic creation in Rosa's telling, but not because of any inadequacy as in section 1. She now speaks of him out of her awareness of how he fails to understand himself:

> *Because he was not articulated in this world. He was a walking shadow. He was the light-blinded bat-like image of his own torment cast by the fierce demoniac lantern up from beneath the earth's crust and hence in retrograde, reverse; from abysmal and chaotic dark to eternal and abysmal dark completing his descending (do you mark the gradation?) ellipsis, clinging, trying to cling with vain unsubstantial hands to what he hoped would hold him, save him, arrest him.* [171]

Rosa does not have the benefit of what Sutpen had told General Compson; yet she imagines exactly right. Sutpen not only does not explain, for example, how he managed to save the plantation in Haiti but he doesn't even see the need for explanation. He does not question the morality of his "design," only why he did not succeed in achieving it. Rosa had recognized his "design" as madness, as a "dream," but had hoped there was some connection, no matter how tenuous, to waking reality: *"some spark, some crumb to leaven and redeem that articulated flesh, that speech sight hearing taste and being which we call human man"* (166). When he makes his suggestion of a trial breeding to her, she reneges on even that possibility and returns to her "demon" explanation. But is that so far wrong? What does one call a person who has no sense of others, who exists from birth to death in a "dream" from which he never wakes to anyone around him? If one's belief in the reality of another person must rest in part on the awareness that person has of himself, how else but fantastically do we characterize one who has no such awareness? What, if not this, is Sutpen's "innocence" all about?

Rosa does not even know the bare "facts" of Sutpen's life which are available to Mr. Compson and Quentin, and she feels hurt by him in a way neither Quentin nor his father can. Yet she develops the "grandeur of soul" to understand without imposition, to use him in justifying herself but without contempt for him, to risk destroying what has kept her alive for forty-three years on the chance that she might find something of him still living, to realize that in judging his mad dream she has also judged her own.

Nevertheless, Rosa's struggle only partially explains the difficulties in the language of section 5. It is impossible not to recognize Faulkner's preoccupations in hers, his language in the way she speaks, his feeling within her actions. At the University of Virginia, Faulkner went even further, saying that all anyone ever really does is talk about himself: "But then, every time any character gets into a book, no matter how minor, he's actually telling his own biography—that's all anyone ever does, he tells his own biography, talking about himself, in a thousand different terms, but himself."[7] The greatness of section 5 is that Faulkner talks about himself through Rosa talking about Sutpen, realizing in fact that it is the only way to talk about himself, not only because Rosa belongs to him as a character in his novel but also because he belongs to her. In committing himself to creating her as a character, he has at the same time committed himself to her creating him as a novelist before his own equilibrating self-consciousness and before his readers. He must accomplish with Rosa what she accomplishes with Sutpen. Thus it is not enough to suggest that Rosa's narrative represents merely one perspective on the Sutpens, her sense of time and history merely one way of coming to terms with the past. Her narrative in section 5 is at the heart of Faulkner's conception of his novel.

Being alive in the present means feeling the loss of the past, the inability ever to comprehend fully history as the object of one's present awareness. Yet that feeling of loss is the guarantee of the future, is finally at one with the future because it, too, is an absence, toward which the present resolves itself. If the past were wholly given to present experience there could be no genuine present or coming-to-be of the future because the future could never become past, could never violate the crystal integrity of a completed object. Historical understanding is possible just because it is never complete, because one's present consciousness can merge with the dehiscence of present into future, can, that is, become aware of itself in time and hence make it possible for one to have a history, just as Faulkner can at once be speaking inside the novel and aware of himself speaking as he shapes the novel from the beginning. Thus the "dream" sense of *Absalom, Absalom!* as instantaneous and eternal is finally at once with its temporal articulation, arising from the awareness of a continual movement of self-transcendence toward the future that like the past is felt as a loss, an absence. The temporal movement of the novel is a present, continual appropriation of the loss of the past which contains within itself both the coming-to-be of the future and the lapse of future into past.

Further, this temporal movement is like the relationship between Faulkner and his characters, beginning with the denial of the loss of the characters to themselves—the attempt to own them, hold them as complete objects before the steady, detached gaze of the author—followed by the realization that such an object is not a character at all. Just as the past requires an incompleteness which is a continual appropriation, so the character who is fully alive within the novel requires an otherness which can never become wholly visible, which demands the author's continual attention to his own movement out of himself toward the character. It is a recognition that the welling up of time as one lives it is identical with the relationship of self and other, an awareness of the loss of self to the past and to another which makes possible a self-transcendence toward the future and toward the possibility of a continued involvement with someone else. It is little wonder that the very language of *Absalom, Absalom!* refuses to stand still, to reveal itself as pattern and artifice whose visible template can be duplicated by the interpreter's effort. For language as it works in literature has undergone the kind of sea change that forever escapes those pale, chiseled determinations we would impose upon its liquid purl .

II

Quentin's intrusion at the end of section 5 marks the sudden, dramatic awareness that the temporal rhythm of the novel is also a tragic one. Like the movement of time itself, experience never fully coincides with itself, and it is Quentin who feels most deeply this inevitable lapse. The "something" he "could not pass" about the Sutpen story is the door through which Henry rushes to meet Judith after he has shot Bon. On the one hand, Quentin knows that Henry had to shoot Bon, that, like Hamlet who could find no peace until the ghost's command was obeyed, Henry could not rest until Bon was stopped. On the other hand, there is Henry's awareness that Bon's murder really wasn't necessary. Quentin's wonder is less with the apparent insolubility of Henry's problem than with the fact that Henry acted at all, facing Judith not only with what he had done but also with what he knew. Given the awareness of such alternatives, such discontinuity, how is it possible to do anything? Knowledge becomes paralysis, action blind.

The final four sections of the novel represent Faulkner's working through of the tragedy and his affirmation of faith in the tragedian, the one whose awareness creates and shapes the whole action. Rosa acts from pain and frustration in going to Sutpen's Hundred and still creates a story whose magnificence contains within it her own limited self and her preoccupations. And likewise, Faulkner as tragedian contains within the magnificence of his novel the tragic acts of all his characters, including his meditation on his own innermost feelings, suppressing nothing, even his egotism and pettiness. One acts from inner necessity and in accordance with the cruelly limited nature of a finite existence wherein only one alternative at a time can be realized, a movement which inevitably loses and negates other alternatives. Yet the action realized engenders not only a loss but also a possibility, just as it is the loss of the present to the past that makes possible a future. One's very finiteness exists only as one is going beyond it. Tragedy inheres in the moment of loss as it is contained within the whole action of the tragedian.

Perhaps the truest measure of Faulkner's greatness is that he allows even this wisdom to be tested, through the alternative creation of the Sutpen story by Shreve McCannon. The problem for Faulkner is to include within his own shaping action Shreve's sense of himself as the artist who, unlike Faulkner, strives to be contemplatively detached from his personal preoccupations, as they would intrude into the story he creates. For Shreve, there is no tragedy that couldn't have been avoided, no feeling of necessity which could not be annulled by stepping back from one's own reaction, by *seeing* clearly enough what is there to be seen. Tragedy is in the response which sees that it didn't have to be that way. Where Quentin radically dissociates knowledge and action, Shreve will demonstrate to him that they can be one and the same. Thus the breathtaking agility of Shreve's intelligence comes as an exhilarating release, not only from the almost claustrophobic intensity of Rosa and Mr. Compson but from Faulkner's activity as well.

In section 6, Shreve, like Mr. Compson before him, is committed to "saving" Quentin by making the most of the difference between past and present, by making Quentin realize that one's present actions are not determined by the actions of those in the past. And if Mr. Compson could not succeed by imagining the Sutpens as qualitatively finer than anyone alive in the present, Shreve would succeed by diminishing the Sutpens to an idiot and a ghost through the force of his own reductive, ironic intelligence. Nevertheless, "something" remains which Shreve recognizes as the key to Quentin's almost physical paralysis. "'No wonder you have to come away now and then'" (217), he tells Quentin at the beginning of section 7. He, too, has realized the necessity to "come away," to step back once more and begin at the beginning with Thomas Sutpen.

The intricacy of section 7 results from the presence of three markedly different ways of exploring the nature of Sutpen's life. Most of the section is ostensibly narrated by Quentin, although he has doubts about whether he is really telling it or already listening once more:

> *Am I going to have to hear it all again* he thought *I am going to have to hear it all over again I am already hearing it all over again I am listening to it all over again I shall never listen to anything else but this again forever so apparently not only a man never outlives his father but not even his friends and acquaintances do* [277]

Mr. Compson is as inescapably present to Quentin as Sutpen to Henry, and by extension, as Sutpen to Quentin. Action not only never offers a decisive break but becomes always more embracing and more oppressive the more one knows about it. This seems to me as close as Faulkner comes in the novel to what Lukács would call a "dissolution of personality." But it is in a special sense indeed, one immediately qualified and measured by Shreve's reaction. For against Quentin's resignation, Shreve's infrequent, yet telling interruptions attempt to restore a form of ironic detachment, half playfully apostrophizing Quentin's "he" with Rosa's "the demon." Under the polyphonic weight of Quentin's speech, Shreve is driven finally to reassert a much more positive control: "'No,' Shreve said, 'you wait. Let me play a while now'" (280).

And as if he has had enough of this deadly "game" of dissolution and control, Faulkner interrupts them both:

> This was not flippancy either. It too was just that protective coloring of levity behind which the youthful shame of being moved hid itself, out of which Quentin also spoke, the reason for Quentin's sullen bemusement, the (on both their parts) flipness, the strained clowning . . . the two of them back to back as though at the last ditch, saying No to Quentin's Mississippi shade who in life had acted and reacted to the minimum of logic and morality, who dying had escaped it completely, who dead remained not only indifferent but impervious to it, somehow a thousand times more potent and alive. [280]

Faulkner is not simply arguing Mr. Compson's point, that somehow Sutpen's character is larger, grander than that of anyone alive in the present. His being "a thousand times more potent and alive" results from the growing awareness of Sutpen possessed by Shreve and Quentin, an awareness of being moved by the very grandeur and terror of his life which they attempt to deny, in Shreve's strained irony and Quentin's repressed outrage.

It is as if both Shreve and Quentin are hypnotized by the devastating results of Sutpen's "design," condemned to a kind of paralysis or a frenetic activity in the face of it, where Faulkner must try through their narratives to re-create and understand what has happened. As Sutpen attempts to "explain" himself to General Compson, his plan was intended to overcome the pain he had felt as a small boy having been turned away from the front door of a Virginia plantation: "that now he would take that boy in where he would never again need to stand on the outside of a white door and knock at it . . . so that that boy, that whatever nameless stranger, could shut that door himself forever behind him on all that he had ever known" (261). Sutpen's dream is to include everyone, to shut the door once and for all on the pain of rejection and the conflict of privilege among individuals. Yet it is built upon the thousands of blacks sacrificed in Haiti, and the last survivor is Jim Bond, a howling idiot who watches Sutpen's mansion burn. It engenders the division of his family against themselves, the conflict between Henry and Bon, the suppression of blacks by the whites, the conflict within Etienne, the participation in a war of secession, and the final irony, his turning away his own son just as he had been turned away. Judith's is the door that opens, for Henry after his murder of Charles. What Faulkner must comprehend, without dissolution and without ironic detachment of any kind, is the quality of such "innocence" that could be at once so magnificent and so petty, so inclusive and yet so inhumanly destructive, that could have begun in such a seemingly generous impulse and ended in such fanaticism.

Unlike Shreve, Faulkner does not dismiss Rosa's characterization of Sutpen as a safe joke. She has recognized what Faulkner insists upon as well, that Sutpen's "innocence" began in his lack of awareness that his design in its very origination was both magnificent and petty, whole and multiple, good and evil. Even as he resolved that no little boy would ever again be turned away, that all would be included, Sutpen thinks of his effort as a combat taking place in a way that is abstractly removed from all direct confrontation between individuals. Like that house itself, which Sutpen can never quite sense as having been made by another human being at a price, his combat is a bloodless schematic, a pattern of him against "them," something greater "than all the human puny mortals under the sun" (238), a war fought by a god or a demon and not an individual. When he relates his experience of the slave rebellion in Haiti, for example, there is no awareness of his having been directly involved in a war or his consideration of the rightness or wrongness of it: "'he was just telling a story about something a man named Thomas Sutpen had experienced, which would still have been the same story if the man had no name at all, if it had been told by any man or no man over whiskey at night'" (247). Confronted finally by a particular individual, his own son rather than a "nameless stranger," Sutpen refuses him admittance.

Rosa's formulation is exact; Sutpen "*was not articulated in this world.*" For it points as well to the responsibility Faulkner has set himself in the very creation of *Absalom, Absalom!*, which is precisely to be "articulated in this world," to avoid, despite the insistent relationship, an attempt like Sutpen's to engender a new kingdom over and above the pain of his life. Faulkner, too, would create in an all-inclusive innocence the violence and suffering of his characters "'riven forever free from brutehood'" (236) by their existence in the luminous dream of his novel, "a thousand times more potent and alive" than in the cruelly limited nature of earthly lives. The very nature of the novelist's task seems to demand that he create such an alternate world, a "Dublin" or a "Yoknapatawpha County" peopled out of the imagination, an autonomous realm, or even a "simulacrum of reality," but graced by the perfection of artistic form. (This edition of *Absalom, Absalom!* contains Faulkner's map, with the inscription at the bottom: "Jefferson, Yoknapatawpha Co., Mississippi. Area, 2400 Square Miles—Population, Whites, 6298; Negroes, 9313. William Faulkner, Sole Owner & Proprietor.") Like Sutpen's dream, a novel, too, appears to be a "design" or an architecture, a creative vision.

Sutpen, however, believes that his design can be distinct from his act of creating it, that if he can make the product of his labor a kind of heavenly perfection, then it does not matter that the "combat" necessary to succeed was conceived and born in the earth, in human blood and destruction perpetuated for generations. Through his creation of Sutpen, Faulkner recognizes the essential falseness of dividing the imaginative life of a novel from life as one lives it. The "design" of *Absalom, Absalom!* is no completed pattern, no "Sutpen's Hundred," no monument to artistic vision. Its life is actual, in a way which implicates Faulkner himself at every point, which in fact "articulates" him in this world. Thus *Absalom, Absalom!* is not an anonymous story which would have been the same story if William Faulkner wrote it or someone else. The terrifying quality of Faulkner's creation of Sutpen is not that, through Sutpen, Faulkner impartially diagnoses the failure of the "Old South" or, as Cleanth Brooks has argued, the spirit of "northern" capitalism in its ambitious sweep. These are indeed present; Faulkner's imagination is diagnostic in the most penetrating sense, to the extent that the complicity between agricultural and industrial capitalism which it adumbrates deserves another essay. But the success of his characterization of Sutpen goes further; it inheres in Faulkner's ability to bring it home, to sense in Sutpen's activity a direct and personal criticism of his own creative effort.

In section 7, Faulkner exposes both Shreve and Quentin for

their corruptness, for Quentin's suppression of himself and Shreve's overriding his feeling for Quentin by his love of his own cleverness. They are unwilling to pay the price Faulkner has paid, which is to suppress nothing, to include even the most painful and intense contradictions. At the end of the section, Faulkner makes a fool of Shreve through the agency of Shreve's own intelligence, the source of his pride, as Shreve is reduced to helpless suspense until Quentin clears up the mystery for him. It is only then, in section 8, that Faulkner can make the move impossible for a Thomas Sutpen, by allowing Shreve and Quentin their triumph in return, the creation of the Sutpen story with full awareness of the feelings which compel their expression and in dramatic contrast to Faulkner's own creation.

While there may be "error of fact" in what Shreve and Quentin say, there is no longer a corrupt consciousness. Both speak out of their own deepest feelings: Quentin that Henry loved his father and Judith and thus had to shoot Bon, Shreve that Bon loved Judith and thus Henry needn't have shot him. And however different, even antithetical to Shreve's creation, Faulkner's own shaping action may be, Shreve is never again reduced to an object of contempt as he had been at the end of section 7. The grandeur of Faulkner's imagination is in its very humility, the willingness to let Shreve's creation judge him even as he has judged Shreve. Faulkner can remain inalterably opposed to Shreve and still recognize that for the opposition to have any meaning or value Shreve must be allowed to exert all the living pressure of his being against Faulkner.

Through over half the section, Shreve's attempts to show Bon's love are punctuated by Quentin's denial, "'But it's not love,'" and Shreve's continual affirmation that it is. Henry's act and not Bon's was the real sin, the destruction of love and not an act of love for his sister. In contrast to Bon's changing the picture, which was an attempt to overcome whatever pain and loss Judith might feel at his death, Henry's shot was a surrender to the necessity of his entire past which kept the purity of an aristocratic ideal Sutpen had made his own by exluding the nigger, even if he is your brother. The violence of Shreve's assertion is felt in his language, in Bon's comment to Henry: *I'm the nigger that's going to sleep with your sister"* (358), and in Shreve's own comment to Quentin: "'why the

black son of a bitch should have taken her picture out and put
the octoroon's picture in'" (358-59). Shreve expresses in as stark
an opposition as possible the language of the Southern tradition
and the reality of love he has tried to reveal to Quentin. His hope
is that the violence can be enough, that it can tear Quentin free
from his preoccupation, show him in Bon's act the knowledge
which can redeem even the destructiveness of Henry's. By the end
of the section, he has gained Quentin's consent:

> "Aint that right? Aint it? By God, aint it?"
> "Yes," Quentin said. [359]

Shreve has come to the conclusion that this final tragedy of
the Sutpens has less to do with the fact that Bon was murdered
than in one's response to that fact. Unless there is the awareness
that Henry's shot could have been avoided, there can be no tragedy,
only waste and destruction. And awareness comes as one sees
completely every facet of the situation, as *both* Henry and Bon:

> Because now neither of them were there. They were both in
> Carolina and the time was forty-six years ago, and it was not
> even four now but compounded still further, since now both
> of them were Henry Sutpen and both of them were Bon, com-
> pounded each of both yet either neither. [351]

For Shreve, the capacity to change, to engender hope from tragedy
inheres in such total awareness which reverses the partiality that
takes sides and destroys its opponent. While Faulkner circum-
spectly indicates throughout section 8 that what Shreve and Quentin
say is "probably true enough," Shreve expresses no such reservations. His faith is contingent upon the complete and immediate
identification of knowledge and action as the key to unlock Quentin's paralysis.

Thus it is with moving sympathy that he speaks to Quentin in
section 9, realizing that to relive the Sutpen story had to have been
worse for Quentin than for himself:

> "Wait. Listen. I'm not trying to be funny, smart. I just want to
> understand it if I can and I dont know how to say it better.
> Because it's something my people haven't got. . . . so that

forevermore as long as your childrens' children produce children you wont be anything but a descendant of a long line of
colonels killed in Pickett's charge at Manassas?" [361]

Just because of his care, he must speak as he does, yet in so doing
he denies the very quality which had allowed him to gain Quentin's
acquiescence at the end of section 8. To admit that it had been
worse for Quentin is to admit that the same knowledge engenders
two different responses, two different actions. Quentin senses it
immediately, correcting not only what Shreve does but also what
he knows: "'Gettysburg,' Quentin said. 'You cant understand it.
You would have to be born there'" (361).

Shreve's bitterness is understandable, as he is forced to realize
that in reality his job may never be finished: "'So it takes two
niggers to get rid of one Sutpen, dont it? . . . Which is all right, it's
fine; it clears the whole ledger, you can tear all the pages out and
burn them, except for one thing. And do you know what that
is? . . . You've got one nigger left. One nigger Sutpen left'" (378).
And his theory of "bleaching out" becomes a grimly ironic parody
of the identification he had attempted to perform for Quentin.
Rather than the grace of love which had closed section 8, Faulkner's
novel ends with the bitterness of Shreve's final question that Quentin cannot answer.

Had Faulkner ended *Absalom, Absalom!* after section 8, it would
not prove the strenuous challenge to criticism that it assuredly is.
Faulkner is clearly not finished with his work until the last words of
the novel, but as an imaginative artifact, as the product of Faulkner's
creation measured against the product of Shreve's creation in section 8, *Absalom, Absalom!* remains a mass of unreconcilable contradictions. For Faulkner has turned Shreve's superlative magic—his
melting of time and history into eternity, flesh into spirit, hate into
love—toward a ruthless logic of division which leaves Shreve and
Quentin themselves at bitter odds with each other. And yet from
the beginning of the novel, Faulkner has been at work to integrate
Shreve's radical alternatives through the realization that the multiplicity of language and character, the shattering and irreducible
conflicts exist only as they are being brought into being out of the
oneness of feeling which animates the novel as a whole. The ending

of *Absalom, Absalom!* is as painful as it is because one remembers the fragile love and beauty which binds individuals together as one, and that love and oneness are as valuable as they are because they can be lost to conflict and contradiction. Faulkner's faith is in the wholeness *and* openness of an action so inclusive that it does not rise above the forces of loss and death but hymns within them the cherished memory of all one loves.

8

Criticism and Community:
On Literary Value

I

I think it is appropriate to conclude this book with some consideration of the idea of literary value, even though critical theory for the
most part seems bored with it. For contemporary literature is often
the one area where it is acknowledged, albeit reluctantly, that
value judgments have any place in the study of literature. As mere
"public critics" previewing the latest sensibility, reviewers are
accorded the dubious honor of trafficking in their likes and dislikes
while more sober scholars go about the proper business of obtaining
information about past literature. If one believes as I do that characterization and evaluation are inseparable, then this situation is
perhaps the worst that can be imagined for any serious consideration
of recent literature. There are many bad reasons for placing value
judgments outside the boundaries of genuine critical thought, most
of them having to do with the idea that criticism should be neutral
and descriptive, that it should say what a poem is or what it means
before assessing its value or significance. I hope chapter 6 has made
clear how an exact and complex critique can be made of the truism
that this stance of contemplative neutrality is itself indicative of a
social and class attitude toward human knowledge. Nevertheless,
there seems to me a good reason for questioning the role and nature
of value judgments which deserves further attention.

When he made the statement that the literary universe is one
where Sade and Jane Austen lie down together, Frye echoed a long
history of belief in the inclusiveness of the literary imagination, as
well as those more immediate feelings which tell us it's "all right" to
exhibit such disparate authors as these in the same course, as an
indication of the "range" of literary experience.[1] Empson is usually

criticized for letting the possibilities of ambiguity and paradox run away with his analyses. Yet the verbal complexity Empson understands marks for him one way of coming to terms with a proposition at least in general terms similar to Frye's: somehow, the choices made in literary works are always inclusive rather than exclusive. Few would side with Iago as a moral creature against Othello, but the point is we don't have to; *Othello* includes both. Unless the idea of value judgments is thought to mean nothing more than a fuzzy assertion that some works are more inclusive than others, then it would seem to run directly counter to the assumption of a unique inclusiveness accorded to imaginative literature.

Indeed, what is often spoken of as the "statemental" or "dogmatic" assertiveness of Marxist criticism has its source in an apparent refusal of such inclusiveness. Given that they are trained to a dialectical thinking which emphasizes choice, conflict, and contradiction, it is not surprising to find Marxists almost alone among contemporary critics in their insistence that some kinds of literature are better than others or, more directly, that one simply cannot accept both Thomas Mann and Franz Kafka. The choice *between* them, Lukács argues, is so essential that it implicates every aspect of one's attitude toward a social world. Value inheres in whether or not a particular work can be seen to advance in any way the struggle of the proletariat. Whatever one thinks of this argument—and it is more subtle than is commonly assumed—it does seem to me to necessitate a response which says straight out what one means by "inclusiveness" and by "value judgments," as if the sorry situation which exists in the study of contemporary literature were not enough incentive.

Indirectly, in my reading of Faulkner, I tried to suggest that even though opposition is fundamental to dialectical thinking, the intense stress of conflict which marks *Absalom, Absalom!* arises out of equally fundamental relationships which also can be realized in dialectical terms. Likewise, implicit in chapter 5 was an attempt to reconcile a Marxist emphasis on choice and conflict with the New Critical belief in the creative power of literature to unify the most disparate oppositions. At this point, I want to return to my characterization of the act of thinking as having three dialectical "moments." Literature, as I argued, can be distinguished from other forms of discourse to the extent that it is dominated by the first "moment," by the upsurge of feeling. Thus, where a poem certainly may contain propositional statements, as well as intricately worked out moral or social positions, these exist poetically only insofar as they are suffused within the dominant feeling of the work. "Inclusiveness" for me describes precisely this dominance of feeling. So it is that Faulkner can recognize in Quentin's expression a feeling of loss like his own, even though his shaping act as author differs radically and profoundly from Quentin's almost catatonic reaction to his experience. The temptation to "identify" Faulkner with one or more of the characters in *Absalom* arises from the way in which even the differences and contradictions among these characters are so thoroughly caught up within the lambent feeling of Faulkner's creative activity.

Certainly rhetorical exhortations and philosophical argument are felt intensely, as for that matter are scientific statements. But here the means of "inclusiveness" are different. *Capital* is as passionate a statement as one might wish; yet we study and evaluate it *primarily* for what it can expose about the actual conditions of capitalistic society and what it can indicate about a direction of change. Friends tell me it is almost impossible to understand Einstein's *General Theory* without some sense of the awe Einstein felt in its demonstration. But again, one studies it primarily to determine its mathematical coherence and its heuristic capacity to predict empirical data. These are not absolute distinctions between "pure" forms of thought, and it is of course possible to learn any number of things, about capitalist society and even about mathematics, from literary works. However, these elements exist poetically as they are felt from within, bodied forth by the inclusiveness of the author's felt, creative act.

On the other hand, the "world" of the poem as its second and antithetical moment, its nonbeing, may be richly evocative of a multiplicity of actual experience, or it may seem as remote as those strangely mystical passages in *Four Quartets;* it may be involved as *Anna Karenina* or as thin as a four-line lyric by Yeats; it may offer the structural symmetry of *Paradise Lost* or the randomness of Frank O'Hara's poetry; it may come to a neatly unified conclusion like *Pride and Prejudice* or remain gaping like *Waiting for Godot.* "Inclusiveness" is not quantitative, nor can it be predicated on this

moment alone without denying some of the very finest literary
works. One poem cannot be more inclusive than another. It either
is or it isn't; it either works as a poem or it doesn't. For me the
legitimate question of inclusiveness asks only whether this "world,"
whatever form it takes, is dominated throughout by feeling. In this
sense at least, Frye is right to affirm the necessary presence of both
Sade and Jane Austen in the literary universe.

However, the further difficulty is that value judgments are involved even in this initial characterization, sometimes in quite
intricate and complex ways. Neither a statement of value nor a
statement that "*a* is a poem" can exist in isolation. They are different, but each implies the other at every point. I have argued at
length against any attempt to divide characterization and evaluation
absolutely, as if they were two discrete acts, and the problem now
seems to me one of determining more precisely how they are related.
One can say that *Capital* is valuable to the extent that it does indeed
have much to say about the nature of capitalist society. That is,
one's sense of its value and one's sense of its inclusiveness work
together in a way that does not seem immediately true of literary
works. Certainly it is not so simple as the argument that one tends
to pronounce "inclusive" those works which confirm one's own
values.

I made the suggestion in chapter 6 that the critic's reading of a
poem involves both a moment of utter identification with the most
intimate feeling of the poem and a moment of critical integrity
which requires him to respect the difference between himself as
critic and the author of the poem. As a consequence, criticism can
be judgmental, even antagonistic, and still realize the fineness and
inclusiveness of the work being studied. I think of Eliseo Vivas writing on Lawrence, out of a very different critical theory from my
own, profoundly distrustful of Lawrence's political and ethical beliefs as they are expressed in the novels and yet capable of understanding the extraordinary capaciousness of Lawrence's genius. Or
there is Leavis in *The Living Principle,* taking a stand against all that
is implied by *Four Quartets* and still able to show more of what
makes Eliot a great poet than the reams of exegetical work that have
been done on the *Quartets.* Even Lukács on Kafka—grandiose, petty,
grudgingly approbative, and dismissive all at once—manages to sug-

gest something of the wholeness of Kafka's work never touched by
the intricate symbolical dictionaries invented by Kafka's interpreters.

I think these examples imply an awareness that the process of
making critical value judgments is as much as anything a process
of clarifying both one's own values and the values embodied in the
poem, as they conflict or as they exist in harmony. Such clarifica-
tion is possible because the peculiar nature of literary inclusiveness
realizes not only choices that are made and the consequences they
have but also the alternatives which have been denied. For me, it is
obvious that Faulkner shapes *Absalom, Absalom!* in a way that
chooses against Shreve's version of the Sutpen story. Yet Shreve's
choice and the consequences it involves are as fully present as
Faulkner's own. Thus it is always possible to imagine a criticism
of the novel which chooses with Shreve and against Faulkner, which
maintains like Shreve that tragedy inheres in the wholeness of
response to a destructive act. The critic's obligation in such a case
is to achieve what Faulkner has achieved, to invoke Faulkner's
choice as his own opposite in the way that Faulkner has invoked
Shreve as his opposite.

Genuine critical value judgments thus become reciprocal. Just as
Faulkner can judge Shreve only to the extent that Shreve's creation
is allowed to judge Faulkner in return, so it is that the critic also
allows the poem to judge him. The idea that one's own critical
methodology—whether a sequence of archetypes, a linguistic "deep
structure" or "genotext," or some understanding derived from one
of the social sciences—can be sufficient to characterize the "latent
meaning" or form of a literary work fails to realize how value judgments are implicated at every point in the act of characterization
and, perhaps even more importantly, the way in which, again, literature "talks back," judges in return the critic who analyzes it. The
difficulty in making value judgments about literature is to respect
that uniquely literary inclusiveness which makes such reciprocity
essential.

However, it is also the idea of reciprocity that seems to me to offer
a way out of the antinomy with which I began this discussion, between an insistence that a poet "neither affirmeth nor denieth" and
an insistence that literature represents a directly political commitment. As I have described the reciprocity of value judgments, it

implies that the poet makes his affirmations in such a way that they include within them what it is he denies. In this sense, his work is far more inclusive than anything permitted by the assumption of contemplative removal embodied in the idea that the poet neither affirms nor denies. For what the latter cannot contain is precisely the act of contemplation itself. Faulkner, on the other hand, as I read him, is obligated to reveal not only what he sees but also his act of attentiveness, not only how he understands Shreve but also how Shreve understands him. Further, it is through the creation of such community that one can realize how literature is political.

The idea of direct political commitment presupposes a scene or a situation on which the author's act impinges: "This is how it is, and this is how we should react to it." Thus, paradoxically, this assumption also depends upon a prior objectification, as much as does the idea of contemplative removal. My idea of reciprocity suggests that the author's creative act takes responsibility both for his own commitment and for the situation wherein it exists. *Absalom, Absalom!* is Faulkner's community through and through. His creative action embodies not only specific commitments but also the situations, the scenes, and the relationships from which those commitments arise. Rather than a question of how one should react to others or to a particular situation, literature as political action begins in the attitude the author takes toward himself as an actor within the community of his work.

If they thought it dignified to answer, most critics would agree that *Absalom, Absalom!* is a "great novel," although, as I argued, the interpretations of the novel often make that assertion hollower than it seems. The more obvious problems of literary value judgments generally arise in connection with contemporary literature. The reason inheres less in the fallacy that it is "so close" to us that we "cannot see" clearly to determine its worth than in the fact that there is little possibility that something on the order of "the weight of tradition" can let us escape responsibility for the choices and distinctions that must be made whenever one writes or thinks about literature. I have had much to say about the gap between recent critical theory and recent literature. Yet there are indeed parallels between the theories of Frye, Bloom, Barthes, and others and the fiction of an author such as Robert Coover. The ideological concerns—the movement of "de-centering," the refusal of any privilege to subjectivity, for example—are as much a part of Coover's fiction as they are of these theories. Indeed, I would hesitate to take recent theory as seriously as I do if it were not apparent that even the attempt to construct self-validating methodologies is indicative of a social situation which extends beyond the boundaries of method itself.

I have made my argument against the criticism; how and in what way could a similar argument be made in relation to a literary work, given what I have said about the special "inclusiveness" of literature? Likewise, I have made much of the relationship between "personal" and "social" in contemporary poetry, using it in my first chapter as exemplary of my own theoretical understanding of poetic action. Yet, while W. S. Merwin's poetry is some of the very finest now being written, few other poets develop such intimidating, aloof, and isolated poems, so spare as to seem almost voiceless rather than polyphonic. To write about authors such as Coover and Merwin together, to make the distinctions my own commitments entail and still recognize the elusive quality and integrity of their work, seems to me perhaps the only sufficient way to conclude an argument about what one means by literary value judgments.

II

If one comes to more recent literature from a novel such as *Absalom, Absalom!*, one of the most conspicuous absences will be the sustained, fine intricacy of personal relationships which makes *Absalom, Absalom!* what it is. There seem to me two particularly important and different realizations of this situation, very roughly divided between fiction and poetry. They are important because both self-consciously deny the primary importance of personality, rather than simply avoiding its possibility, and they are as different as the fanciful, spiraling cumuli of Robert Coover's fiction from the austere chill of W. S. Merwin's poetry. Merwin is haunted, as is Coover, by a need to break up the solidity of the subject, to introduce within the field of personality a radical dislocation which severs its tenacious, grasping hold on itself. Yet it is Merwin, too, who of all contemporary poets most directly resists the paralyzing fictions of artifice which have moved to occupy the center of contemporary writing such as Coover's a center left vacant by the absence of subject, of personality.

I don't, of course, intend that my division between poetry and fiction be omnipresent, or even that the absence of personal relationships must be always and everywhere a problem in discussing contemporary literature. My sense of the critic's job is that he is obliged to perform as fully as possible a passage which can accompany and sustain the movement into the future of those works he loves, and there must be as many ways to do this as there are works of literature and people who read them. Yet it is this assumption itself which requires another, and one that is very much a part of my response to Merwin's poetry. It is the possibility of a profoundly indirect, though intimate, community between poet and critic. A good poem is never wholly caught in the past or in its own present but opens toward a future as well. Thus the problem faced by the critic when he begins to speak is that he has already a very real audience which is the poem itself. His voice does not curl out of silence but gathers itself in the swell of a lunar current being transformed into the sparkling crest of speech by the poet's creative awareness. If with enough love and skill he can engender his critical effort, he will then create a silence within it which allows him to sense the immigrant presence of the other within his own movement of thought and to be freed from the fear that unless the coordinates of his speech mesh exactly with the poem chaos must intrude. Merwin's poetry thus may well appear isolate and unpeopled, but criticism of it need not be, and it can learn its freedom from the creative action of the poems themselves.

The criticism of fiction, on the other hand, has developed for the most part quite a different possibility. Here is a passage from Robert Coover's story called "The Hat Act":

> *Wild shouting etc. (as before).*
> Large man reaches inside lovely assistant's tight green shorts, rolls his eyes, and grins obscenely. She grimaces and wiggles rear briefly.
>
> *Wild shouting etc. (as before).*
> Large man withdraws hand from inside lovely assistant's shorts, extracting magician in black cape and black silk hat.

Thunder of astonished applause.
Magician bows deeply, doffing hat to audience.

Prolonged enthusiastic applause, cheering.
Magician pitches lovely assistant and first large man into wings.
Inspects second large man, lying dead on stage. Unzips him and
young country boy emerges, flushed and embarrassed. Young
country boy creeps abjectly offstage on stomach.[2]

This has to do with sex at least, if not love, but if you've read the
whole story you know already that the people within it aren't very
important. Even the muse, the lovely assistant, must die for the
story to succeed. Coover's stories make criticism focused on themes
such as love and sex an obviously redundant exercise, and thus
initially they seem to escalate the continuing twentieth-century
saga of Artist versus Critic. How do you handle critics who insist
on the value of insight and passion and darkly interior psychological
understanding everywhere? If you want to bother at all, you can
show that such things are no more difficult, and no more *central,*
than any other magician's fiction, and probably not as entertaining.
Nately's whore is better than Kurtz's horror any day. Nobody
pretends she's real, and why should they when possibilities are
infinite? Coover would reveal criticism which still affirms a depth
psychology of personality as nothing more than a con game, a
magician's trick sanctioning the most cruel and distorted pleasures
at the expense of others. "Stereotype" and "substance" are for
Coover one and the same.

In this last respect especially, Coover's work can stand as repre-
sentative of a certain kind of fiction, associated with John Barth,
Thomas Pynchon, William Gass, and Donald Barthelme among
others. The most immediately obvious quality of their fiction is
that it contains already the labor of critical ingenuity our scholarship
has been trained to exercise on literary constructions, and thus
there is indeed something perverse about the increasing accumulation of articles and monographs about Pynchon's work in particular.
It is as if young Stencil left Malta to become a critic. For Pynchon's
novels, like Coover's stories, deliberately accentuate the fictive acts
of the author, playfully collapsing such privileged categories of
distinction as "stereotype" and "substance," fairy tale and realism,

popular culture and "great literature," even, in "The Hat Act," author and reader.

My initial response was to be appalled at such a headlong and idiosyncratic betrothal of unreality, a marriage between an author and an imaginary reader who has been freed from his stereotypical vision by the fanciful movements and contours of the story's advance. The "stereotype" audience is already "in" the story, and the point of "The Hat Act" is you, the imaginary "real" audience. It was not until sometime later that I realized Coover's fiction has been accompanied by a remarkably similar critical maneuver, convinced of its own solidity and definition and, paradoxically, developed out of certain aspects of modern literature. For the connections between recent criticism and "modernism" have been obscured by the "modern/postmodern" disjunction which relegates Eliot and Yeats—and perhaps soon (who knows?), Joyce as well—to that myth of the totalizing imagination, through the creation of an autonomous work of art intent on imposing value and order on the chaos of experience. Coover is already aware of the next step, that "postmodernism" needs the myth it reduces, just as the magician needs an audience or, as Derrida has said of Lévi-Strauss, the *bricoleur* needs the myth of the engineer. Yet there is more to the relationship between "modernism" and "postmodernism" than this recognition.

For my purposes, the striking and pertinent fact about Joyce's *Ulysses* is not the bewildering multiplicity of voices and characters but that there is no voice and no character who challenges Joyce, no presence of a fully *different* awareness, such as Ursula Brangwen in *Women in Love* or Shreve McCannon in *Absalom, Absalom!,* who creates another novel within the one Faulkner is writing and which Faulkner takes as seriously as his own. Eliot's poetry, for all its wholeness and balance, is like *Ulysses;* there is no other human presence beyond the poet himself. Eliot and Joyce made great literature out of their meditation on this seemingly inexhaustible stretch of consciousness, penetrating its most intimate recesses with a patience that did not scruple to criticize what at the same time was so carefully elaborated. The criticism with which I am concerned is predicated on this Eliot-Joyce pole of modern literature, but pushed to a finality, stripped of their essentially *critical* integrity which made them realize the elusive multiplicity of their own speaking voices. What is left is to anchor value only in the *absence* of different and competing voices. Thus the literary work becomes a vestibule in the whiteness of the page, where to enter is to be borne away beyond the necessity of all possible beginnings, lodging one's own speech in its interstices. One does not expect another awareness in the work to be taken as seriously as the author's, and as a consequence, there is no need to take seriously the possibility of a poetic awareness which "talks back," which challenges one's own.

Common sense, of course, says that the author has a voice as well as we do, and so his voice must be done away with. Here is Northrop Frye in *Anatomy of Criticism:*

> The axiom of criticism must be, not that the poet does not know what he is talking about, but that he cannot talk about what he knows. To defend the right of criticism to exist at all, there-fore, is to assume that criticism is a structure of thought and knowledge existing in its own right, with some measure of inde-pendence from the art it deals with.[3]

There is an appeal to structure and order, to a doubling back which would lay bare the existence of a work by repudiating one's ex-perience of it, but deeper than that and justifying such a movement of thought is another, a claim to a first-order primary speech. It is a claim inherited from the poetic revolution of the twenties, the staggering possibilities for the making of metaphor which culminate in Frye's statement that "everything is potentially identical with everything else."[4] It is for that visioned potential that one denies particular voice to the artist, making his work an unfleshed pres-ence, tall in our midst but ghostly, awaiting our bones to knit in the spaces and move, marching the work into the world of Identity. Here there would be no question of any silence or any dissonance; the poem or story "begins" when we begin to speak, and we begin to speak when we forget ourselves and trace out the articulate edgings of an anonymous structure. And perhaps this is the perfect form of criticism for "The Hat Act." Coover is talking to no one within the story, but to us. When we can forget, and when we can assume the unlimited potential of that imaginary axis, then and only then does the story have a voice. It can even be a voice of love, wrapped in a wide, dark world with no edge or encumbrance between author and readers. It is this, or it is the particular and degrading sexuality of what happens in the story.

My conviction is that such an aesthetic cannot be adequate to W. S. Merwin's poetry. Each of Merwin's last three books, *The Lice, The Carrier of Ladders,* and most recently *Writings to an Unfinished Accompaniment,* is like a purgatory, an escape from this infernal pattern of archetypal return, the movement from discrete and particular psyche, content, to potential identity, form, and back again.[5] There can be a sense of sameness about these books, if only because the pressure of disciplined escaping remains the vital, turning force of Merwin's work. Here is "Memory of Spring" from *The Carrier of Ladders:*

> The first composer
> could hear only what he could write

Its subject is the secret of the power of metaphor, the dramatic simplification and fusion that is "first," primary, what "to compose" means at its root. For a critic like Frye, it is the condition for both criticism and literature, but Merwin hears as well its accompaniment, the silent winter it brings in its wake. And that is the essential ambiguity of the poem: escape is both necessary and contingent, necessary because every metaphorical heart looks final but beats dicrotally, leaving a dissonance even between the maker of the title and the maker of the poem; and contingent because escape itself is already a memory, unpunctuated by the fleeting, present awareness which shapes the poem at the awesome edge of hearing what is felt cannot be written and yet cannot be escaped.

"Surf-Casting," in *Writings to an Unfinished Accompaniment,* mocks even the discipline itself:

> It has to be the end of the day
> the hour of one star
> the beach has to be a naked slab
>
> and you have to have practised a long time
> with the last moments of fish

sending them to look for the middle of the sea
until your fingers
can play back whole voyages

then you send out one
of your toes for bait
hoping it's the right evening

you have ten chances

the moon rises from the surf
your hands listen
if only the great Foot is running

if only it will strike
and you can bring it to shore

in two strides it will take you
to the emperor's palace
stamp stamp the gates will open
he will present you with half of his kingdom
and his only daughter

and the next night you will come back
to fish for the Hand

The peculiar violence of the poem, in contrast to "Memory of
Spring," inheres in the suddenly sharp collpase of the speaker of
the poem into the "you," the fisherman, in the last stanza. It's as
if in trying to prove, through the scrupulous, disciplined, critical
mocking of his pretensions, that there indeed must be a "you,"
a something there to mock and thereby to escape from, the poet
instead discovers the something he is tracking to be the discipline,
the escaping itself: "if only the great Foot is running." The point
was to have been that if one is looking, listening, fishing for an
archetypal palace, then of course it would be found. The result is
the realization that the very discipline of escape is what creates both
source and goal as one and the same, that what is needed is an
escape from escaping.

Thus it is in sharp contrast to fiction and the criticism of fiction
that I want to suggest Merwin's poetry is directed less toward es-

caping the limitations of the subject, the self and its idiosyncracies, than toward a renunciation of the peculiar psychic greed which could constitute the nuclear identity of a personality. And this is a movement which eventually precludes any possibility of resolving the self into whatever anonymous whole beyond and enveloping it. With the French structuralist thinkers in the lead, reinforced by Althusser's reading of Marx, it is becoming increasingly easy for contemporary thought to disavow itself of the notion of a substantial subject as the core of the individual's existence. But I think the result merely re-creates the motive for the subject on a grand scale, on the order of a "total form" of literature, or more subtly this, from Michel Foucault's *Archaeology of Knowledge:* "Must I suppose that in my discourse I can have no survival? And that in speaking I am not banishing my death, but actually establishing it; or rather, that I am abolishing all interiority in that exterior that is so indifferent to my life, and so *neutral,* that it makes no distinction between my life and my death?"[6] Here, projected as the death of the subject is at the same time the birth of something far worse, a greed for possession and dominance which claims the power of life and death itself for the terms of one's own understanding.

The extent of Merwin's renunciation is most direct in *The Lice,* published in 1967 and one of the most important books of poetry to appear in the sixties. The year also marked the national emergence of The Doors and Jimi Hendrix, the March on the Pentagon, the publication of Ihab Hassan's study of Henry Miller and Beckett, and it was in this sibilant whir of imminent apocalypse that Merwin had realized already the falseness of escaping one order of finality merely to institute another. *The Lice* is filled with disgust at all things human, but with an accompanying awareness of the impossibility that our humanness can ever be dissolved into the vast, unspoken darkness of a waiting kingdom. Here is "Avoiding News by the River":

> As the stars hide in the light before daybreak
> Reed warblers hunt along the narrow stream
> Trout rise to their shadows

Milky light flows through the branches
Fills with blood
Men will be waking

In an hour it will be summer
I dreamed that the heavens were eating the earth
Waking it is not so
Not the heavens
I am not ashamed of the wren's murders
Nor the badger's dinners
On which all worldly good depends
If I were not human I would not be ashamed of anything

The poem is wrapped to itself, the very tensile energy of the first stanza never allowed escape but nerved in stone at the end: "If I were not human I would not be ashamed of anything." No degree of mere technical facility can obviate that conclusion, as there can be no magical attempt to flush a purity free from the turbulent and shameful muck of human affairs. When asked his idea of happiness, Alfred Hitchcock, our great formalist of the cinema, replied that happiness would be as a clear horizon, no clouds, no shadows, nothing. There is no projection of such a clear empyrean for Merwin, only the invisibly shadowed and ribbed inertia of living as best one can. This is the end of "The Last One," perhaps the finest poem in *The Lice:*

Well the next day started about the same it went on growing.
They pushed lights into the shadow.
Where the shadow got onto them they went out.
They began to stomp on the edge it got their feet.
And when it got their feet they fell down.
It got into eyes the eyes went blind.

The ones that fell down it grew over and they vanished.
The ones that went blind and walked into it vanished.
The ones that could see and stood still
It swallowed their shadows.
Then it swallowed them too and they vanished.
Well the others ran.

The ones that were left went away to live if it would let them.
They went as far as they could.
The lucky ones with their shadows.

The Lice is as deep an expression of fatalism and despair as one is likely to find in contemporary literature, almost untouched by the playfulness found in the work of Coover or Barth or Barthelme. But Merwin has recognized the illusion that at least in art, at least in the saving artifice of the master craftsman, there can be escape, and that has proven to be a liberating discovery. While it contains many poems as bleak as those in *The Lice, The Carrier of Ladders,* published in 1970, is an attempt at exploring an alternative to dissolution or aggrandizement. It is the possibility of living one's life as a continual transformation through being observed, being touched, being judged even by what is around us, a recognition that at the very point of personal identity there is an otherness which presses continually upon us.

Here is "Ascent":

> I have climbed a long way
> there are my shoes
> minute larvae
> the dark parents
> I know they will wait there looking up
> until someone leads them away
>
> by the time they have got to the place
> that will do for their age
> and are in there with nothing to say
> the shades drawn
> nothing but wear
> between them
>
> I may have reached the first
> of the bare meadows
> recognized in the air
> the eyes by their blankness
> turned
> knowing myself seen by the lost
> silent
> barefoot choir

Frye speaks quite blithely in *Anatomy* and in *The Critical Path* about the need to be a spectator to one's own life.[7] Yet the value of being able to observe one's actions can be realized only if, like Merwin in "Ascent," we see with eyes that are not ours and only if we do not assume as though by magic the vantage and distance of an impersonal eye surveying a layered field. There is no objective structure or anatomy on earth which can coerce such vision into existence, because its essential nature is that it does not exist; it is being pulled into existence to the extent that we are able to think about what is around us thinking about us.

There is still enough of a drive toward dissolution in *The Carrier of Ladders* for Richard Howard's comment to have some validity, that "the real goal of these poems, what they are developing toward, [is a] darkness, [an] unconditional life . . . which must be characterized by its negatives, by what it is not, for what it is cannot be spoken," as in the last stanza of "The Well":[8]

> It is a city to which many travellers
> came with clear minds
> having left everything even
> heaven
> to sit in the dark praying as one silence
> for the resurrection

The radical discovery of *Writings to an Unfinished Accompaniment,* on the other hand, is that such unconditional, undifferentiated life can never be a goal but, precisely, an accompaniment. It is what sustains the poet's effort but what cannot itself be directly grasped. *Unfinished* here is not something waiting to be finished, a broken immediacy waiting to be consummated or a potential to be fulfilled, but a supersession of the very notion of finishing, of finality. Thus the opposition which informs *Writings to an Unfinished Accompaniment* is no longer between identity and difference but between oneness and identity. The movement of identity cancels all doubleness and division in the reification of its own source as a goal, a stable substance or structure or power to be possessed or whatever—"if only the great Foot is running." Merwin's accompaniment has become a vital, flickering absence whose elision is the desire to possess and control a oneness which makes all likeness

possible, while there can be nothing which is like unto it. This is
"Division":

> People are divided
> because the finger god
> named One
> was lonely
> so he made for himself a brother like him
>
> named Other One
>
> then they were both lonely
>
> so each made for himself four others
> all twins
>
> then they were afraid
> that they would lose each other
> and be lonely
>
> so they made for themselves two hands
> to hold them together
>
> but the hands drifted apart
>
> so they made for the hands two arms
>
> they said Between two arms
> there is always a heart
>
> and the heart will be for us all
>
> but the heart between them
> beat two ways
> already for whoever
>
> was to come
>
> for whoever would
> come after
>
> one by one

This is no poem of formal purity; the audacity of the first stanza
cannot be justified either by caprice or by artifice, only by the

pressure of the deepest poetic impulse. So the sure delicacy which, despite an insistent meter, can pause deftly between the last beat of "divided" and the first beat of "because." Hence the lines are neither rhythmic mush, ebbing one accent into the next until halted at "finger," nor declamatory, full of "pregnant pauses." Or again, it is the delicacy which resuscitates the sound of the first beat of "finger" as a counter within the portentous, resonant, back-throat hum of "god/named One." This way in which the rhythm complicates itself is perfectly realized toward the end of the poem: "but the heart between them/beat two ways." It's almost a form of tmesis. The first e in "between" and the e in "beat" have no heard rhythmic value themselves, yet their inaudible stretch allows the initial edge of the b and t sounds to gain a split precision from the lulling drift of the n and m whose movement, in turn, gathers cohesion from its crest into "beat." The words and sounds are hoarded in the cupped pause which sinews each flexion of abrupt line and spaced stanza into tentative prominence, but without losing the simplicity and forward thrust of the whole.

It is possible to hear poems only because the poet hears himself, as does Merwin, who listens silently and attentively so that there is no possibility of dissolving into the oracular and incantatory rhythms of his own voice just because it can be oracular and incantatory. The promise of such community, of a speaking and a listening which shapes every line and every word, is that although the very central pulse of the poem thus "beat two ways," there need be no disgust or contempt for what is human and inevitably divisible in our humanness. The discovery of "Division" is that whatever audience the poem might have, each reader will be more than just an ear or a voice. He will be able to think as finely and imaginatively as the poet himself, and he will hear, as the poet hears, the oneness of his voice doubled in the silences and the surfaces which that voice shapes and is shaped by, a development absolutely impossible to know in advance.

Eliot once said of Pound that his hells are for the other people, and the moral quality of Eliot's insight is brought poetically alive in "Division." More often than not in *The Lice*, Merwin's poems are hells created for an imagined audience, for a mass that comes after the poem and whom he had promised to leave behind in

"Lemuel's Blessing," the 1962 poem that inaugurated the first major change in his work. It is this distance, this aloof contempt, which is the greatest temptation to dominance and possession, and for a poet such as Merwin who is so finely aware of the waste we make continually, it is the most insidious and pervasive quality of all. But the problem is not that our lives are so encrusted with stock responses, with trash and debris, that nothing with any value can endure. It is rather that we are so distant from the actuality of our lives, from our present existence as including our nonexistence as essential to it, that we see only trash and debris, only what is immediate, existent, and present before us. The truly conventional response is the belief in convention, and once that fiction is abandoned in the fragile, labile reality of an interior community such as in "Division," there no longer can be any pretense of raging or coaxing an imaginary audience into acquiescence.

"Division" is at one with itself only as it echoes its own loneliness, and it is truly alone because Merwin is so aware of what is not present in the poem, the necessary absence of who is to come, a creative awareness as intricate as his own. The order of achievement represented by "Division" marks a genuine escape from the self-immolation of shuttling between two fictions, between a discrete and lonely psyche and a purely potential identity, which Merwin's poetry has promised since *The Lice.* "Division" is the kind of purgatory which carries with it, but does not succumb to, the knowledge of hell. Yet it is without the realization of Beatrice and without that marvelous freedom Dante possesses of learning his own transparence in the community of others. The very possibility is mirrored only briefly and transiently in what is perhaps the best poem in *Writings to an Unfinished Accompaniment,* "To the Rain." It is not Merwin writing and speculating to himself about an unknown audience, hoping that some one of them might make himself known to the poem. That is what the rain shames the poet out of in the first two stanzas:

> You reach me out of the age of the air
> clear
> falling toward me
> each one new

> if any of you has a name
> it is unknown
>
> but waited for you here
> that long
> for you to fall through it knowing nothing

What follows is a hymn to an active audience within the poem, an audience who never speaks but whose clarity blazes like the rainbow's incipience at the edge of the sun, guiding the voice one does hear. Here is the whole poem:

> You reach me out of the age of the air
> clear
> falling toward me
> each one new
> if any of you has a name
> it is unknown
>
> but waited for you here
> that long
> for you to fall through it knowing nothing
>
> hem of the garment
> do not wait
> until I can love all that I am to know
> for maybe that will never be
>
> touch me this time
> let me love what I cannot know
> as the man born blind may love color
> until all that he loves
> fills him with color

Any and every structure is what one already sees and knows, like a vision dangled before the eyes, a toy to be desired or despised. And that vision is blind. True seeing is an action whose love shapes the invisible intercession of clearness into color and color into the very age of the air. It is in the eye, but it is also in the rainbow's retina hidden in the clear touch of the rain, the immeasurable richness inhering in the autonomy of reciprocal creation that refuses to be reduced to a spectacle, its garment of invisibility shed. This, too, is a kind of greed perhaps, although I like to think it is the real thing, a love so fierce that it cannot be satisfied either with the mimetic desire of what it projects another to be or with the disinterested arrogance of presuming another merely existing to himself. Its rage is for the sameness, the contact between oneself and another to be so fully and intricately realized that the difference can assume infinite value and magnitude.

III

It is easy enough to say that poems like "Division" and "To the Rain" offer only a shadow of the richly human world present in *Absalom, Absalom!* or *Women in Love* or *Anna Karenina*. Measured against Coover's work, the poems may have their attractions, but of a minimal sort. I am convinced such devaluation rests on an inherent privilege accorded to the second and antithetical moment of literary works, to the "world" of the poem. Certainly there can be little question that Merwin's lines, which often seem barely a catch of breath, realize almost nothing of the existential density of these novels. It is only if one reads "Division" and "To the Rain" as *acts* and not just worlds, as being, nonbeing, and becoming, that it is possible to sense the fullness of Merwin's creation. His own question in "Gift," the last poem in *Writings,*

> what does it not remember in its night and silence
> what does it not hope knowing itself no child of time
> what did it not begin what will it not end

can then be answered positively. The poems forget nothing; they are incomparable examples of literature at its most inclusive.

Nevertheless, there is a caveat to be entered here, an infernal and disturbing memory in these purgatorial poems which tells us that we have reached a point where even the best poets can feel they have only a certain talent, a gift, to rely on, which may or may not develop any further. Merwin hardly needs the accompaniment of criticism to remind him that there are risks as well as virtues in the spare economy of his language, a real danger as well as a genuinely poetic integrity inherent in his decision to follow through the movement of escape begun in "Lemuel's Blessing." Indeed, criticism should bear its burden of responsibility as well. The disinterest in actual literature marked by the consuming goal of methodological purity has consequences for what authors do. Literature can continue to exist only in our performance of it, not on paper and not in textbooks purporting to have consolidated our gains. With much recent literature, and I think largely because of these strategies, we face already the situation Merwin limns for his own poetic "gift" in "The Place of Backs":

When what has helped us has helped us enough
it moves off and sits down
not looking our way

after that every time we call it
it takes away one of the answers it had given us

it sits laughing among its friends with wrong names
all of them nodding yes

if we stay there
they make fun of us
as we grow smaller because of the melting of our bones

One returns here to Coover, who understands this fatal self-destructiveness of Artist versus Critic perhaps better than anyone, where as "mimetic rivals" they divide and merchandise the gifts of the imagination in ever-diminishing quantities and where a "selfless" marketplace of perfect anonymity thus may seem to offer the only respite, everyone with his back to everyone else.[9] Value judgments of any sort would only perpetuate the conflict, endow the mimetic rivalry with the stamp of "free enterprise." For the dark side of every attempt at realizing literary value in contemporary culture must be the persistent threat of reducing literature to a commodity. Yet there are, at least, two ways of reading the end of "The Hat Act," which has Coover releasing the country boy—as I must now release Coover—who has been throughout the story the butt of all the jokes. He comes on stage with "the last word," a sign that reads in large letters:

THIS ACT IS CONCLUDED
THE MANAGEMENT REGRETS THERE
WILL BE NO REFUND

Perhaps it is that Coover remains the magician of artifice to the end, and this is his best trick of all, the one that melts all our bones, dissolves all our reality and our fictions into their dark cradle. But perhaps, instead, this ending is a question that can be released into and borne against the rhythm of both beginnings and endings in a way that allows us to act the value of our love to the fullness of risking even the very real thought of its being only an artifice, a commodity, after all. I won't presume to speak for Coover, whether the risk is worth it. Yet I do think Merwin's poetry offers the strength to affirm the possibility as no longer paralyzing nor one that must be escaped.

Notes

Preceding the notes for chapters 1–6 are lists of the principal works cited in those chapters, with the abbreviations I have employed. For works not originally in English I have used published translations whenever available, as cited in the lists; otherwise the translations are my own.

CHAPTER 1

AK   Michel Foucault. *L'Archéologie du savoir.* Paris: Gallimard, 1969. Translated by A. M. Sheridan Smith as *The Archaeology of Knowledge.* New York: Random House, 1972.

C   Donald Hall. *Contemporary American Poetry.* 2d ed. Baltimore: Penguin Books, 1972.

"D"   Jacques Derrida. "La Différance." *Bulletin de la Société français de philosophie* 57, no. 3 (July–September 1968). Translated by David B. Allison as "Differance," in *Speech and Phenomena and Other Essays on Husserl's Theory of Signs.* Evanston: Northwestern University Press, 1973.

IB   Joseph Riddel. *The Inverted Bell.* Baton Rouge: Louisiana State University Press, 1974.

LW   Linda Wagner. Review of *The Inverted Bell* by Joseph Riddel. *Contemporary Literature* 16 (1975).

NAP   Murray Krieger. *The New Apologists for Poetry.* Bloomington: Indiana University Press, 1963.

PDM   Paul De Man. Review of *The Anxiety of Influence* by Harold Bloom. *Comparative Literature* 26 (1974).

"Three"   E. D. Hirsch. "Three Dimensions of Hermeneutics." *New Literary History* 2 (Winter 1972).

1. The reference is to "Examples of Wallace Stevens," in *Language as Gesture* (New York: Harcourt, Brace and Co., 1952), pp. 223–24.

2. Riddel refers to Derrida's "Structure, Sign, and Play in the Discourse of the Human Sciences," in *The Languages of Criticism and the Sciences of Man,* ed. Richard Macksey and Eugenio Donato (Baltimore: Johns Hopkins University Press, 1970). The essay was published by Derrida as "La Structure, le signe, et le jeu dans le

discourse des sciences humaines," in *L'Ecriture et la différence* (Paris: Seuil, 1967).

3. Quoted by Robert Scholes in "Metafiction," *Iowa Review* 1, no. 4 (1970): 100.

4. My description of "feeling" as suprapersonal owes a great deal to Merle Brown's argument in the first chapter of his *Wallace Stevens: The Poem as Act* (Detroit: Wayne State University Press, 1970). See also his *Neo-Idealistic Aesthetics* (Wayne State, 1966), in particular chapter 5.

5. W. S. Merwin, *Writings to an Unfinished Accompaniment* (New York: Atheneum, 1973), p. 8.

CHAPTER 2

"ACF"   Benedetto Croce. "L'Arte come creazione e la creazione come fare." In *Nuovi saggi di estetica*. Bari: Laterza, 1920, 3d ed. 1948.

ASC   Benedetto Croce. *Ariosto, Shakespeare, e Corneille*. Bari: Laterza, 1920. 4th ed. 1950; reprint 1968.

BC   Gian N. G. Orsini. *Benedetto Croce*. Carbondale: Southern Illinois University Press, 1961.

"CT"   Benedetto Croce. "Il Carattere di totalità dell'espressione artistica," in *Nuovi saggi di estetica*.

GA   Benedetto Croce. *Breviario di estetica*. In *Nuovi saggi di estetica*. Translated by Patrick Romanell as *Guide to Aesthetics*. Indianapolis: Bobbs-Merrill Co., 1965.

GG   H. S. Harris. *The Social Philosophy of Giovanni Gentile*. Urbana: University of Illinois Press, 1966.

NAP   Murray Krieger. *The New Apologists for Poetry*. Bloomington: Indiana University Press, 1963.

NIA   Merle Brown. *Neo-Idealistic Aesthetics: Croce-Gentile-Collingwood*. Detroit: Wayne State University Press, 1966.

PA   Giovanni Gentile. *La Filosofia dell'arte*. Milan: Treves, 1931. 2d ed., Florence: Sansoni, 1950. Translated by Giovanni Gullace as *The Philosophy of Art*. Ithaca: Cornell University Press, 1972.

"PLB"   William Wordsworth. "Preface to the Second Edition of the *Lyrical Ballads*." In *Criticism: The Major Texts*, edited by Walter Jackson Bate. New York: Harcourt, Brace and World, 1952.

"VMH"   Benedetto Croce. "Ciò che è vivo e ciò che è morto della

filosofia di Hegel." In *Saggio sullo Hegel e altri scritti.*
Bari: Laterza, 1948.

WW   Cleanth Brooks. *The Well-Wrought Urn.* New York:
Harcourt, Brace and World, 1947.

1. The reference is to "The Later Poetry of W. B. Yeats," in
Language as Gesture (New York: Harcourt, Brace and Co., 1952),
p. 94.

2. Two noteworthy exceptions to what I have argued here are
Emilio Agazzi's *Il Giovane Croce e il marxismo* (Torino, 1962)
and Michele Abbate's *La Filosofia di Benedetto Croce e la crisi
della societá italiana* (Torino, 1955). Agazzi's exhaustively docu-
mented study not only traces in detail the origins of Croce's thought
but also demonstrates the importance of Croce's reading of Marx
and Labriola. Yet the emphasis on the "young Croce" is important.
Indeed, Agazzi goes so far as to say that the distinction between
"a consciousness of the particular and a consciousness of the general
or universal" (p. 487) amounts to an absolutely inflexible division
between "*art* and *science*" which persists throughout Croce's career.
In fact, the distinction between "particular" and "general" was
reformulated any number of times. And while it is true, to say the
least, that Croce had little sympathy with or understanding of what
a scientist does, Agazzi's insistence on an uncomplicated ideological
continuity is, again, a form of idealization which fails even to realize
the historical change and development of Croce's thought in
response to the varying pressures from his experience with literature,
with the ideas of others, and with the radical change in Italian
political life.

Like Agazzi, Abbate works from a very real context of Italian
social and intellectual life. The problem is that in the crucial chapters which describe Croce's "idealism" this context is not allowed
to mediate between the "materialism" of Marx and the "idealism"
of Croce. Directly juxtaposed to each other, Marx's language and
Croce's language are so immediately and strikingly different that one
wonders how the one could have read the other. And indeed, such
unmediated juxtapositions only work to enforce those abstract
arguments where, from one perspective, Marx looks to be merely
"mechanical" and, from the other, Croce appears nebulous and
unreal. Abbate's own awareness of how Croce's "idealism" was
forged in opposition to *positivism* of a determinate kind should
have warned him that any such simple juxtaposition was impossible.

I think the strength of Abbate's argument is to show how Croce's thinking never really calls into question the position of his own class, how in fact Croce is too quickly insistent on "class" as merely an abstract concept. The argument parallels my own contention that Croce fails to achieve a genuinely critical awareness of his own present act of thinking through the nexus of distincts. But this inability to turn one's thinking back on itself critically, or to realize critically the relationship between one's own class and others, is not a failing to be attributed solely to the bourgeoisie as Abbate seems to think. To believe so merely abrogates the responsibility to be self-aware about one's own work.

CHAPTER 3

AC   Northrop Frye. *Anatomy of Criticism*. Princeton: Princeton University Press, 1957. Reprint. New York: Atheneum, 1969.

CE   Roland Barthes. *Essais critiques*. Paris: Seuil, 1964. Translated by Richard Howard as *Critical Essays*. Evanston: Northwestern University Press, 1972.

"D"   Jacques Derrida. "La Différance." *Bulletin de la Société français de philosophie* 57, no. 3 (July–September 1968). Translated by David B. Allison as "Differance," in *Speech and Phenomena and Other Essays on Husserl's Theory of Signs*. Evanston: Northwestern University Press, 1973.

F   Tzvetan Todorov. *Introduction à la littérature fantastique*. Paris: Seuil, 1969. Translated by Richard Howard as *The Fantastic*. Cleveland: Case Western Reserve University Press, 1973.

"HMD"   Claude Lévi-Strauss. "How Myths Die." *New Literary History 5* (Winter 1974).

"NF"   William Wimsatt. "Northrop Frye: Criticism as Myth." In *Northrop Frye in Modern Criticism,* edited by Murray Krieger. New York: Columbia University Press, 1966.

PH   Fredric Jameson. *The Prison-House of Language*. Princeton: Princeton University Press, 1972.

RC   Claude Lévi-Strauss. *Le Cru et le cuit*. Paris: Plon, 1964. Translated by John and Doreen Weightman as *The Raw and the Cooked*. New York: Harper and Row, 1969.

"RE"   Northrop Frye. "The Road of Excess." In *The Stubborn Structure,* edited by Max Black. Ithaca: Cornell University Press, 1970.

SM   Roland Barthes. *Système de la mode*. Paris: Seuil, 1967.

    SP Jacques Derrida. *La Voix et al Phénomène*. Paris: Presses Universitaires de France, 1967. Translated as "Speech and Phenomena," in *Speech and Phenomena and Other Essays on Husserl's Theory of Signs*. Evanston: Northwestern University Press, 1973.

"SSP" Jacques Derrida. "La Structure, le signe, et le jeu dans le discourse des sciences humaines." In *L'Ecriture et la différence*. Paris: Seuil, 1967. Translated as "Structure, Sign, and Play in the Discourse of the Human Sciences," in *The Languages of Criticism and the Sciences of Man*, edited by Richard Macksey and Eugenio Donato (Baltimore: Johns Hopkins University Press, 1970).

  S/Z Roland Barthes. *S/Z*. Paris: Seuil, 1971.

"Three" E. D. Hirsch. "Three Dimensions of Hermeneutics." *New Literary History* 2 (Winter 1972).

"TW" Roland Barthes. "To Write: An Intransitive Verb?" In *The Languages of Criticism and the Sciences of Man*, edited by Richard Macksey and Eugenio Donato. Baltimore: Johns Hopkins University Press, 1970.

  VI E. D. Hirsch. *Validity in Interpretation*. New Haven: Yale University Press, 1967.

  WW Cleanth Brooks. *The Well-Wrought Urn*. New York: Harcourt, Brace and World, 1947.

1. "But I should not like the effort I have made in one direction to be taken as a rejection of *any* other possible approach. Discourse in general, and scientific discourse in particular, is so complex a reality that we not only can, but should, approach it at different levels and with different methods. If there is one approach that I do reject, however, it is that (one might call it, broadly speaking, the phenomenological approach) which gives absolute priority to the observing subject, which attributes a constituent role to an act, which places its own point of view at the origin of all historicity— which, in short, leads to a transcendental consciousness" (my italics). *The Order of Things* (New York: Random House, 1970), p. xiv.

CHAPTER 4

  AI Harold Bloom. *The Anxiety of Influence*. Oxford University Press, 1973.

"AL" Northrop Frye. "The Archetypes of Literature." In *Fables of Identity*. New York: Harcourt, Brace and World, 1963.

   CP   Wallace Stevens. *The Collected Poems of Wallace Stevens.*
          New York: Knopf, 1955.
  "CT"   William Saunders. "Reaching beyond Desire: Charles Tomlin-
          son's Poetry of Otherness." Dissertation, University of
          Iowa, 1975.
  "FC"   Ian Hamilton. "Four Conversations." *London Magazine,* No-
          vember 1964.
   LK   Bertrand Russell. *Logic and Knowledge.* Edited by Robert C.
          Marsh. London: Allen and Unwin, 1956.
  PDM   Paul De Man. Review of *The Anxiety of Influence* by Harold
          Bloom. *Comparative Literature* 26 (1974).

1. In fact, in *A Map of Misreading* (Oxford University Press, 1975), Bloom "admits" that perhaps the anxiety of influence is a feature of almost all Western poetry: "The affliction of belatedness, as I have begun to recognize, is a recurrent malaise of Western consciousness, and I would now recant my previous emphasis on the anxiety of influence as a Post-Englightenment phenomenon" (p. 77).

2. Quotations from Tomlinson's poetry are from *Seeing Is Believing* (Oxford University Press, 1960); *The Way of a World* (Oxford University Press, 1969); *The Way In* (Oxford University Press, 1974); *Written on Water* (Oxford University Press, 1972). Poems discussed in detail are given in an appendix to this chapter.

3. See Merle Brown's reading of this poem in his *Wallace Stevens: The Poem as Act* (Detroit: Wayne State University Press, 1970), pp. 46-48.

4. Calvin Bedient, *Eight Contemporary Poets* (Oxford University Press, 1974); and William Saunders, "Reaching beyond Desire: Charles Tomlinson's Poetry of Otherness" (diss., University of Iowa, 1975).

5. In conversation with William Saunders.

6. I have appropriated Coleridge's term "outness," as well as Owen Barfield's discussion of its meaning in his *What Coleridge Thought* (Middletown: Wesleyan University Press, 1971), pp. 59-68.

7. I am indebted for this suggestion to Merle Brown's "Intuition versus Perception: On Charles Tomlinson's 'Under the Moon's Reign,'" forthcoming in *Journal of Aesthetics and Art Criticism.*

CHAPTER 5

   AC   Northrop Frye. *Anatomy of Criticism.* Princeton: Princeton
          University Press, 1957. Reprint. New York: Atheneum,
          1969.

Cap   Karl Marx. *Capital.* Vol. 1. Translated by S. Moore and E. Aveling. New York: Kerr, 1906.

CC   Raymond Williams. *The Country and the City.* Oxford University Press, 1973.

Engels Frederick Engels. Letter to J. Bloch. In *Marx, Engels, Lenin on Historical Materialism.* New York: International Publishers, 1974.

HCC   Georg Lukács. *History and Class Consciousness.* Translated by Rodney Livingstone. London: Merlin Press, 1971.

"IMP"   Northrop Frye. "The Instruments of Mental Production." In *The Stubborn Structure,* edited by Max Black. Ithaca: Cornell University Press, 1970.

MF   Fredric Jameson. *Marxism and Form.* Princeton: Princeton University Press, 1971.

SM   Roland Barthes. *Système de la mode.* Paris: Seuil, 1967.

SMeth Jean-Paul Sartre. *Search for a Method.* Translated by Hazel Barnes. New York: Random House, 1968.

"TC"   Georg Lukács. "The Twin Crises." In *Marxism and Human Liberation,* edited by E. San Juan, Jr. New York: Dell, 1973.

1. Perry Anderson, "Components of the National Culture," *New Left Review* 50 (July–August 1968): 53, 55.

2. See my discussion of the "heresy of paraphrase" in chapter 2.

3. *Finnegans Wake* is "a single voice—a voice offering to speak for everyone and everything . . . a surrogate, a universal isolated language. . . . Given the facts of isolation, of an apparently impassable subjectivity, a 'collective consciousness' reappears, but in an altered form. This is the 'collective consciousness' of the myth, the archetype. . . . In and through the intense subjectivities a metaphysical or psychological 'community' is assumed, and characteristically, if only in abstract structures, it is universal; the middle terms of actual societies are excluded as ephemeral, superficial, or at best contingent and secondary. . . . Social versions of community are seen as variants of the 'myth'—the encoded meaning—which in one or another of its forms is the only accessible collective consciousness. There is the language of the mind—often, more strictly, of the body—and there is this assumed universal language. Between them, as signs, as material, as agents, are cities, towns, villages: actual human societies" (*CC,* 245–46).

4. The terms "known community" and "knowable community" are developed most explicitly in chapter 16 of *The Country and the City.*

CHAPTER 6

C   Jean-Paul Sartre. *Critique de la raison dialectique*. Vol. 1. Paris: Gallimard, 1960–.

Engels   Frederick Engels. Letter to Margaret Harkness. In *Marx, Engels on Literature and Art,* edited by Lee Baxandall and Stefan Morawski. New York: International General, 1974.

EP   Karl Marx. *Economic and Philosophic Manuscripts of 1844.* Translated by Martin Milligan. New York: International Publishers, 1964.

M   Wilfred Desan. *The Marxism of Jean-Paul Sartre.* New York: Doubleday, 1965.

MF   Fredric Jameson. *Marxism and Form.* Princeton: Princeton University Press, 1971.

WL   D. H. Lawrence. *Women in Love.* Modern Library, 1950.

1. Even if one wants to go further, to posit the problem as a relation between Lawrence and an "actual landscape," the resolution remains the same. Indeed, part of the greatness of *Women in Love* is that it refuses any easy distinction between "art" and "life," between how Lawrence lives his life and how he writes the novel, or between how Lawrence writes the novel and how Birkin lives his life within the novel. Whatever "actual landscape" Lawrence faced is no more neutral than the landscape in *Women in Love.* People have come here; they have inhabited it in a certain way, and Lawrence is at work with all the creative intelligence he can summon to articulate the meaning of those relationships. One certainly may quarrel with Lawrence's realization but hardly dismiss it by fiat, as if mountains possessed some pristine and nonhuman meaning all their own.

2. See my discussion of contradiction and opposition in chapter 2.

3. See my discussion of Derrida in chapter 3.

4. Of course neither assumption can de facto paralyze critical practice in the hands of a sensitive and intelligent critic such as Eliseo Vivas. His analysis of the "Moony" chapter in *Women in Love* (*D. H. Lawrence: The Failure and the Triumph of Art* [Bloomington: Indiana University Press, 1960]) as the making of a "constitutive symbol" is enormously suggestive; it makes you read the novel again in a new way, as does Jameson's quite different discussion of symbolism in *Marxism and Form.*

5. I am indebted for this idea of the importance of the epigraph

to my colleague William Johnsen. Indeed, Johnsen had argued earlier in his dissertation that the "then" of the first line of "Prufrock" "implies an antecedent; the antecedent the reader sees is the speeches of Statius and Guido above and before the poem. . . . The antecedents of Statius and Guido suggest that an imaginary listener inspires Prufrock's confession" ("Toward a Redefinition of the Modern" [diss., University of Illinois, 1970], p. 105).

CHAPTER 7

1. *New Literary History* 2 (Winter 1972): 250.
2. *The Meaning of Contemporary Realism,* trans. John and Necke Mander (London: Merlin Press, 1963), p. 26. However, one can find support for Lukács's contention in unexpected places. There is Yvor Winters, of quite different political persuasion: "The most damnable fact about most novelists, I suppose, is their lack of intelligence: the fact that they seem to consider themselves professional writers and hence justified in being amateur intellectuals. . . . I cannot read the neat but simple Mr. Hemingway, nor the inarticulate (though doubtless profound) Mr. Faulkner, and I can see no reason why I should be asked to try" (*The Function of Criticism* [Denver: Swallow, 1957], p. 39). And there is R. P. Blackmur, hardly one to be considered an ideological foe of that "modernism" Lukács finds so questionable: "I merely inquire why he [Faulkner] blurs the operation of the intelligence, and I can only suggest as an answer that he has the kind of sophistication which will accept only a low degree of order, the order of actions whether of the psyche or of the conflict of interests and loyalties before they have been understood and so have lost some intimacy" (*A Primer of Ignorance,* ed. Joseph Frank [New York: Harcourt, Brace and World, 1967], pp. 25–26).
3. C. Hugh Holman, "*Absalom, Absalom!*: The Historian as Detective," *Sewanee Review* 79 (1971), 542–43; Melvin Backman, *Faulkner: The Major Years* (Bloomington: Indiana University Press, 1966), p. 88; Olga Vickery, *The Novels of William Faulkner* (Baton Rouge: Louisiana State University Press, 1964), p. 86.
4. William Faulkner, *Absalom, Absalom!* (Modern Library, 1964), p. 22. Further page references are given in the text.
5. Frederick L. Gwynn and Joseph L. Blotner, eds., *Faulkner in the University* (Charlottesville: University of Virginia Press, 1959), p. 88.
6. Vickery, *Novels,* p. 101.
7. Gwynn and Blotner, *Faulkner in the University,* p. 275.

CHAPTER 8

1. "It is an elementary axiom in criticism that morally the lion lies down with the lamb. Bunyan and Rochester, Sade and Jane Austen, *The Miller's Tale* and *The Second Nun's Tale,* are all equally elements of a liberal education, and the only moral criterion to be applied to them is that of decorum." *Anatomy of Criticism* (1957; rpt., New York: Atheneum, 1969), p. 114.

2. "The Hat Act," in *Pricksongs & Descants* (New York: New American Library, 1969), p. 251.

3. Frye, *Anatomy of Criticism,* p. 5.

4. Ibid., p. 124.

5. Quotations from Merwin's poetry are from *The Lice* (New York: Atheneum, 1967); *The Carrier of Ladders* (Atheneum, 1970); and *Writings to an Unfinished Accompaniment* (Atheneum, 1973).

6. Michel Foucault, *The Archaeology of Knowledge,* trans. A. M. Sheridan Smith (New York: Random House, 1972), p. 210.

7. See Frye, *Anatomy of Criticism,* p. 348; and Frye, *The Critical Path* (Bloomington: Indiana University Press, 1971), p. 129.

8. Richard Howard, "A Poetry of Darkness," *Nation,* December 14, 1970, p. 634.

9. I take the phrase and the idea of "mimetic rivalry" from René Girard's discussion in *Mensonge romantique et vérité romanesque* (Paris: Editions Bernard Grasset, 1961); translated by Yvonne Freccero as *Deceit, Desire, and the Novel* (Baltimore: Johns Hopkins University Press, 1965).

Index

Abbate, Michele, 239-40*n*2
Actual Idealism, 46, 48, 51-53
Aesthetic synthesis, 39, 40-45.
  See also Croce, Benedetto
Agazzi, Emilio, 239*n*2
Anderson, Perry, 146
Archetype, 63, 70-71, 74-75. *See also* Frye, Northrop
Ariosto, 39, 48, 53-54
Autonomy, poetic: and New Criticism, 6, 8-10; and poetics, 8-9; and Eliot, 9; defined, 24; in Croce's *Estetica,* 25; in Brooks, 25-26; and self-referential poetic language, 25-26, 27-29; and dialectic, 30; confusion in Croce's definition of, 32, 45-46, 54; and division, 157
Auto-affection, 90-91, 93-94. *See also* Differance

Backman, Melvin, 189
Balzac, Honoré de, 78-79, 149, 160
Barfield, Owen, 242*n*6
Barth, John, ix, 14, 122-23, 221-22
Barthelme, Donald, 221-22
Barthes, Roland, 21, 75; *S/Z,* 12, 78-79, 153; *Critical Essays,* 59, 77-80; on "system" and "message," 59, 78-79; relation between metalanguage and object-language in, 63, 78-83; and "presence," 64-65; and the uncertainty of meaning, 75, 83; and history, 77; and difference, 77-78, 81-83; on Balzac, 78-79, 149; *Système de la mode,* 80-83, 148-49; "To Write: an Intransitive Verb?", 81-83; and Picard, 148; division between creation and criticism in, 148-49; relationship

to recent fiction, 218-19
Bedient, Calvin, 103
Blackmur, R. P., 7, 10, 26, 146, 147, 245*n*2. *See also* New Criticism
Blake, William, 15, 70-71, 187
Bloom, Harold: and misunderstanding, x, 96-99, 109; *Figures of Capable Imagination,* 5; *The Anxiety of Influence,* 12, 96-103, 109, 114, 122, 184; on Hartman and Wordsworth, 97; and history as influence, 99-100; and misreading, 100-03; relationship to recent fiction, 218-19; *A Map of Misreading,* 242*n*1
Bly, Robert, 11
Brooks, Cleanth, 25-26, 27-29, 31, 75-76, 189. *See also* New Criticism
Brown, Merle, 36, 49, 51-52, 242*n*7. *See also* Croce, Benedetto

Circle, of the Spirit, 32, 40-43, 45-46. *See also* Croce, Benedetto
Class, 158-61, 163-66, 173-74, 175-80, 181-84. *See also* Jameson, Fredric; Sartre, Jean-Paul
Collingwood, R. G., 74
Conrad, Joseph, 24
Coover, Robert, ix, 218-24, 235-36; "The Hat Act," 220-24
Criticism, and methods of interpretation, 57-58, 141-42, 188-92, 196
Croce, Benedetto: and New Criticism, 20, 32-33; and Gentile, 20, 48, 51-53; *Estetica,* 25, 31, 41; on poetic autonomy, 25, 53-54; *Breviario,* 31, 33, 38-45, 50, 51; *Nuovi saggi di estetica,* 31, 48-49,

70; *Fearful Symmetry,* 70-71; confusion between dialectic and classification in, 70-71, 74-75; *The Critical Path,* 73; and distance, 96-98; "The Archetypes of Literature," 98; "The Instruments of Mental Production," 148; and mythic community, 148-49; on imaginative inclusiveness, 213-14; relationship to recent fiction, 218-19; and metaphor, 223

Gadamer, H.-G., 66
Gass, William, 221-22
Gentile, Giovanni, 36, 59, 77; and Croce, 20, 31, 48, 51-53; "reform" of Hegel's dialectic, 46-48; *The Philosophy of Art,* 47, 54-55; and fascism, 48; *Sommario di pedagogia,* 52, 53; *Sistema di logica,* 53
Girard, René, 246n9

Hall, Donald, 10-11, 13, 17-18
Hardy, Thomas, 141
Harris, H. S., 53
Hartman, Geoffrey, 97
Hegel, G. W. F., 31, 33-38, 46-48, 53, 57, 89, 176, 181. *See also* Croce, Benedetto; Gentile, Giovanni
Heidegger, Martin, 66
Hill, Geoffrey, 5, 11
Hirsch, E. D., x, 77; *Validity in Interpretation,* ix, 58-59, 65-68; "Three Dimensions of Hermeneutics," 19, 68-70, 188; conception of meaning, 20, 58-59, 65-70, 147-48; conception of type, 62, 65-70; on Frye, 70
History: and freeplay, in Derrida, 87-89; and differance, 88-89, 94; and definition of modernism, 95-96; and influence, in Bloom, 99-100; in Sartre, 171-74; and dialectic, 181-82

Holman, C. Hugh, 189
Howard, Richard, 229
Hume, David, 110
Husserl, Edmund, 20, 56, 59, 89-94, 109. *See also* Derrida, Jacques

Image, in Croce, 39
Influence, 96-103, 109, 113-14, 115-16, 119-20, 122-23, 124, 126-29. *See also* Bloom, Harold
Intuition: in Croce, 25, 32-33, 34, 43-45, 45-46, 50-51; in Husserl, 91-93

Jameson, Fredric: and structuralism, 21, 76, 86; *The Prison-House of Language,* 76, 86; on Barthes, 80-81, 83; on Derrida, 86; *Marxism and Form,* 142-43, 158, 162-66, 169, 176-83, 184-85; on symbolism and class analysis, 163-65; on Sartre, 172-74; and class conflict, 176-83
Johnsen, William, 244-45n5
Joyce, James, ix, 13, 153, 222-23
Judgment: in Croce, 32-33, 44, 49

Kant, Immanuel, 3, 57, 59, 89, 109
Kinnell, Galway, 11, 15
Krieger, Murray, 6, 19, 20, 25-26, 59. *See also* New Criticism

Lacan, Jacques, 183
Lawrence, D. H., ix, 163-65, 185, 222, 244n1
Leavis, F. R., 5, 7, 10, 146, 216. *See also* New Criticism
Lévi-Strauss, Claude, 9-10, 20, 59-60, 61-62, 64, 76, 84-88. *See also* Derrida, Jacques
Locke, John, 110
Lukács, Georg: *History and Class Consciousness,* 54, 143-45, 148, 150-51, 158, 180, 183-84; critique of "rationalism," 143-45; interview